OWL VERSUS BLADE

STEEL CITY
RIVALS

OWL VERSUS BLADE

STEEL CITY RIVALS

ANTHONY CRONSHAW

WITH PAUL A. ALLEN

JOHN BLAKE

Published by John Blake Publishing Ltd,
3 Bramber Court, 2 Bramber Road,
London W14 9PB, England

www.johnblakepublishing.co.uk

www.facebook.com/Johnblakepub [f]
twitter.com/johnblakepub [t]

First published in paperback by Pennant Books in 2010
This edition published in 2012

ISBN: 978-1-85782-817-7

British Library Cataloguing-in-Publication Data:

A catalogue record for this book is available from the British Library.

Design by www.envydesign.co.uk

Printed in Great Britain by CPI Group (UK) Ltd

Papers used by John Blake Publishing are natural, recyclable products made
from wood grown in sustainable forests. The manufacturing processes conform
to the environmental regulations of the country of origin.

Every attempt has been made to contact the relevant copyright-holders, but some were
unobtainable. We would be grateful if the appropriate people could contact us.

In memory of Neil and Shaun,
gone but never forgotten

Matthew David Cryer 1990-2008

Please see www.justice4matthew.com – **this fund has been
set up in the memory of Matthew as a lasting memorial
to the wonderful, bright, cheerful, good natured, talented
and enthusiastic young man he was.**

AUTHOR PROFILE:
ANTHONY CRONSHAW

Anthony Cronshaw was born on 3 November 1955; he had little choice about following in his father James's footsteps when it came to supporting the Owls, as Bramall Lane was strictly out of bounds. He first went to school at Shirecliffe Infants and Junior School. When he was 11, his father remarried, to Marie, and the family moved to the Birley Estate. For the first time in his life, Anthony had a real mother. His brothers Mark and David and sister Donna completed the family line-up.

By the early 70s, Anthony had left school and for the most part of his adult life he drifted from one job to another.

Anthony married Christine on 2 July 1983, and on 23 November 1988 their daughter Samantha was born. These years were happy ones in more ways than one because the Owls were on the up and, by the time Samantha started school, Wednesday had enjoyed probably their most productive period for many a year.

He wrote his first book *Wednesday Rucks and Rock 'n' Roll* in 2002 and has made contributions to other football-related books. *Steel City Derby* is his biggest challenge to date and he has enjoyed every minute of putting it together.

EDITOR PROFILE:
PAUL A ALLEN

 Paul Allen is the author of *Flying With The Owls Crime Squad*, and for 10 years he was a known face within the Sheffield Wednesday hooligan gangs. In 1995, Paul turned his back on football hooliganism, and also in a way on Sheffield, as he moved to pastures new in Ontario, Canada. Today, he works as a Health & Safety Consultant in the healthcare sector, but he still looks forward to visiting his home city whenever he can.

CONTENTS

INTRODUCTION

The city of Sheffield sits nestled between seven hills, and has the lifeblood of five rivers to feed it. The town had already become a giant of the Industrial Revolution long before it achieved city status in 1893, and for centuries has carried a reputation for quality steel and steel products unmatched by any other city in the world. But Sheffield is not only a giant of industry, it is also a giant of the sport of Association Football, and its pedigree in the development of the game, loved around the world, is just as impressive as its industrial achievements, although maybe not as well known.

The world's oldest football club (Sheffield FC), oldest ground (Sandygate Road), first ever football tournament (Youden Cup), first floodlit match (Bramall Lane – 1878) and first ever county Football Association (Sheffield & Hallamshire FA) are among the gifts that the Steel City has given to the world of sport. The city is also one of the few in England that can boast two professional teams. But it is also a city so often ignored by the mainstream media, especially where its football teams are concerned. Sheffield may lack the glamour of London, or Manchester, but what it lacks in glamour it makes up for in grit and determination. The people of Sheffield have an intense inbuilt streak of stubborn pride. Maybe that comes from hundreds of years of fierce independence from the path of conformity, or maybe it is just pig-headedness. Either way, the citizens of Sheffield are not afraid to say what they think or to embrace the things they love, and to hell with the consequences.

STEEL CITY RIVALS

One thing that the people of Sheffield love with a passion is the game they helped to build – football. They love the game, and they love their football teams, Sheffield Wednesday and Sheffield United, even though history shows that the clubs rarely give back, in terms of success, anywhere near what they take, but we love them just the same. I recently stumbled across a website where some 36 per cent of people surveyed said that the football rivalry in Sheffield does not match that in other large British cities. All I can say to that is those surveyed have obviously never taken in the spectacle of a full-blooded Steel City derby. They have never felt the passion flooding down on to the field from both the blue and red side of the stadium. They have never seen the looks of joy and despair on the faces of those hard-nosed South Yorkshire folk at the final whistle, when their team has won or lost. A Steel City derby can match the passion of almost any sporting fixture anywhere in the world, and it is a fixture that can deeply divide families and workplaces, almost to breaking point.

In this book, we examine the history of the Steel City derby, both on and off the field of play. We will look at the bitter rivalry played out by 22 men chasing a ball on the pitch, and by hundreds of warring football supporters chasing each other off it. In every context, the struggle for supremacy, between red and blue, is absolute and, to the people of Sheffield, it is never just a game!

THE BIRTH OF A RIVALRY

The great city of Sheffield that we know today has a wonderful rich history that can be traced back over 1,000 years. The area, which has developed into a thriving 21st-century metropolis, has seen settlement since the ice age, but it wasn't until the Norman Conquests that large numbers of people really started to come together at the confluence of the Sheaf and the Don. In future years, these two rivers would bring great prosperity to the town through the water power they provided to the fledgling cutlery and edge-tool industries. By the late 1600s, Sheffield was a picturesque place with a population of around 2,500. A third of them, however, were so poor that they relied on their families and neighbours for help to survive. At the time, most of the population was concentrated around the town centre close to the two aforementioned rivers, and even as early as the mid-17th century Sheffield had established itself as the main centre for cutlery production in England, and this would spark further expansion in the coming decades.

By the beginning of the 18th century, the area was expanding at great speed, and, between 1678 and 1736, the population had risen from a meagre 3,000 to a staggering 14,531. The good folks of Sheffield must have been thirsty buggers because 161 public houses had a full licence and this did not include the alehouses and beer-offs that also did a roaring trade.

Drunkenness, however, was a major problem; many punters ran up healthy bar bills, and those who were slow to settle it would end up in the debtors' prison, which was situated on Pudding Lane, a road now known as Kings Street. The situation got so bad that another two prisons had to be built, one on Scotland Street and the other on Tudor Street.

Sheffield was also a very dangerous place after dark and many areas of the town were reputed to be meeting places for counter-feiting and forging. Around this period, such activity was classed as treason, and one Henry White was arrested for being in possession of a number of counterfeit shillings. White was convicted and sentenced to be transported for 15 years, which probably meant he was sent to Australia, but he was lucky they did not hang him. The public house that he was caught in was none other than the illustrious Hen and Chickens on Castle Green, so nothing's altered there then in all these years.

By the mid-1800s, Sheffield had built its own canal and had been connected to the railway system, which would come back to throw a spanner in the works of Wednesday some 50 years later, when a line was run through the middle of their stadium! The Sheffield Canal became the lifeblood of the fledgling cutlery and steel industry, and provided all the timber and coal to fuel the thirsty furnaces. It was not only the furnaces that were thirsty, but also the population, which by now numbered 135,000, and they too were well provided for with some 700 licensed premises.

During this period, it was cricket that kept the sporting-mad public of Sheffield occupied, and in 1821 Darnall Cricket Club built an 8,000-seater stadium. Unfortunately, it was three miles out of town and by 1829 it was a white elephant; in contrast, the ground at Hyde Park, which was much closer to the town centre, prospered.

The Wednesday Cricket Club was founded in 1820, but, with the rapid expansion of the town, which was growing at an alarming rate, cricket facilities were being gobbled up for housing and work premises. It was the brainchild of Michael J Ellison, who played for Sheffield Cricket Club, to approach the Duke of Norfolk, who had eight-and-a-half acres of land that was sitting idly on the southern edge of the town, with a view to renting the said land for the purposes of developing a cricket ground that could be used by many of the town's teams; the added bonus was that it was totally smoke free, unlike many other places in the town.

A meeting was arranged for all the major teams in the area, most of whom attended, at the Adelphi Hotel on Monday, 30 January 1854 close to where the Crucible stands today. It was agreed to pay the Duke an annual rent of £70 and take out a 99-year lease on the ground. A committee was formed and shares were issued at £5 each. With the formalities about the leasing of the land over, work began on building 10ft-high walls around the perimeter, and it was decided that the ground would be called Bramall Lane after the Bramhall family who were file makers in the area.

With the addition of a covered gallery and refreshment bars, the ground was ready for action, and the following clubs took advantage of their new surroundings: Broomhall, Caxton, Milton, Sheffield, Shrewsbury and, of course, Wednesday. Yorkshire County Cricket, which was also founded during the Adelphi meeting, based themselves at the Bramall Lane ground and played Sussex, in their very first competitive match, on the site in August 1855.

In 1862, the first ever football match was played at Bramall Lane, between Hallam and Sheffield, the oldest football club in the world, Sheffield having been founded in 1857 and Hallam some three years later. The game was staged in aid of the Lancashire Distress Fund, which came about because of the demise of the cotton industry due to the American Civil War, but the game was not a good advert. There was a mass brawl after William Waterfall was struck by Major Creswick. Waterfall went ballistic and punched the major several times. After tempers cooled, Waterfall was asked to go in goal, instead of being sent off – now that's one rule that would really spice up the game today.

In a famous meeting some seven years later, on 4 September 1867, also at the Adelphi Hotel, a certain John Pashley proposed the Wednesday Football Club be formed, to keep the members of the cricket club together during the cold winter months, and the motion was seconded by William Littlehales. Subsequently, Ben Chatterton was elected the first club president, and John Marsh was chosen as the very first secretary and captain of the team; the colours of blue and white, which still stand today, were also chosen at this meeting.

Wednesday held a practice match at their first ever ground, at Highfields, on 12 October 1867, followed a week later with a first ever competitive game, which resulted in a victory over the Mechanics at Norfolk Park.

The first competition the fledgling club entered was the Cromwell Cup in 1868, and, after beating Mackenzie in the semi-final, they came across the much fancied Garrick in the final at Bramall Lane. The game finished goalless in front of 600 fans, and so it was decided to play next-goal winner. Wednesday went on to win the game, and so lift their first ever trophy.

The year 1868 saw Wednesday play only friendly games against such teams as Pitsmoor, Mechanics and Broomhall. By 1870, the club had relocated to Myrtle Road, and a game a year later, against MacKenzie, was abandoned after only 20 minutes because the ball burst and no one had a replacement. The disillusioned players, from both teams, headed for the pub to drown their sorrows.

Football was growing all around the country during this period, and 1872 would prove to be a pivotal year in the history of the sport when the Football Association introduced the Challenge Cup. The battle for the trophy survives to this day, and is the world's oldest sporting knockout competition.

With the success of the FA Cup, the Sheffield Association introduced a Cup competition for local sides in 1876, and 25 teams entered, including Wednesday. First up for Wednesday were Parkwood Springs who were beaten at Myrtle Road; further victories over Kimberworth, Attercliffe and Exchange set up a final encounter with Heeley, and a then massive crowd in excess of 8,000 flocked to Bramall Lane to witness a classic encounter.

Heeley soon went 3–0 up, but Wednesday rallied, and stormed back to win 4–3 after extra-time, lifting this prestigious trophy at the very first time of asking. Coincidentally, the trophy is still played for today in the guise of the Senior Cup.

Wednesday were now the top team in the area and the trophy cabinet was full to bursting. In 1880, the FA Cup was entered for the first time, but the club were eliminated in the quarter-finals by Darwen. The following year, they went one better and reach the semi-final, only to lose to Blackburn Rovers. By 1882, the club was once again on the move, this time to Robert's Farm near Hunters Bar, where they again made a losing appearance in the quarters of the FA Cup, this time falling to Notts County.

In 1883, Wednesday split from the cricket section, and went their own way; the reason being that the football side of the club was making all the money and the cricketers were spending it.

Wednesday hired the Lane for matches until 1887, when they purchased the Olive Grove ground, which they had on a seven-year lease from the Duke of Norfolk. The club spent a further £5,000 sprucing the place up and played their first ever game in September, when Blackburn Rovers were the visitors, and the game ended 4–4. The ground was just off Queens Road and the players changed in the Earl of Arundel and Surrey public house before making their short walk to the football ground. It was also in 1887 that the club turned professional with the first players being paid around five shillings for a home game, and seven shillings and sixpence if they travelled away. Initially, Wednesday were totally against turning professional and several players defected to the newly formed Sheffield Rovers, but Tom Cawley was a die-hard Wednesday player, and even though he'd made the move to the Rovers he got the players together and offered Wednesday one more chance to change their minds.

At a hastily assembled meeting, Wednesday reluctantly agreed to the players' demands, and turned professional. The other alternative would have been disastrous, and really does not bear thinking about, given the history of the club we know today; soon after this, Sheffield Rovers disbanded, when most of their newly acquired players went back to play for Wednesday.

Olive Grove saw its fair share of crowd trouble in the early years; in October 1890, a game against Crewe, which Wednesday lost 6–4, saw disturbances, and the recipient of the crowd's hostility was none other than the so-called umpire, Mr Wake, who also happened to be a Wednesday supporter. Before linesmen were introduced, an official from each club would assist the referee, and by all accounts poor old Mr Wake was not having a very good day. Wednesday had been 5–2 down but pulled it back to 5–4 before Crewe scored a blatantly offside sixth, and, despite the home team's appeals that the umpire should raise his flag, Mr Wake ignored their protests and waved away the players. This incensed the Wednesday supporters, and when the game ended the crowd stormed on to the pitch, surrounding Wake, and he had difficulty reaching the safe haven of the dressing rooms because the crowd was jostling him. Instead of keeping his head down, he stood in the doorway and started to argue with the irate supporters, while puffing on his pipe. This really put their backs up and it was only the quick intervention of two police officers that saved his skin as they bundled him into a waiting cab.

After that incident, the club feared sanctions from the Football Association in the shape of a heavy fine, but worse was to come. The following January, the crowd attacked the referee, a Mr Wright from Derby, after he too refused to cancel out a goal in Wednesday's 2–1 defeat at the hands of Newton Heath. At the final whistle, the crowd made a beeline for the official, jostling him and pelting him with mud before club officials came to his aid.

These incidents were probably in retaliation for the game at Newton Heath when Wednesday players were attacked by rival supporters. Brayshaw was hit with a stick, and Ingram was bundled into the crowd. After the game, all those associated with the Sheffield club had to make a hasty retreat or face retribution at the hands of a baying mob.

By 1889, even the FA Cup was not immune to crowd disturbances. The semi-final tie between Preston and West Brom, held at Bramall Lane, was delayed because of marauding Preston fans. They ran from the Shoreham End to the Bramall Lane side of the ground causing trouble. West Brom complained that their players and supporters had been intimidated, causing them to lose the game, but the result stood.

Twelve months later, the Grove was eventually closed for two weeks, but this time it was due to the behaviour of the players. Wednesday had two players sent off, in an FA Cup tie with Small

Heath, for serious rough play. Wednesday still won the game 2–0 but, as there were no games scheduled during this period, it was hardly a severe punishment.

The first 20 years or so in the history of the Wednesday Football Club had been ones of moderate success. They were by far the biggest club in Sheffield during this period, but by the end of the 1880s their cosy period of unchallenged dominance within the town was about to be put to the test. A new kid was about to enter the playground, and the seeds of an intense rivalry, which persists to this day, would be sown. The Steel City would never be the same.

THE FIRST DERBY MATCHES

The year was 1889 and the expansion of Sheffield had continued relentlessly over the previous 20 years; the town was, by now, a bustling city in the making, an honour which would be bestowed by Queen Victoria in 1893. The population had risen to almost 400,000, many of whom made their living in the thriving cutlery and steel industries. The work was hot, dusty and dangerous, and when the long shift was over they liked nothing more than having a drink in one of the 514 public houses and 651 alehouses that were scattered around the city. According to the government of the time, Sheffield had more drink-related incidents than any other city of a similar size. Workers would even send out the firm's lad or apprentice to bring them ale while they worked because the work was often dirty, and the air full of dust. Nothing lubricated their parched throats better than a gallon or two.

As well as a love of the ale, the folk of Sheffield also loved their football and, in 1889, Sheffield United Football Club was formed. The scene was now set to have two rival teams vying for the affections of the football-mad people of the town. In the early years of the rivalry, the support for the two clubs mainly came from around the city centre and the surrounding areas such as Heeley and the Park, and it would not be long before the two teams would lock horns in the first of many Steel City derbies.

The very first meeting of the clubs was played at Olive Grove on 15 December 1890. It was a Monday, which was known locally as

Saint Monday because it was a customary rest day for all those who worked in the cutlery industry. Further research leads me to believe that rest had nothing to do with the name, and the workers just liked to get pissed on that particular day of the week. It was also the customary Bull Week where workers put in as many hours as humanly possible, so they got a good wage to last them over the Christmas period. A crowd of around 10,000 descended on the Grove and witnessed a Wednesday victory in awful conditions because of the fog and smoke.

United had joined the Midlands Counties League, which included the likes of Rotherham Town, Lincoln City, Burslem Port Vale and Gainsborough Trinity. Wednesday were currently bottom of the much stronger Alliance League, which had teams such as Nottingham Forest, Newton Heath, Small Heath and Darwen, but, while Wednesday struggled, United were having a very good season and had lost just three of 23 games.

Wednesday kicked towards the town first half, but it was United who started the brightest, and after 20 minutes Robertson scored the first ever goal in a Sheffield derby. As the game went on, the visibility was fading fast, and the crowd were having difficulty picking out the ball. This seemed to spur Wednesday on and, in the second half, Woolhouse equalised. Further drama was to unfold with only five minutes remaining as Winterbottom scored the winner to give Wednesday victory in the first meeting between the clubs.

Wednesdayites must have partied in the surrounding boozers, and made their envious rivals' lives a misery when they finally sobered up and returned to work the following day; with the two sets of supporters living in each other's pockets, some fans must have come to blows, and the teams' respective grounds were also no more than a mile apart, if that.

The return game at Bramall Lane on 12 January 1891 saw a crowd of around 14,000 and things were going well for Wednesday after Billy Ingram and Bob Brandon had put them two to the good, but United rallied and, before Wednesday knew what had hit them, goals by Watson and Howell had levelled matters. To add insult to injury, with only a few minutes remaining, Calder scored when he was clearly in an offside position, but the goal stood, much to the annoyance of the players and supporters of Wednesday. United had won 3–2 after being 2–0 down, and now it was United's turn to gloat, much as the Wednesdayites had done at the end of the previous fixture.

After just one season in the Midlands League, United tried to join Wednesday in the Alliance, but were soundly rejected, and rumour had it that it was Wednesday who swayed the vote in favour of keeping United out. With that door closed, they joined the Northern League and enjoyed the company of Middlesbrough, Sunderland Albion, Darlington and Newcastle West End.

During the following season, another friendly was organised for 26 October 1891, and Wednesday travelled the short distance to Bramall Lane. The crowd numbered some 22,900 and Wednesday were well and truly spanked 5–0. This led to Unitedites issuing what can only be described as the original calling cards, which read:

In Loving Remembrance of
THE SHEFFIELD WEDNESDAY FOOTBALL TEAM
Who were sadly put to rest on Monday, October 26th
At Bramall Lane
Poor old Wednesday were fairly done,
When United beat them five to none;
Although they lost, they did their best,
So let them quietly take their rest.
(Friends of the above club kindly accept this intimation)

The cards were condemned by the *Telegraph* because they felt that they would create ill-feeling between the rival supporters. There was already tension between Wednesday and United supporters, and this culminated in scuffles breaking out during the game; even United's players got involved on the Shoreham after leaping the fencing, and the 40 police officers on duty helped restore order. It was only 1891, and already the Olive Grove boot boys were causing mayhem on the Shoreham! What a picture that would have been, seeing the Wednesday boys giving the Unitedites a good kicking, and the coppers and the players must have received a few digs too. One more outbreak of violence occurred before the game finished in favour of the triumphant United team.

The cards printed by the jubilant Unitedites were left in the local hostelries, and when Wednesdayites picked them up they must have nearly choked on their beer. People were having them posted through their letterboxes, and even at work they were not safe from these dreaded cards. Wednesdayites took it on the chin, though, and let United have their moment of glory because everyone knew who the top team in the city were – just as they do today.

The defeat was a hard pill to swallow, however, and the committee called an emergency meeting where it instructed all the players to regularly attend training sessions and get their act together. This seemed to do the trick because, when United made the short trip to Olive Grove on 16 November, Wednesday played as though their lives depended on it, and ran out comfortable 4–1 winners, with Woolhouse and Spikesley getting two each. Needham grabbed United's consolation. The crowd had been 11,500 and Wednesdayites present responded by dishing out their own funeral cards that read as follows:

In pitiful remembrance of
Our idols,
THE SHEFFIELD UNITED FOOTBALL TEAM
Who departed their football life,
Struggling to the end,
At Olive Grove on Monday, November 16th 1891
When United died, they struggled hard
Enough to live a brighter and longer life;
Do as they would, they could not ward
Neat kicks by Wednesday, and thus the strife
Ended, thus closed famous United's reign;
Sheffield now mourns their death the more,
Dying as they did – ne'er to rise again
And kick for fame at Wednesday's door.
Yes, United had lost four to one.

Now the boot was on the other foot, and Wednesdayites vigorously set about the task of rubbing Unitedites' noses in it. I would like to wager that the pubs were awash with the bloody things and the local printers were doing a roaring trade. You've got to give United credit though for coming up with the idea nearly a century before the famous ICF introduced theirs.

Wednesday had been trying for years to gain entry to the Football League, but the original 12 members kept giving them the knock-back and the club had resigned itself to playing in the Alliance League. It was rumoured at the time that Blackburn Rovers had been angered when Wednesday poached a certain Tom Brandon, and they had got all the other clubs to keep the Sheffield club out; however, on 13 May 1892, the club finally made it into the Football League, and went straight into the expanded First Division. Sadly for our red and white brethren, United had to settle for second best, and were placed in the Second Division, which, would you believe, still rankles with them today.

Wednesday immediately made plans to improve the facilities, and they set about levelling the pitch, which at the time had a 6ft slope on the railway side. A new stand was to be built, which would include dressing rooms and baths, plus a refreshment bar at the rear. I wonder how a balti pie would have gone down at the Grove.

During this period, three games were played between Wednesday and United. The first came on 17 October 1892 at Olive Grove, and the game ended 1–1 in front of a crowd of around 17,000. A month later, Wednesday won 3–1 at the Lane, but the game was a bit on the rough side, and United had to play most of the second half with only 10 men. The final match in this trilogy was the Wharncliffe Charity Cup Final, at Olive Grove, which ended goalless, and the crowd was a very poor 4,000. The two clubs had been ordered to play the charity game by a Mr JC Clegg after Wednesday had refused to play the previous season.

The Football League Division One now had 16 teams and Wednesday were rubbing shoulders with the best; during that first season they managed 12 victories out of their 30 games, and, with

United making a solid start to life in the Second Division, football in Sheffield had never been better.

Wednesday started the 1893–94 season brightly with victories over Notts Co and Accrington before three straight defeats brought them back to earth. This was the prelude to a six-game unbeaten run, which stretched until Blackburn Rovers turned them over 3–0 at the Grove. This was followed by a 5–3 victory at Everton, and by the end of the year the club had enjoyed victories over Aston Villa, 5–3, and Newton Heath, 5–1.

Across the city in the Second Division, United had also started well, winning three out of their first four games. After eight matches, United had amassed 10 points. Bootle, 8–3, and Port Vale, 10–0, were swept aside as United went for promotion at the first attempt. Meanwhile, back at the Grove, Wednesday started the New Year with a 6–0 thrashing of West Brom, but then went on a disastrous run of games losing seven on the bounce, and were facing the prospect of changing places with United.

United, on the other hand, had still only been beaten three times, and, as the teams entered the last month of the season, Wednesday were in trouble.

On the final day of the season, United were guaranteed a test match game. Promotion and relegation was decided on these games when the top three in the Second played one of the bottom three in the First. Wednesday pulled out all the stops to beat Notts County, and so avoid being left in the bottom three. Small Heath had pipped United to the title, but lost their test match to Newton Heath, and, when United beat Accrington 1–0 in Nottingham, it meant they would be joining Wednesday in the top division.

THE SHEFFIELD DERBY: DIVISION ONE 1893–94

The first ever Sheffield derby in the Football League was played at Bramall Lane on 16 October 1893 and it was another rough affair. This time it was Wednesday who were reduced to 10 men, and the game finished in a 1–1 draw with Hill scoring for United and Spikesley scoring for Wednesday. The following month, on 13 November, United won 2–1 at the Olive Grove with goals from

Drummond and Hammond while Miller netted for Wednesday, who also missed a penalty when Howlett saved from Brandon.

United would end the season as Sheffield's higher-placed team when they finished 10th to Wednesday's 12th, although the FA Cup saw Wednesday reach the semi-final.

It was also in 1893 that Sheffield was granted a City Charter, which was a fitting tribute to our glorious city that was built on seven hills and five river valleys. Sheffield has seen many conflicts dating back to the Romans where they built a fort at Templeborough to keep an eye on the Brigantes over the road at Wincobank. I wonder what the travelling Italians would have made of the Roman Ridge boozer a few years back.

THE SHEFFIELD DERBY: DIVISION ONE 1894-95

United and Wednesday had enjoyed victories on four occasions each in all games that had been played since 1890, so, as the teams got ready to go head to head for the 1894–95 season, things were evenly balanced in the Steel City.

United were the first to achieve a League double with a 3–2 success at Olive Grove. The scorers were Hill, Hammond and Howell for the reds, while Spikesley and Davis replied for Wednesday. The return game at Bramall Lane saw United run out 1–0 winners thanks to a Mr Watson. As in the previous season, it was United who finished higher with a top-six finish compared to Wednesday's eighth, but once again the FA Cup saw Wednesday reach the semis.

Wednesday seemed to leave their League form at home when it came to the FA Cup because they'd only managed one victory out of the final 11 games, but in the Cup the blue and whites defeated the Cup holders Notts County 5–1, Middlesbrough 6–1 and Everton 2–0.

For the semi-final game, over 8,000 Wednesdayites travelled to Derby for the meeting with West Brom, but sadly it ended in defeat just like the previous season, and Wednesdayites began to wonder if their club would ever lift the FA Cup.

THE SHEFFIELD DERBY: DIVISION ONE 1895-96

Wednesday won the first derby at the Olive Grove 1–0, thanks to Bell, and the return game at the Lane was on Boxing Day 1895. A crowd of over 19,000 saw a final score of United 1 Wednesday 1, with Watson and Brady scoring the goals, but it was in the FA Cup where the real drama unfolded as the boys in blue and white brought back the first bit of silverware to the Steel City when Wolverhampton were defeated 2–1 in the FA Cup Final. The Wednesday line-up that day featured Massey, Earp, Langley, Brandon, Crawshaw, Petrie, Brash, Brady, Bell, Davis and Spikesley. Fred Spikesley scored 12 of the 17 goals that brought the Cup back to Sheffield, and, after finishing behind United for the last two seasons, Wednesday finally found the key to unlock the major trophy cabinet. It was also a brand-new trophy because Aston Villa had let somebody nick the original after they had stupidly displayed it in a Birmingham shop window. Wednesday enjoyed a civic reception back in Sheffield after their victory, which was delayed because Wednesdayites in their thousands thronged the town centre, and the parade took far longer than expected.

Not only had Wednesday won the FA Cup but they had also regained their place as top dogs with a top-seven placing, while United had slumped to 12th.

THE SHEFFIELD DERBY: DIVISION ONE 1896-97

With Sheffield's first piece of historic silverware in the bag, Wednesday now set their sights on the League title heading into the 1896–97 season, but unfortunately they found it difficult to turn Cup form into League points, and on Boxing Day at the Lane a poor performance saw United triumph 2–0 with Priest and Howell doing the damage. In the return game at Olive Grove, the game would end in a stalemate with Brandon scoring for Wednesday and Needham replying for United.

The referee had to have a word with the Wednesdayites because of their poor behaviour. The Wednesday hooligans, dressed in their flat caps and mufflers, were well ahead of their times and all dressed accordingly. When they'd had their fun, like throwing missiles at the lump of lard that was Fatty Foulke in the United goal, they could blend in with the crowd. The police had them under surveillance, but it was bloody hard work dragging that tripod around and the flash of magnesium kept giving the game away.

The authorities knew that crowd disorder was on the increase, but mainly it was the players and officials that were bearing the brunt of the supporters' frustrations; rarely did rival fans clash, but when they did I bet it was a lively affair.

Travel on the railways started to make life a little easier for the away fan, but I bet if my mate Shaun had been around in those days he would have booked a horse-drawn carriage to take the boys from the Travellers at Wadsley Bridge to most of Wednesday's away games. I could just see them now outside the boozer feeding the horses for a nice little trip over the Pennines to face Burnley.

Back in Sheffield, the two grounds were so close together it was more than likely that trouble flared after the local encounters in the surrounding hostelries when the drink had been flowing. Probably the most popular with the Wednesday supporters would have been the Earl of Arundel and Surrey, the Bridge Inn on London Road, the Myrtle Inn, which sadly closed in 1970, and the Ball Inn where United used to have their training ground.

Unitedites, on the other hand, had an abundance of places where they could wet their whistle. The closest probably would have been the Railway Hotel, which is still open today, the Sheaf House, where Wednesday were once on the verge of purchasing a piece of land that ran adjacent to the property, and the numerous more that littered London Road.

THE SHEFFIELD DERBY: DIVISION ONE 1897–98

It was United who got their hands on the League title first when in 1897–98 they lifted the trophy for the first and last time in their history. The first Steel City derby of United's Championship-winning season was played at the Olive Grove on 16 October 1897 in front of a crowd of 24,000, paying record League gate receipts of £620, but that was as good as it got for Wednesday who lost out to a single goal scored by Bennett. The return game at the Lane, on 27

December, saw Spikesley score for Wednesday and Earp put through his own goal for United. It was a record attendance of 37,389 and the gate receipts were a staggering £962.

Wednesday finished fifth, their top finish so far, but it could not hide the fact that their fiercest rivals had pipped them to the coveted trophy.

THE SHEFFIELD DERBY: DIVISION ONE 1898–99

Wednesdayites went into the 1898–99 season on a bit of a downer because not only had United pipped them for the Championship, but also the lease for the ground had expired, and, after all that good work getting the place into shape, the landlords, who were the Railway Company and Sheffield Corporation, needed to extend the Northern Line straight through the middle of the stadium. They allowed them to fulfil their fixtures but they had to vacate by the following season.

United and Wednesday met for their final game at the Olive Grove ground on 3 October 1898 and the game ended in another 1–1 draw with Hemmingfield scoring Wednesday's last ever Olive Grove derby-day goal while Priest netted for United.

Boxing Day at the Lane brought more success for United who won 2–1 thanks to Morren and Beer, while the consolation goal for Wednesday was netted by Hemmingfield, the crowd was a fantastic 32,500. In less than 10 years, attendances for the Steel City showdown had risen from a few hundred to the numbers seen for this game, which just goes to show the passion for the game that existed in the city, and which exists to the present day.

While United were on the up, the soon-to-be-homeless Wednesday were on the brink of losing their top-flight status. Wednesday had looked at acquiring a 20-year lease on the nearby Sheaf House ground, but Mappins Brewery who owned the land suddenly upped the rent, and Wednesday had to look elsewhere. Just imagine if they had been successful and managed to get their hands on Sheaf House, the two grounds would have been amongst the closest of probably any clubs in the world. Two other sites were looked at, in Carbrook and Owlerton, with the latter being a popular choice but the hardcore of Wednesdayites lived in Heeley and it was thought that Carbrook would be easier to get to.

Carbrook Hall had been built in 1623, but had been a public house since 1855. There was vast land surrounding the place so it would be ideally suited for a football ground. When Wednesday played Aston Villa, voting slips were handed out, and about 10,000 were returned, with Carbrook getting 4,767 votes compared to Owlerton, which polled 4,115.

The Villa game was a strange one because, with 10 minutes remaining, and Wednesday leading 3–1, the match was abandoned, and when it was played to a finish, some five months later, the game only lasted 10 minutes and Wednesday added a fourth to win 4–1.

Even though Carbrook seemed the perfect option and the fans had voted in favour of it, it appeared that the board at Wednesday chose Owlerton as the cheaper option. So, in April 1899, it was decided at a special general meeting that shares would be issued to raise the £5,000 needed to purchase the plot of land at Owlerton.

(Carbrook would eventually be transformed into a massive industrial area, housing the giant steelworks that produced the finest special steels, which would make the name of Sheffield famous throughout the world.)

Wednesday waved goodbye to the Olive Grove in April, when Newcastle United were the visitors, and, in addition to losing their home, they had already lost top-flight status. When work started on their new home, in June 1899, Wednesdayites were hoping for a swift return to Division One.

Wednesday had waved goodbye to Sheffield 2, and headed for the more glamorous surroundings of Owlerton. The club had acquired a piece of land on the banks of the River Don, but it was not an easy place to get to and lacked public transport. Undeterred, however, Wednesdayites trekked to the new ground in their thousands, and, in the very first game at Owlerton, 12,000 saw their heroes defeat Chesterfield by a score of 5–1.

NEW HOME, NEW CENTURY, OLD RIVALRY

The 1899–1900 season was Wednesday's first in their new home, and it was also the year that Sheffield recorded its first ever FA Cup derby when the teams met at Bramall Lane on 10 February 1900. The match was a second-round tie, and had to be abandoned in the second half due to heavy snowfall, with the score standing at 0–0. The attendance was a very impressive 32,381, and the gate receipts were £1,183. The clubs attempted to replay play again five days later, but, after they'd opened the gates, the snow was too deep so the match was postponed. When the match was finally played, the pitch was a sea of mud, and the game was an ill-tempered affair, but it was Wednesday, through Brash, who took the lead. It was not to be Wednesday's day, though, and, after their goalkeeper was injured, and Spikesley went off with a knee injury, an equalising goal for United, by Almond, took the game to a replay at Owlerton. For the replay, and United's first ever visit to Wednesday's new home, the blue and whites would be without Massey, the goalkeeper, Spikesley and Millar, who had been kicked off the park two days earlier.

The press would go on to describe the return encounter as a disgrace, and, when Thickett broke the leg of the youngster Lee, the game would descend into an orgy of kicking, but it wasn't just the ball that was being kicked. United scored through Needham, and it then proceeded to get worse for Wednesday, as Pryce was sent off for nearly breaking Hedley in two, and they ended up with just eight men after Langley made sure that Bennett did not finish the game.

Beer made the final score 2–0 to United, but the sad fact of all of this was Lee's career was ended before it had begun, and he never played again. He died in 1906 aged just 29 years of age. The FA held an inquiry, and this resulted in Langley being banned for a month and Pryce getting two weeks.

Despite the defeat to United in the Cup, the first season at Owlerton would prove to be a successful one as Wednesday returned to the top flight as Second Division Champions.

THE SHEFFIELD DERBY: DIVISION ONE 1900–01

The Steel City rivalry was rekindled on 15 December at the Lane, and, again, United won 1–0, thanks to a goal by Field in front of a crowd of a healthy 25,000. When the team from S2 made their first visit to Owlerton in the 1900–01 season, a crowd of 11,000 witnessed a 1–0 Wednesday victory.

The silverware count now showed that United had got one League title and one FA Cup success compared to Wednesday's solitary FA Cup triumph, and that was not the only sour statistic which Wednesdayites were forced to taste. The count of Steel City derby victories, in the League, stood at seven wins for the reds, and only two wins for the blues.

Crowd disturbances were again rearing their ugly head, and this time it was the players of Bury who bore the wrath of Wednesdayites, after they had deposited their team out of the FA Cup at Owlerton. At the end of the game, they were attacked with an array of missiles and several players were cut. The Wednesday supporters chased them along Penistone Road towards the railway station, but, thankfully for the S6 club, the incident was not reported to the FA and Wednesday breathed a sigh of relief.

THE SHEFFIELD DERBY: DIVISION ONE 1901–02

Wednesday, nominally, could claim to be the dominant force in Sheffield after they had finished in a higher League position than United the previous season, and, when the clubs met on 2 November, Wednesday triumphed thanks to the only goal of the game being scored by Wilson. The return game at the Lane, though, would see United run out easy 3–0 winners thanks to Bennett (2) and Priest. Both games drew crowds in excess of 27,000.

United would finish the season on another high when they again won the FA Cup, defeating Southampton 2–1 in a replay, after the first game had finished 1–1. This had more than made up for their previous season's loss at the hands of Tottenham Hotspur.

Wednesday, once more, finished higher than United in the table, but that elusive Championship was still out of reach.

THE SHEFFIELD DERBY: DIVISION ONE 1902–03

The beginning of the 1902–03 season was keenly anticipated by Wednesdayites, and for once the players responded. That elusive first League Championship would be claimed. A win was even clinched at Bramall Lane for the very first time, when Spikesley, Wilson and Davis did the business while Priest and Lipsham replied for United. A League double was, sadly, not on the cards though and United would claim some revenge when they won 1–0 at Owlerton shortly before Wednesday were crowned Champions. That defeat was not the only one Wednesday suffered during the run-in, and a disastrous spell of form, which saw them win only one out of the last four games, gave Sunderland the chance to nick the title. Thankfully, Sunderland lost to Newcastle United in the final game of the season and the Championship was safe.

The downside to the Championship-winning performance of 1903 was when the team travelled to Sunderland, and the players were attacked after the final whistle. As the team left the ground on their horse-drawn carriage, an unruly mob pelted the vehicle with a shower of missiles. It was now becoming commonplace after a home defeat for the supporters to mob up and vent their frustration on the opposing players and officials, but the authorities seemed to be burying their head in the sand, and charges were few and far between.

THE SHEFFIELD DERBY: DIVISION ONE 1903–04

Wednesday were once again in rampant mood at the start of the 1903–04 season, and a second successive League title would eventually make its way back to S6, but both Sheffield clubs would have solid seasons. The first League meeting of the teams was a table-topper a couple of months into the season, and both teams took a share of the spoils with Lipsham bagging United's goal, and that man Wilson again grabbing the Wednesday response. The gate was another good one, with 34,500 turning up. The point saw United stay top and Wednesday second. The return game at Owlerton finished one goal short of a massacre as Wednesday ran out 3–0 winners, thanks to Chapman (2) and Simpson.

THE SHEFFIELD DERBY: DIVISION ONE 1904–05

The 1904–05 season would see the end of the career of probably the first ever Wednesday legend Fred Spikesley. Spikesley had made 321 appearances and scored 115 goals, one of them being the first ever League goal scored against United by a Wednesday player. He made his debut in 1892 after signing in the Bull and Mouth public house on Waingate, and was paid a massive £3 a week. He was nicknamed the 'Olive Grove Flyer', and scored both goals when Wednesday beat Wolves in the 1896 FA Cup Final.

Wednesday were hoping for a hat-trick of titles, but a 3–1 defeat at Owlerton by United on 10 December did not help matters. The crowd was a very low 16,000 and, with Wilson scoring for the Wednesday, and Brown (2) and Donnelly for United, the day belonged to the red side of the city. The trip to Bramall Lane was just as bad with the score 4–2 in United's favour. Donnelly, Brown, Priest and Drake scored for United while Stewart (2) notched the Wednesday response.

THE SHEFFIELD DERBY: DIVISION ONE 1905–06

The 1905–06 season would prove to be eventful in more ways than one. First, Wednesday travelled to Bramall Lane and, thanks to Chapman and Stewart, won 2–0. Second, because of crowd trouble after the Preston game, Owlerton would be closed for 14 days from 26 February, but seeing as how the next home fixture was not until the visit of Woolwich Arsenal, on 24 March, this was not exactly a very severe punishment. Preston players were pelted with numerous missiles, and, like Bury previously, several players were cut. Owlerton was becoming a very hostile ground to visit, but again the FA seemed to be a bit limp when it came to dealing with matters of this nature, and the feeble punishment handed down was a testament to their dithering.

When United visited on 18 April, it was Wednesday's turn to achieve a very first double over the old enemy when Davis netted from the penalty spot in the 80th minute, and how the Wednesday support must have celebrated.

THE SHEFFIELD DERBY: DIVISION ONE 1906-07

The first derby of the 1906–07 season game was played at Owlerton and ended 2–2 with Wilson (2) doing the honours for Wednesday while United had Brown and Needham to thank. Later in the season, Wednesday pulled in a record crowd for the Cup quarter-final with Liverpool, when 37,830 turned up to witness a 1–0 victory.

Wednesday then took thousands to Birmingham for the semi-final with Woolwich Arsenal and they were not disappointed, as their favourites won the game 3–1 to set up a final tie with Everton. In the meantime, there was the small matter of another derby game, but this time United, thanks to Drake and Lipsham, stole the show, 2–1 with Maxwell grabbing the Wednesday consolation, in front of a crowd of only 12,000.

Although Wednesday slumped to a very lowly 13th, their worst finish since returning to the top flight, there was the added bonus of Cup glory as the team triumphed over Everton to bring the Cup back to Sheffield, and this also meant that Wednesday now edged in front of United as far as trophies were concerned, winning four to United's three.

THE SHEFFIELD DERBY: DIVISION ONE 1907-08

Wednesday again continued their quest to be top dog in the city and on 9 November the blue and whites came, saw and conquered at Bramall Lane in front of a very good crowd of 30,694, running out 3–1 winners thanks to Brittleton, Chapman and Stewart, while Levick grabbed United's consolation.

At Owlerton, Wednesday again won 2–0 thanks to Wilson and Maxwell. A respectable fifth-place finish was achieved behind the champions Manchester United.

In Sheffield, the population had risen to about 450,000, and we now had a university, in addition to a city-centre abattoir, called the Killing Shambles, situated on Waingate. Horse-drawn trams were still the order of the day, and this mode of transport would take you to the match and deposit you at Hillsborough Corner, where you could wet your whistle in the Hillsborough Inn, Shakespeare and the Rose Inn. It was once reported that the landlord of the Burgoyne Arms on Langsett Road, a man called Hales, was nearly 8ft tall and weighed 29 stone. Now the current landlord is a very good friend of mine and we used to travel to many a game in the 70s, but he's nowhere near 8ft!

The horses' days were just about numbered though, as the city started integrating the electric version and the four major routes passed through the Wicker with one terminating at the Norfolk Arms in rural Handsworth. On the outskirts of the city lay the villages of Hackenthorpe and Beighton, and it was in Hackenthorpe that a certain Thomas Staniforth had a foundry making farming and gardening implements. Mr Staniforth obviously thought well of his workers because he had built them cottages adjacent to his factory on Main Street, just opposite the Blue Bell. Staniforth eventually sold out to Stanley Tools who ceased production on the site in 1980.

Today both areas are football crazy, whether its Bramall Lane or Hillsborough that is your chosen destination, but back in the early 1900s a trek to either ground must have taken forever. In Hackenthorpe they would meet outside the New Inn on Sheffield Road and ready the hounds and horses for a bit of fox hunting, while the good folk of Beighton would congregate outside the George and Dragon.

THE SHEFFIELD DERBY: DIVISION ONE 1908–09

Sheffield's football fanatics had to wait until Christmas Day for the first derby of the season when a crowd of 28,000 descended on

Owlerton to see Simpson score the only goal of the game for Wednesday, before, amazingly, 24 hours later travelling to the Lane; United exacted swift revenge, winning the game 2–1 with Hardinge and Peart scoring for the reds, and Bradshaw getting the Wednesday reply. The crowd was 38,408 so in a matter of two days nearly 70,000 had witnessed the two games. Again it was Wednesday who finished the better, with another top-five finish, while United could only manage 12th.

THE SHEFFIELD DERBY: DIVISION ONE 1909–10

The first Steel City encounter of 1909–10 saw one of the best Sheffield derbies so far when a crowd of 30,000 witnessed an end-to-end game that not only had six goals shared but also brought in gate receipts of £821. United scorers were Simmons (2) and Brelsford while Kirkman (2) and Chapman replied for Wednesday.

United then came to Owlerton, and won 3–1 thanks to Hardinge (2) and Evans, with Brittleman getting Wednesday's consolation.

THE SHEFFIELD DERBY: DIVISION ONE 1910–11

Wednesday would do their third League double over United in the 1910–11 season, winning at Owlerton, 2–0 thanks to a double by Chapman and then a McLean goal edging the game at Bramall Lane.

Even though Wednesday had made a loss of £2,000 the previous season, they took a party of 14 on an end-of-season tour of Sweden and Denmark. First, they defeated Gothenburg 5–0 before turning over a Sweden Select XI 2–0. They then moved on to Denmark where they overcame the national side 3–2. Wednesday played a total of five games in seven days and won them all.

THE SHEFFIELD DERBY: DIVISION ONE 1911–12

For the first time in history, both games finished by the same score. The first meeting of the teams, at the Lane, finished 1–1 with Kitchen scoring for United and Wilson for Wednesday. At Owlerton, Wilkinson scored for the visitors with Glennon replying for the hosts.

The Sheffield public were really enjoying their football, and over the festive period 33,000 travelled to Owlerton to see Wednesday beat Sunderland 8–0 on Boxing Day.

A grand total of 547,000 supporters had visited the homes of Wednesday and United during the season for League games with United having slightly the higher aggregate attendance by some 7,000. Football really was the lifeblood of the townsfolk who enjoyed the release on the terraces after working hard all week in the Steel City.

THE SHEFFIELD DERBY: DIVISION ONE 1912–13

The 1912–13 season would see another Wednesday legend leave Owlerton, in the form of Harry Chapman. Harry had played 299 times and scored 100 goals, with seven of them coming in the Sheffield derby. He had been with Wednesday 10 years, and had two Championship medals and one FA Cup medal to his name. Sadly, he would die just three years later from tuberculosis, aged 38.

It was also during this season that George Robertson presented the club with a mascot in the shape of an owl. The powers that be hoped this would not detract from their current nickname of the Blades, but, when the owl was placed in the roof of the North Stand in October 1912, Wednesday not only beat United 1–0, thanks to Glennon, but also had success over Liverpool and Oldham, and the owl stayed. From this point on, the club became known as the Owls, and United were welcome to claim the discarded Blades moniker.

The Blades nickname had described both Sheffield teams in the early years, especially when they played away, and the gentlemen of the press would also use the Cutlers. In the 1890s, you were either a Laneite or a Groveite, or if the two clubs were playing each other the newspapers would bill it as 'the clash of the Blades'. When Wednesday moved to Owlerton, they still regarded themselves as the Blades, but the success of the new Owl mascot would prompt a change, and not only of the club's nickname, but also of the ground they called home. The 1–0 defeat would be United's last Sheffield derby at Owlerton as the club changed the name to Hillsborough.

Wednesday also won the return leg at Bramall Lane 2–0 thanks to Robertson and McLean.

THE SHEFFIELD DERBY: DIVISION ONE 1913–14

Again, it was Wednesday who achieved the double over their city rivals: a goal by Glennon did the trick in front of 42,912 at Bramall Lane, a record attendance, with gate receipts totalling £1,192, and, in the return at the newly named Hillsborough, the Owls won 2–1 thanks to Glennon and McLean. The gate was a very impressive 39,000, so for the very first time the games had attracted over 80,000 paying customers.

When 43,050 came to Hillsborough to see Wednesday and Wolves fight out an FA Cup replay, with 12 minutes remaining, and the Owls winning 1–0, a sudden surge at the Penistone Road End of the ground saw the newly built retaining wall collapse, sending spectators and debris falling on to the fans below. The game was held up while 75 fans were taken to hospital. After a lengthy delay, the referee played out the remaining minutes, with Wolves minus their goalkeeper Peers, who had fainted at the sight of the injured and was in no fit state to continue. Wednesday held on to win, but Wolves put in a complaint to the FA saying the tie should be replayed; this was rejected and Wednesday went through, with the club compensating the injured fans to the tune of £500.

THE SHEFFIELD DERBY: DIVISION ONE 1914–15

Conflict in the Balkans plunged the country into war with Germany in 1914, but the FA decided to play out the season against the wishes of the majority of the country.

Wednesday and United met on 5 September 1914 at Bramall Lane with Wednesday winning 1–0, thanks to Wilson. On 2 January, the return match at Hillsborough ended 1–1 with Davies scoring for United and Wilson for Wednesday.

Although the fans in attendance did not know it then, this was to be the final Football League derby until 1919.

BETWEEN THE WARS

THE SHEFFIELD DERBY: DIVISION ONE 1919–20

After being starved of serious football for the past four seasons, the Sheffield public were again ready to resume the city rivalry, and on 27 September, at Hillsborough, Wednesday won 2–1 courtesy of Campbell and Gill, with Tummon scoring for United. The relief of the Sheffield public was plain to see and the attendance was in excess of 30,000. At the Lane, United won 3–0 with goals by Masterman, Kitchen and Tummon.

Now the Sheffield derby was put on hold for another six seasons but this time it had nothing to do with the Germans. Wednesday had been relegated, and it would be August 1926 before the Steel City rivals would meet again in the League. The two clubs did meet each other in the FA Cup of 1925 at Bramall Lane, when United won the game 3–2, and went on to lift the trophy beating Cardiff City 1–0 at Wembley.

Sheffield by 1925 was in the grip of gang warfare; some 40 years before the Shoreham and East Bank boys were gearing up to confront one another, it was probably the granddads of the soon-to-be OCS and BBC who got caught up in the fights that occurred most weekends in and around the city centre.

It had all started some 10 years earlier, when nearly 70,000 men were out of work, and at the mercy of the Board of Guardians, the predecessor of today's Social Security. Many fellows had that much time on their hands that drink seemed a solution to all their problems, and it was reported that many citizens of Sheffield had been cautioned for being in a state of drunkenness. The average man got about 30 shillings a week to keep his wife and kids, and to supplement their income many acted as bookies' runners. Of course, it had been illegal to gamble in the United Kingdom since 1853, but it was possible to phone a bet through to an agent. However, this method was only for the very wealthy, as few families back then had a phone in their home, with most folk even having to trek outside to use the toilet, which was often shared with all the neighbours.

It was not just betting on the horses that was rife. Betting on men having races and bare-knuckle fights was also popular, but the most lucrative was the tossing ring, where men would bet fortunes on the toss of a coin. These were situated at Tinsley, Wadsley and the Five Arches and the man in control would cream off around 2/6d in the pound. The most famous tossing ring was at Skye Edge and this led to the most savage gang battles in our city's history. People would travel from Barnsley, Doncaster and Rotherham, and it was even reported that the legendary Sheffield United goalkeeper Bill Foulke was a regular punter.

The police with the aid of the army, who were on the lookout for deserters from the First World War, descended on Skye Edge in force and the good folk of the Park looked on in amazement to see soldiers with bayonets drawn far from the front. No one escaped and, with the deserters rounded up, the others were dragged before the courts and fined.

In 1919, the Mooney Gang had taken control of the very profitable Skye Edge tossing ring, but this riled the Park Brigade who believed that they had the rights because they lived on the doorstep.

Heavily outnumbered, the Mooney firm lost control, and this led to tit-for-tat reprisals and the Sheffield gang wars were born. Many men on both sides were slashed with razors and shot at. Scores more carried life preservers, so called because these short heavy coshes, which were sometimes filled with lead, probably saved a few lives.

My mate Scotty told me that his granddad, Ernest, served a six-month custodial sentence for his part in the flare-ups. Ernest was a fully paid-up member of the Park Brigade and proud of it.

With the earnings from the tossing rings gone, many of the smaller gangs like the Neepsend Gas Tank Gang and others went about harassing the publicans and business people of the city. The city centre was rapidly becoming a no-go area for many law-abiding citizens. This all came to a head on the eve of the celebrations for Sheffield United returning with the FA Cup on Tuesday, 28 April 1925. As 10,000 people went wild when Billy Gillespie raised the Cup on the balcony of the town hall, the coroner was opening the inquest into the death of William Plommer who had been savagely beaten to death on Princess Street, near to Norfolk Bridge, by members of the Park Brigade. This led to an all-out war on Sheffield's gang culture. Well over 8,000 people crammed into Burngreave Cemetery to pay their respects to Mr Plommer, and a certain PJ Sillitoe was given the task of cleaning up the city. Sillitoe formed the Special Duties Squad, whose aim was to fight fire with fire, and by 1927 the job was done. There was the odd flare-up between the Smithfield and Junior Park Brigade, but nothing on the scale of previous years. A local boxing promoter, it was rumoured, unsuccessfully tried to get George Mooney, leader of the Mooney Gang, and Sam Garvin, leader of the Park Brigade, to fight for a £100 purse. It was also said that the crowd would have been bigger than any Cup tie between Wednesday and United.

THE SHEFFIELD DERBY: DIVISION ONE 1926–27

United won the first League meeting between the clubs for six years, at Hillsborough, by a score of 3–2 with Johnson (2) and Hoyland doing the damage; Trotter (?) scored for the Owls. The gate was a very good 43,282 and when Wednesday travelled to the Lane 59,555 watched United win 2–0 with Tunstall and Mercer getting the goals.

THE SHEFFIELD DERBY: DIVISION ONE 1927–28

It was off to the Lane to witness a 1–1 draw in front of 42,512 with Tunstall netting for the Blades and Trotter for the Owls. At

Hillsborough, 41,646 witnessed a 3–3 draw courtesy of Wilkinson (2) and Harper for Wednesday and Blair (2) and Partridge for United.

The clubs also played each other in the FA Cup this season, in the fifth round. The game at Hillsborough finished 1–1 with Wilkinson scoring for Wednesday and Partridge for United.

The game attracted a massive attendance of 57,076, while the replay at Bramall Lane crammed in 59,447, when United ran out easy winners 4–1, with Johnson becoming the first player to score a hat-trick in a derby game.

The four games had attracted a staggering 200,681 and it was now boom time as far as the Sheffield derby was concerned.

THE SHEFFIELD DERBY: DIVISION ONE 1928–29

Wednesday were again Champions in 1928–29 and turned United over 5–2 at Hillsborough, thanks to Hooper (2), Allen (2) and Rimmer, while United replied through Gibson and Tunstall. The attendance was 44,699, while at the Lane a crowd of 44,576 watched a 1–1 draw with Hooper scoring for the Owls and Phillipson for the Blades.

THE SHEFFIELD DERBY: DIVISION ONE 1929–30

Wednesday and United shared the spoils in the first derby of the season with the game at the Lane finishing 2–2, Tunstall (2) hitting the back of the net for United and Seed and Allen for Wednesday. The gate was 47,039 while, at Hillsborough, 54,459 saw a 1–1 draw thanks to Dunne for United and Burgess for Wednesday.

Wednesday had once again done back-to-back Championships, just as they had almost 30 years before and now had four to their name; the disappointment of a few years earlier was a distant memory and the crowds were the best they had ever been.

It was also in this season that the club became Sheffield Wednesday for the very first time. A meeting was held to officially change the name from The Wednesday Football Club, and the certificate was signed in London on 3 August 1929.

THE SHEFFIELD DERBY: DIVISION ONE 1930-31

Wednesday travelled to Bramall Lane as League Champions, and settled for a 1–1 draw with Gibson netting for United and Burgess for Wednesday. The return game at Hillsborough saw United win 3–1, thanks to Dunne, Oxley and Tunstall. The Owls' consolation came courtesy of Ball. Wednesday's hopes of a third straight League title did not materialise, although they did finish a very creditable third.

THE SHEFFIELD DERBY: DIVISION ONE 1931-32

The Owls had the better of the encounter at Hillsborough, winning 2–1 thanks to Ball and Stephenson, with Dunne scoring for United. At the Lane, it finished 1–1 with Barclay for the Blades and Ball for the Owls.

The attendance at Hillsborough was 35,823, while at the Lane it was 39,006, clearly showing that football in Sheffield was still pulling in the crowds even as the world entered a severe economic downturn.

THE SHEFFIELD DERBY: DIVISION ONE 1932-33

At Hillsborough, the rivals shared six goals as Ball, Rimmer and Hooper bulged the old onion bag for the Wednesday and Barclay, Oswald and Dunne replied for United. Over at the Lane Wednesday won 3–2 with Starling, Stephenson and Ball netting for Wednesday and Dunne scoring both United's goals. It was Ball's fifth goal in as many derbies and he was now chasing Andrew Wilson's record of 11.

THE SHEFFIELD DERBY: DIVISION ONE 1933-34

This was a very good year for the blue and white half of the city because United were relegated. Oddly enough, though, both Steel City derby fixtures would go the Blades' way; the first meeting saw the Owls lose to a single goal by Williams in front of 28,049 at Hillsborough, and they were then totally outplayed at the Lane, with Boyd hitting the only derby-day League hat-trick in the history of the fixture. He was complemented by Stacey and Pickering with

Wednesday's solitary contribution coming from Burrows. A crowd of 32,318 were in attendance to see this rout and, even though Wednesday tried with all their might to keep United in the top flight by allowing them to achieve another double, they only managed another 10 victories and finished bottom of the pile, thus ending a run of 37 seasons in the top flight.

The next Steel City derby game would not take place until the 1937–38 season, and this time it would be a Second Division fixture, as Wednesday soon followed their near neighbours out of the top flight. But, while the Sheffield derby had been put on hold, Wednesday had managed to add two notable achievements. First, in the shape of a new record attendance when 72,841 crammed into Hillsborough to witness an FA Cup tie with Manchester City. The match ended in a 2–2 draw, and, although Wednesday would lose the replay 2–0, the boys from Sheffield 6 only had to wait another 12 months to add another piece of silverware in the form of the FA Cup as Wednesday dispatched West Brom 4–2 in the Final.

When the euphoria of the Cup triumph had died down, many expected Wednesday to kick on and challenge for major honours, but this was not to be and, by the end of the 1936–37 season, Wednesday had joined the Blades in the Second Division.

THE SHEFFIELD DERBY: DIVISION TWO 1937–38

This was the season that the football-loving public of our great city witnessed the first ever Sheffield derby outside the top flight, on 16 October 1937, when the sides met at Hillsborough. United just edged it thanks to Eggleston. The crowd was a massive 52,523, and the return at the Lane was also watched by a very large crowd of 50,827. United made it another double when Barton and Dodds won it for the Blades; Drury scored for the Owls, but this was scant consolation as Wednesdayites drowned their sorrows in the local hostelries.

THE SHEFFIELD DERBY: DIVISION TWO 1938–39

With the Germans on the rampage again, the country was readying itself for another war. There was, however, the small matter of another two Steel City derbies before Wednesdayite and Unitedite would join forces again to fight Germany.

The first was played at Bramall Lane, and ended scoreless in front of 44,909. On 4 March 1939, most of the 48,983 in attendance at Hillsborough sang the praises of Fallon who hit the winner in the last 12 minutes to clinch the points for the Owls.

Wednesday and United had been neck and neck with the eventual Champions Blackburn Rovers all season, but it was the Owls who missed out, and the Blades joined Rovers in the top flight.

In September 1939, the Germans would invade Poland, and once more the British Empire would mobilise to confront tyranny, and the 1939–40 football season would be cut short after only a couple of games.

THE FORTIES AND FIFTIES

How the city had missed the derby encounters in the Football League, and, when the games resumed after the war, United were in the First Division and Wednesday were plying their trade in the Second. It was the Blades who finished the 1946–47 season on a high, after finishing sixth, while the Owls endured their worst ever League position and finished 20th, just avoiding the drop into regional football.

The 1947–48 season again saw the Blades top dogs, but Wednesday improved no end and finished fourth. The following year, it was United who helped restore the Steel City encounter by getting themselves relegated, and as a result most Sheffielders could not wait for the 1949–50 season to begin.

THE SHEFFIELD DERBY: DIVISION TWO 1949–50

This was one of the most breathtaking seasons the two clubs had yet witnessed. Wednesday had won the first encounter at Hillsborough thanks to goals by Jordan and Quigley with Hutchinson replying; the gate was 55,555 and who could blame them for turning up in their thousands, as this was the first encounter for well over 10 years. At Bramall Lane, United evened things up with a 2–0 victory, but it was not enough to dampen the spirits of all Wednesdayites, because, even though Brook and a chap called Warhurst made it a red day in front of 51,644, it was Wednesday who went on to clinch promotion by having a superior goal average of 0.008 of a goal.

Wednesday's stay with the elite only lasted 12 months, and on the last day of the 1950–51 season the Owls had to claw back four goals on Chelsea. A bumper crowd of 41,166 saw the Wednesday demolish Everton 6–0, but Chelsea netted four and down went the Owls, by 0.044 of a goal, to rejoin the Blades in Division Two.

THE SHEFFIELD DERBY: DIVISION TWO 1951–52

Once more the Sheffield derby was back on the sporting calendar, after a one-year hiatus, and there were also plenty of mini-derbies with the Yorkshire contingent now swelled to include not just the Sheffield sides, but also Leeds United, Hull City, Barnsley, Rotherham United and Doncaster Rovers.

Wednesday travelled to Bramall Lane in the first Steel City derby, and the crowd was again a huge one, 51,075. The Wednesdayites present saw the team get off to a flying start, scoring within two minutes, but by the hour mark it was level at 2–2, and in the last 30 minutes United scored a further five to record the highest ever derby score line of 7–3. On target for the Blades were Hawksworth (2), Brook (2), Ringstead (2) and Smith, with Woodhead (2) and Thomas hitting the back of the net for the Owls.

At Hillsborough, Wednesday were again humiliated and Ringstead (2) and Hutchinson saw to it that a debut derby goal by one Derek Dooley was scant consolation. This match was also witnessed by a record derby crowd of 65,384, but, although it was United's day in the Steel City games, it was Wednesday's season as the Owls returned to the top flight as Champions.

THE SHEFFIELD DERBY: DIVISION ONE 1953–54

It would be two more seasons before the rivalry resumed, and the two clubs, by this time, were far too close to the foot of the table to make the games enjoyable. United won the first encounter at the Lane 2–0 while Wednesday enjoyed a 3–2 triumph at Hillsborough.

The final League table would make grim reading for both clubs, however, as Wednesday finished 19th, and the Blades were one place below in 20th.

OWL VERSUS BLADE
THE SHEFFIELD DERBY: DIVISION ONE 1954–55

Wednesday dropped out of the top division in 1955 after United had once more achieved the double. In the first meeting, Waldock gave the Blades a 1–0 victory at the Lane, while in the return fixture Marriot scored a last-minute consolation after Ringstead and Cross had given United a two-goal lead.

I came into this Wednesday world halfway through the 1955–56 season while my future heroes were languishing in the Second Division. To make matters worse, while I was having my arse slapped for the very first time by some Blade-loving midwife, my team had been turned over in the County Cup at Hillsborough by United, to the tune of 5–2. I even thought that the nurses were taking the piss as I lay in my cot, but after this minor setback I knew I was born to be a blue.

THE SHEFFIELD DERBY: DIVISION TWO 1958–59

The Sheffield football public now had to wait until the 1958–59 season for hostilities to be renewed when, once more, Wednesday returned to the top flight as Champions. The 1950s was a period in the Owls history known as 'the Yo-Yo years' as promotion seemed inevitably to be followed by relegation, and the cycle continued. The encounter at Hillsborough resulted in the Owls winning 2–0 in front of 46,404, while, over at the Lane, Wednesday again tried in vain to let United join them in the top flight with a 1–0 loss, but Fulham had other ideas and squeezed United into third place to the dismay of all Wednesdayites.

The 40s and 50s had seen the Owls dominate the local scene, and, during the 11 seasons that spanned the period, Wednesday had finished higher in the League on no fewer than nine occasions. While I was blowing the candle out on my first birthday cake, the unfortunate Blades were treading the boards in the Second Division. I was nearly into my third year before the Sheffield derby was back on track, but again United had let the city down, and by 1960 we had left them floundering in the lower league.

The 50s saw the return of gang culture to the streets of Sheffield with the emergence of the Teddy Boy, who liked nothing better than smashing up cinemas. This may come as a shock to any followers of Leeds United, who for many years have classed themselves as the original seat smashers. The Teds, as they were called, enjoyed themselves in such places as the Barleycorn and the Locarno, where they would rock'n'roll to the likes of Buddy Holly, Bill Haley and Gene Vincent. The dress included tight-fitting jeans or drainpipe trousers, crepe-soled shoes or winkle-pickers with the customary velvet-collared drape jacket. Their main rivals were the college-type Beatniks, who were a more peace-loving outfit than the rampaging Teds, and their taste in music was more jazz and the Blues.

THE SWINGING SIXTIES

The 60s would herald a new dawn for the city of Sheffield, as the doom and gloom of putting the city back into shape after parts of it, including Bramall Lane, had been decimated by German bombs. The whole place was changing for the better and, while new housing was springing up in the suburbs, the old back-to-back houses were going to be swept away.

THE SHEFFIELD DERBY: THE FA CUP QUARTER-FINAL 1960

The first game up in this decade was an FA Cup quarter-final tie, and many Wednesdayites flocked to Bramall Lane hoping for victory; they were not disappointed because a Wilkinson double did the business and saw the Owls through to the semis.

The result really pissed off the Blades because scuffles broke out as many Wednesdayites were leaving the Shoreham. In previous years, red and blue had stood side by side at both Hillsborough and Bramall Lane, but times were a-changing.

Wednesday, at the beginning of the 60s, certainly held the upper hand in the city, and finished fifth in the First Division, while United just missed out on promotion from the Second. In addition, the Owls had a victory over their fierce rivals in the Cup quarter-final at the Lane, in front of a very lively 59,692. United consoled themselves with another victory in the County Cup Final when this time Rotherham United were firmly dealt with, and so, as we waved goodbye to the 1959–60 season, those of us over at Sheffield 6 were strutting round town in the knowledge that Wednesday were once more top of the city hit parade.

The 1960–61 season saw Wednesday chase Tottenham Hotspur all the way to the Championship and settle for their highest League position since last winning the title back in 1930.

On the FA Cup front, both clubs steadily progressed to the latter stages, but this time, when the draw for the last eight was made, another Steel City quarter-final was not forthcoming. Wednesday drew Burnley at Hillsborough, while United faced a tough trip to St James' Park to face Newcastle United.

The Owls were held to a 0–0 draw in front of 55,000 while United were victorious in their tangerine shirts thanks to a Billy Russell hat-trick. When the draw was made for the semi-finals, United got Leicester City, while the winners of the replay at Turf Moor faced Tottenham Hotspur. Excitement at the prospect of an all-Sheffield FA Cup Final began to grow in the city, and Wednesday must have been confident because they had already triumphed in the League 4–3 at Burnley. Sadly, it was not to be, and the Lancashire club won 2–0. It was now left to the Blades to carry the city flag all the way to Wembley.

The first two games finished goalless and, when the teams met for the third time in nine days, Leicester City won 2–0 to break the hearts of all Unitedites, who must have been longing for a trip to the twin towers. But this had been a good season for the football-loving public of Sheffield and once more the Steel City derby was back on the agenda.

THE SHEFFIELD DERBY: DIVISION ONE 1961–62

The 1961–62 season kicked off brightly with Wednesday winning three out of four of their opening games, and Wednesday were in a very confident mood as they travelled to the Lane, but it was the Blades, and Doc Pace, who did the damage in their 1–0 victory. The crowd that day was 38,497, with first blood to United.

The following month, the Owls were enjoying the company of Roma in the Fairs Cup, while the Blades were making steady progress in the League Cup.

★ ★ ★

While I was embarking on my first steps through the education system, my father and his mates were enjoying life in the fast lane. Sheffield was a very lively place, and the centre had just about been restored to the way it was before it suffered at the hands of the German bombers. One such famous Sheffield landmark was the Marples public house that stood on the corner of Fitzalan Square. This pub was originally called the Old London Mart, but many knew it locally as the Marples. Sadly, it was bombed on 12 December 1940 with the loss of over 60 lives. It was restored in 1959 and became a popular meeting place through the 60s and 70s before it finally closed its doors a few years ago. The sad part in all this is that it is now a fucking German motorbike shop! Those in the planning department ought to hang their heads in shame when allowing this once-famous Sheffield landmark to be surrendered to the Germans.

As we moved into 1962, Wednesday had progressed to meet Barcelona in the next round of the Fairs Cup. In the FA Cup, both clubs progressed to the fourth round, but, before Cup fever could once again grip the citizens of Sheffield, there was the small matter of another derby encounter. The blue half of the city was confident that the Owls could avenge the earlier defeat at Bramall Lane, but it was not to be, and once again it was that man Pace who was a thorn in Wednesday's side as he grabbed both United's goals in their 2–1 success.

In the Fairs Cup, Wednesday enjoyed a stunning 3–2 Hillsborough victory over the might of Barcelona, but went out of Europe 4–3 on aggregate after succumbing 2–0 in the second leg.

THE SHEFFIELD DERBY: DIVISION ONE 1962–63

Everyone was looking for the clubs to push on, and bring a bit of silverware back to the city at long last as the dawn of the 1962–63 season broke the clouds of a long boring football-less summer. I myself was exiled in Shirecliffe during this period, just a stone's throw away from the temple of the gods that was Hillsborough, but at the tender age of six I did not figure in my father's match-day ritual of enjoying a beer with his mates before and after the game.

Both teams enjoyed a bright start to the season, and, as 6 October approached, which would bring another encounter between the clubs, this time at Bramall Lane, it was Wednesday who just edged out United 14 points to 13. The game at the Lane ended in stalemate, 2–2, with G Shaw and Pace netting for the Blades and Layne (2) for the Owls.

The months of October and November were disastrous for the Owls as they failed to win a single game, and as we moved into 1963 things could only improve on the football front. Wednesday did manage to get back to winning ways with a 3–0 victory at West Brom, in one of the few games played in the month of January due to atrocious winter weather.

The season kick-started itself at the end of February with both Wednesday and United enjoying a modicum of Cup success. The Owls run was short-lived, though, as Arsenal dumped them out at Highbury, while United again enjoyed a trip to the fifth round before suffering at the hands of Southampton.

As the season came to a finale, it was left to the Steel City derby to bring the 1962–63 campaign to an end when the Blades travelled to Hillsborough. It was Wednesday this time who had the better of things, winning 3–1, with David Layne (2) and McAnearney turning things around after Pace had given United an early lead.

A funny aside to the season was that Wednesday had been invited by the Fairs Cup Committee to take part, once more, in the Fairs Cup, along with Birmingham City and Everton, but the English FA and Football League requested that Burnley and Sheffield United should join Everton. The Fairs Cup people did not take too kindly to the arrogance of those from England and only Everton were allowed to play. Wednesday and United had already had talks with the Europeans, and it was decided that the clubs would alternate with Wednesday going first and United enjoying European football in 1963–64. The following season, the Fairs Cup Committee once again invited the Owls, but this time the English FA and Football League gave their blessing, and instead of twiddling their thumbs at home Wednesdayites enjoyed another jaunt into Europe. If it had not been for those beautiful people at the FA, Sheffield United would have been enjoying European football for the first time, but it was not all doom and gloom for the Blades, as they were now free to concentrate on winning the County Cup.

THE SHEFFIELD DERBY: DIVISION ONE 1963–64

It was now my turn to add my name to the millions who have entered our famous arena, and it would not be long before I tasted the atmosphere of a Steel City derby for the first time. Wednesday played at the Lane on 14 September, and enjoyed a share of the spoils once more when playing out an entertaining 1–1 draw. By the end of the month, United had only lost one game and had opened up a six-point margin on the Owls.

Wednesday picked up and, by the time I had celebrated my eighth birthday, were climbing the table. I'd probably been to about half-a-dozen games so far, but the thought of being involved in my first ever Sheffield derby had not really crossed my mind.

As we approached the big day, on 18 January, the Owls were reeling from a shock Cup exit at the hands of Newport County, witnessed by a crowd of 42,898, including my good self. The Owls produced a magnificent performance that had them dancing all the way along Penistone Road. Wilkinson (2) and Layne had done the trick on my debut.

The following week, United entertained Swansea Town in the fourth round of the FA Cup, and the boys from school asked me to tag along, but I knew that my father would not let me go to *that* place, and so, if I was to pull a fast one, I would need financing. I told him I was going to watch the reserves at Hillsborough, and he happily forked over the cash. With money in my pocket, this eight-year-old made his way to the Lane to cheer on Ivor Allchurch and his Swansea team. We watched the game from the Bramall Lane End, and we roared every Swansea attack. The Welsh supporters must have wondered what these four ankle-biters were doing in amongst them but we were just soaking up the magic of the FA

Cup. The game ended 1–1 and the Swans asked if we were attending the replay. If my dad found out I'd been to the Lane, I'd have my arse tanned, so a trip to South Wales was a definite no-no. In the end, some neighbour grassed me up and my backside was slapped, not so much for going to the dark side, but because I'd lied to my father and that was unforgivable.

THE SHEFFIELD DERBY: DIVISION ONE 1964–65

The build up to the 1964–65 was extra special to me because my father had given his permission for me to travel to Bramall Lane for the derby, but this had to wait until after Christmas because the game was pencilled in for the day after New Year's Day. I was now nine years old and still living in the Wednesday heartland of Shirecliffe. I would travel down Herries Road with my best mates Wesley, Christopher and John.

By this time, Sheffield was in the grips of the swinging sixties and the older lads such as Ernest and Graham would head for the bright lights of the capital whenever the Owls were visiting the likes of Chelsea, Spurs or Arsenal. Once in London, they would discard their bags in the left luggage and head for the game; win, lose or draw, they would then head back to the station and have a quick wash and brush-up, change into their finest sharp suits and hit the hot spots of Soho and Carnaby Street. These Northern lads had to have their wits about them because it was also during this period that the streets of London had more gangsters than we had chip-shops, so getting a bit too familiar with a bit of Cockney skirt could get you well and truly stitched up.

Back in Sheffield, our night scene consisted of the Esquire Club, but that was alcohol free! The King Mojo was out on its own as the number-one club for the youth of the city, and the Black Cat was not far behind. There was also the Locarno, which only a few years earlier had been a haven for the Teddy Boys. Now Elvis and Eddie had been replaced by the Kinks and Small Faces, and the smell of Brylcreem had gone for ever, unless you happened to visit the Barleycorn on Cambridge Street.

Wednesday had started the season brightly under the guidance of new manager Alan Brown, with victories against Blackburn and Arsenal, but on the seafront Blackpool had inflicted a first defeat.

The Owls were in confident mood on the day of the first derby game. The crowd was a respectable 32,684, including my very own gang of four. While the older supporters were enjoying their pre-match pints in the surrounding hostelries, and paying around 6d for the privilege, myself and the boys were scanning the match-day programme, which incidentally cost the same as that foul-tasting liquid the oldies were supping, and parked ourselves on our usual vantage point, which was that ledge that ran down to the corner where the East Bank meets the North Stand.

The game itself was like all local derbies, a tense affair. Wednesday had the better of the opening 20 minutes, but failed to capitalise on it, and as the game petered out towards half-time a certain Alan Birchenall put the Blades in front on his debut. After the break and the customary cup of Bovril, Wednesday pressed hard for the equaliser, and came close when Fantham, Quinn and Finney brought the best out of Hodgkinson, but it was the Blades, and the man they nicknamed the Sherman Tank, Birchenall, who grabbed the headlines when he headed in United's second from a corner. To make matters even worse for the Owls, Pearson was booked for a deliberate trip on Joe Shaw.

After the game, United had gone top six, while Wednesday floundered in 14th place, so it was the red side of the city that was smiling for once. As we walked away from Hillsborough and past the cinema on Wordsworth Avenue, people were already queuing for the latest offering to be shown on the silver screen, which included The Beatles' *A Hard Day's Night* and the legendary *How the West Was Won*.

Well, this was my very first Sheffield derby defeat, and it left a bitter taste in my mouth. We were not happy at all until we got back to the Five Arches and got out the tennis ball, with a view to replaying the game outside the pub. This time, the Owls won convincingly, and our half-time refreshments of a bag of crisps and a bottle of pop, courtesy of my gran, went down well.

Despite the fact that we'd been beaten by the Blades, I could not wait for my next visit to Hillsborough and would be constantly glancing through my ever-increasing pile of programmes. It was like a drug, and in September 1964 I nearly overdosed with six home games in the month.

After the defeat at Hillsborough, Wednesday desperately needed to go to the Lane and regain some pride. The Owls were not doing too badly in the League, and in 18 games the boys from Sheffield 6 had only tasted defeat at Manchester United, Aston Villa and Spurs, while Chelsea were the only club to secure maximum points at Hillsborough.

As Father Christmas paid his annual visit in 1964, we had the Beatles with 'I Feel Fine' topping the charts at Christmas, their sixth number one. The popular public houses in and around the town were the infamous Black Swan, Barleycorn and the Buccaneer. The Adelphi, where the original meeting to form Wednesday Football Club was held in 1867, was especially popular for Wednesdayites, and so were the many pubs that stretched along Penistone and Infirmary Roads. Before you were ready to hit the pubs and clubs, you could pick up a ready-made suit from the likes of Barney Goodman for around £9, and for the same price you could enjoy a family holiday at Pontins in Prestatyn. Bloody hell! My summer holidays were spent playing on Shirecliffe tip, or, if we were really lucky, Gran would take us across the city to Millhouses Park, but usually we were bunged a couple of bob and headed for the open-air baths in Longley Park.

We were now into 1965 and a trip across to Bramall Lane was just around the corner for most Wednesdayites, except me. My father would not let me go across the city after all because I had been a naughty boy, and had been caught shoplifting in Woolworth's. Most of the kids that went to my school were bang at it in good old Woolies, whether in town or at Hillsborough Corner. They had introduced self-service and us ankle-biters had taken them up on their offer – literally. Looking back, I cannot believe I'd been stupid enough to jeopardise my trip to the Lane for a handful of pick and mix. While the rest of my mates were catching the Shirecliffe flyer to town, I was stuck in Gran's watching *Grandstand*, while Granddad was knocking out the zeds after returning from the Kings Head. I'd been to my other grandparents, at 120 Hoyland Road, in the morning and loved knocking the ball about in the back yard. Granddad would be puffing away on his pipe while carefully cutting up the old newspapers into squares, which he would thread through a piece of string and hang behind the toilet door. I think that is where I get my artistic ability from, watching Granddad George perform some kind of shithouse origami.

They also had a coal cellar, and it was my job to count the bags of coal that the nutty-slack man deposited down the coal chute because Gran did not trust the bastard. I didn't mind, but I would re-emerge as black as the ace of spades and be thrown in the tin bath for a good scrubbing.

The game was now under way and I was wondering how my mates were getting on in my absence. Wednesday were lucky early on when Birchenall had a goal-bound shot cleared off the line by Mobley. The Owls were attacking the Shoreham, and the game was more than livening up. With 32 minutes on the clock, Birchenall put United ahead against the run of play. Wednesday drew level soon after when Hickton powered one home on 40 minutes, and the teams went into the break level.

Wednesday upped the tempo in the second half, but it was the Blades, through Matthewson, who regained the advantage. Then Birchenall put Jones clean through and he missed an absolute sitter. This miss would come back to haunt the Blades as Wednesday got their just reward when Fantham equalised, and, with only seven minutes remaining, he slotted home the winner to send the Wednesdayites crazy.

While I had been exiled in Sheffield 5, my boys had done me proud, and we had done the old enemy good and proper. Unfortunately, Wednesday added only one more away victory during the rest of season, and that was at Blackburn. On the other hand, the home form was good which guaranteed a top-eight finish.

On the Sheffield front, Wednesdayites would frequent the Albert on Cambridge Street and sink pint after pint of jungle juice, the popular name at the time for a pint of Stones Bitter. When they were not brawling at the regular dances in the City Hall, they would head further down Cambridge Street and use the Barleycorn, which had its fair share of Irish customers. The Paddies would come in and down a pint, then place the upturned glass on the bar and offer to fight anyone present. These bully-boy tactics used to put the wind up some members of the Saturday-night crowd, but Ernest told me of one Wednesdayite, called Big Dal, who would have more Paddies on their arses than anyone around.

Sheffield could be one hell of a rough place and some of the establishments were not for the faint-hearted. One such place was Glossop Road Baths, where they would cover the pool with wood and turn it into a dancehall come the weekend. Trouble would always be plentiful in and around the area, and it was not uncommon for people to fight and use cellar grates as weapons. Ernest also told me of a night in the Brown Bear in 1960 after Wednesday had defeated United in the quarter-final of the FA Cup at Bramall Lane. Peter Swan and Doc Pace had been at each other's throat all game, and, with Swanny being a no-nonsense centre-half, he was kicking lumps out of the skilful Pace. He kept him under wraps all afternoon, nullifying him as a force; later that night, when Ernest and the lads popped into the Bear for a pint, who should be stood at the bar having a right chinwag and a pint but Peter Swan and Doc Pace.

THE SHEFFIELD DERBY: DIVISION ONE 1965–66

Wednesday went into the season with high hopes of building on the eighth position from the previous season. United, on the other hand, were confident of retaining the County Cup, which they held after defeating Doncaster Rovers. It was also the year that the World Cup was coming to England, and Hillsborough was chosen as one of the venues. The Owls kicked off the campaign in a change of strip and the stripes had been replaced by a blue body with white sleeves.

In one of the games leading up to the derby, Wilf Smith had been named the Owls' first ever substitute at Old Trafford, but it was

David Ford who had the honour of being the first to take to the field, when he replaced the injured Don Megson at Sunderland.

Away from football, a semi-detached house in Stocksbridge would have set you back about three grand at this time, and the ladies of our good city were also getting excited as *The Sound of Music* was due to be released on 3 October.

I was again exiled on the day of the first derby, and Bramall Lane was out of bounds, but many Wednesdayites did make the trip across the city and swelled the gate to an impressive 35,655. Strong sunshine and a stiff breeze welcomed the players. United had the better of the opening exchanges with Jones going close, but as the game wore on Wednesday sprang into life. Barry Wagstaff then became the first ever substitute in the Sheffield derby, but the game was becoming very scrappy as it moved into the half-time break. United had a goal cancelled out because Reece was offside, but, when the game resumed for the second half, United came out the stronger and it was inevitable that Birchenall would add to his growing list of goals against the Owls. He netted his fourth goal in three games and he was fast becoming a right pain in the arse. United had once again stolen the spoils, and to make matters worse they sat proudly at the top of the League while Wednesday were in a lowly 15th place. Again we had been done by our old enemy.

It was not nice at school when we returned from a derby game, because the playground would be covered in blood due to the kids scrapping, and with Unitedites at ours being a bit thin on the ground they took a bit of a beating. The kids were only emulating what was going on in the football grounds, because hooliganism was rife up and down the country. Football fans were rampaging and smashing up city centres every week, and Sheffield was no exception.

My very first experience of football violence was at Hillsborough in November, just three days after my 10th birthday, when those men with the funny voices (Liverpool) had come on to the East Bank and Wednesdayites got a bit pissed off that we were losing 2–0. Fights broke out, and over 13 supporters were arrested, including one for assaulting a police officer, who had his nose broken. The average fine was around the £20 mark, but the fan that broke the policeman's nose was remanded in custody. The fans rampaged after the game, and the ones with the funny voices smashed up their train on the way back to Merseyside.

There was also trouble around the country. At Brentford, Millwall fans threw a hand grenade into the opposing fans, but fortunately for all those concerned it was a dud. And at Old Trafford Manchester United supporters attacked the Blackburn team bus.

Back on the field, Wednesday achieved victories over Arsenal, Blackburn, Fulham and Sunderland, but only four were drawn during this period, and the Owls tasted 11 defeats. United had faired a little better, but Wednesday were doing quite well in the FA Cup after victories over Reading, Newcastle United and Huddersfield. The Blades had gone out to Wolves; mind you, they had reached the County Cup Final after defeating Barnsley, so it was not all gloom for your average Blade.

Wednesday were on a roll now and, with the prospect of a trip to Wembley on the horizon, the Owls went into the derby full of anticipation that they could avenge the defeat at Bramall Lane. My pals and I made our way to our usual vantage point, and cheered as the teams were announced.

The crowd was 34,045 and the Kop was full to bursting. We didn't have to wait long as Fantham screamed one in from 20 yards after only seven minutes. Wednesday were in complete control now, and how they never added to the tally I'll never know, but against the run of play United scored, with our old foe Mr Birchenall scrambling home the loose ball in the 39th minute.

The game was end to end in the second half, and, as we moved into the last 20 minutes, the next goal would probably decide the game. Once again, it was the scourge of Sheffield 6, Alan Birchenall, who ran on to a through ball before slotting it past the helpless Springett. Wednesday pressed for the equaliser, and got their just deserts in the 74th minute when Eustace headed home from a corner, and the spoils again were shared. We settled for a 2–2 draw, which was not the result we were hoping for but at least we had not lost.

After that game, the League season kind of whimpered out,

although Wednesday did make it to the FA Cup Final, after a famous Villa Park victory over Chelsea in the semi, but defeat against Everton, especially after being 2–0 up, was not a happy experience for this 10-year-old. England, at least, did go on and win the World Cup, so as we waved goodbye to another season I was full of anticipation that next year was going to be the year of the Owl.

Sheffield was still in the grip of Beatlemania, who only three years earlier had been persuaded by Pete Stringfellow to play the Azena at Gleadless. It cost him just over £100 to put it on, and they played to a packed house. The date of the gig was February 1963, and two months later they notched up their first number one with 'From Me to You'.

A new venue called the Heartbeat was opened in the city, where, for five shillings, you could wine, dine and dance. If you fancied a bit of the orient, the Rickshaw on West Street became the first ever Chinese restaurant in the city to hold an alcohol licence. When the pubs closed, the lads would head for the Chinese, but a chow mein and fried rice was not really on their minds; it was the fact that they could booze after hours without paying to go into a club.

After the disappointment of the previous season, which had soured in more ways than one after I had queued for semi-final tickets, and then got left at home. I was not going to make the same mistakes again. Added to this was the fact that Gran had promised that Granddad would accompany me on my travels for a very first Wednesday away game, if we were lucky enough to have a Cup run and be drawn away from Hillsborough. It would just be my luck that we'd go out in the first round at home.

THE SHEFFIELD DERBY: DIVISION ONE 1966–67

United had lost their first four games before securing their first points in a 1–0 victory over Fulham, and, on the eve of the Sheffield derby, had only eight points, compared to Wednesday's magnificent 10.

Wednesday had Sam Ellis, Graham Pugh and Jim McCalliog making their first derby appearance. Like all derby games, this one started slowly, but sprang into life after seven minutes when Woodward put the

Blades into the lead. Jones scored soon after to put United two up in the first 20 minutes. Wednesday were now shaken into life, and came close on several occasions, while at the other end Springett was doing his utmost to keep the likes of Jones and Birchenall at bay. Graham Pugh on his derby debut pulled one back just before half-time, so there was some hope of pulling it round after the half-time interval.

The game produced little chances after the break but, just when we thought all was lost, Jim McCalliog, another Wednesday derby-day debutant, saved the day when he popped one in with just over 20 minutes remaining.

At the club, Wednesday had a new mascot called Ozzie Owl, while, off the pitch, before the second Sheffield derby, Wednesdayites had been busy writing offensive slogans around the Bramall Lane ground.

Hooliganism was now at fever pitch around the country; Derek Dougan was attacked by a spectator at Millwall, and when the Owls visited Burney several coaches had their windows put through, showering the occupants with glass. Wednesday were also having their fair share of problems, and many coaches were bricked as they journeyed up either Halifax or Penistone Road. As a result of the spiralling violence, the Minister for Sport Denis Howell wanted to get tough and decided to ban offensive weapons, such as banners, bottles and cans, from football grounds. There was also talk of replacing the terraces with seats, and giving all games a certificate like those at the cinema. This would mean that games with the most potential for violence could be rated X, meaning that only over-18s could attend.

Wednesday were just above United in the table on the day of the second instalment of the derby, but it was the Blades, thanks to Bill Punton, who came out on top. Punton would score the only goal of the game to the delight of most of the 43,490 present.

THE SHEFFIELD DERBY: DIVISION ONE 1967–68

This season introduced the skinhead to the terraces, and Wednesday and United had their fair share of these boot boys. When they were not rampaging around the terraces of Hillsborough and Bramall

Lane, they would congregate in the city centre, with the favourite hang-outs being Pond Street, Castlegate and the newly opened Hole in the Road. The favourite uniform of the 'skins', as they became known, consisted of the Ben Sherman or Fred Perry shirt, Levi jeans, with customary turn-up, the must-have braces and the heavy industrial boot or Doc Martens. If you were really in the money, a sheepskin coat would be your crowning glory. They would seek out their main combatant, the greasers or greabos, just like the mods had done with the rockers, but the skins had another enemy in the shape of the ever-increasing Asian population that had settled in the east of Sheffield. Attracted by the steel industry, and the jobs associated with it, many immigrants from the Indian sub-continent, and also countries such as Aden, came to the city, and the majority set up home in the east-end neighbourhoods such as Attercliffe, Brightside, Darnall and Tinsley. So-called 'Paki-bashing' became a sport of choice for many Sheffield skins during the late 1960s and early 70s, and many a foray down Attercliffe Common was made by those seeking guaranteed confrontation.

On the football front, Wednesday travelled to the Lane for the first encounter which proved to be a lively one, both on and off the terraces. As the game kicked off, more fans were being ejected as rival fans clashed, but the majority of the 36,258 sat back and enjoyed an end-to-end encounter. The first half ended without either side breaking the deadlock, and, as the game limped towards another derby stalemate, big John Ritchie broke the deadlock with 15 minutes remaining; this was to be the Owls day, and if truth be known these days on enemy soil were few and far between. This was only their 10th victory away from home since that very first League meeting back in 1893, while the Blades had enjoyed 14 victories at Hillsborough and Olive Grove.

After that successful trip to the Lane we were now gearing up for the visit of Sheffield United to honour a Wednesday legend. This was our chance to say a final farewell to probably the greatest goalkeeper ever to play for Sheffield Wednesday.

Ron Springett had been a great servant for the Owls and had played for us on 384 occasions and for England 33 times. Indeed, if it had not been for another favourite son of Sheffield, Gordon Banks, our Ron would have played in the World Cup in '66.

A crowd of 23,070 turned up to honour one of our longest-serving players, and the Owls won, thanks to Whitham, Ritchie and Eustace while Reece and Woodward replied for the Blades. Ron played until half-time when he was replaced in goal by his brother Peter. Amazingly, he then appeared in the famous blue and white after he came on as substitute to replace Jack Whitham.

As Old Father Time turned the page from 1967 to 1968, Wednesday sat comfortably in fifth place, while United were bottom and fans of the two teams now geared themselves up for the next instalment of the Steel City derby.

This game finished like many more before them. Hodgkinson had been outstanding in the United goal and restricted Wednesday to only one goal, which was scored by Johnny Fantham. United then equalised through Hill, and the game ended in a 1–1 draw. Something, however, was missing from this game, and it delighted all the Wednesdayites; United had gone and done it again by transferring two of their brightest stars in Jones and Birchenall. With relegation staring the Blades in the face, the board at the Lane had gone for the easy option and profited from the sale. Unitedites were incensed and had been kicked where it hurts in their darkest hour.

THE SEVENTIES

Our first encounter against our old rivals in the new decade was a tribute to long-serving Owls defender Gerry Young who had served the club so well over a number of years. The game ended 3–3 with Whitham (2) and Warboys scoring for the Owls, and Dearden, Currie and Staniforth for the Blades. Sporadic outbreaks of off-the-field revelry marred the game to an extent, but we will return to that later, and, as the first full season of a new decade opened, the Steel City braced itself for the first derby game in the Second Division since 1959.

THE SHEFFIELD DERBY: DIVISION TWO 1970–71

It was at this game that, as a 14-year-old, I was parading round Bramall Lane with a white coat on, and a tray hanging off my shoulders. It was going to be my best pay day ever, and the dozy old sod who calculated your drinks and boxes of wagon wheels was well off the mark in his estimation of what these Shirecliffe and ex-Shirecliffe boys had secreted away. It was a 'one from them one for you' policy that we had adopted, if you know what I mean.

Bloody hell, it was well before kick-off and I'd replenished my empty tray on numerous occasions from the little storeroom that was nestled away under the cricket pavilion. One or two of the boys who had been brazen enough to go on the Shoreham or Bramall Lane End came back with empty trays and penniless. Myself and my old mate Wesley were too clever and stayed pitch-side, working side by side, and making sure their money was in our hands before we handed over the goods, but some of the Blades on the Shoreham were that thick that they never checked their change.

Kids were coming back and telling of fighting on the Shoreham, but Wes and I were too busy scamming the customers to worry about football violence. We saw no profit whatsoever in kicking the shit out of one another while there was money to be made. How times had changed four years down the line, when I exchanged my white smock for a denim jacket and bovver boots.

As the game kicked off, I placed myself out of harm's way and continued making money throughout the proceedings, just to the right of the massed Wednesday supporters. Many Wednesdayites had gone on the Shoreham, and our boys did more than sing and chant, unlike their counterparts had done at Hillsborough six months earlier.

On the field, Colquhoun and Dearden had put United into a commanding 2–0 lead, but the Owls rallied in the second half, and goals by Craig and Sinclair had brought the scores level. In my excitement, I nearly lost the contents of my overloaded tray. But I knew something would come along and spoil the day, and it did, in the shape of John bloody Tudor. Tudor, who was on as a substitute, hit the winner in the 73rd minute. I consoled myself with the knowledge that United might have come away with both points, but yours truly had fleeced them left, right and centre.

By the return game on 12 April 1971, the country had gone decimal and it was now 70p to get into Baileys. The game itself was a 0–0 draw, the first time ever in a derby game at Hillsborough, and the police made 13 arrests, mainly for fighting in and around the ground. Those unfortunate enough to have their collars felt copped for a fine around the £35 mark. A crowd of some 47,592 watched the game, and this was to be our last meeting of any note until December 1979 by which time we had both dropped to the depths of the Third Division.

Sheffield was again going through another transitional period and the city was now tram free. The Pond Street and Bridge Street bus stations were becoming battlegrounds for warring football supporters most Saturday afternoons. The city also had a new landmark, which was aptly named the Hole in the Road, complete with its famous fish tank. This too saw its fair share of confrontations between Wednesday and United fans.

1971–72: The Owls and Blades played a benefit match at Bramall Lane which ended 2–2. Woodward and Currie bulged the onion bag for the Blades, and Downes and Prendergast replied for the Owls.

1972–73: Another benefit game at the Lane saw 23,540 turn up to watch old boy David Ford score for United, while Joicey netted for Wednesday.

1973–74: Hillsborough was the venue for the County Cup Final, United's favourite trophy, and the Owls won 4–3 on penalties after the game had finished goalless. The crowd was not bad as these matches go, with 18,869 turning up.

1974–75: Wednesday and United never faced each other this season, which was a very rare occurrence; since their first meeting, 85 years earlier, there had only been eight seasons when the Owls and the Blades did not cross swords in one form or another.

1975–76: A benefit match was played at the end of the season, but only 6,495 turned up, and the game finished goalless. It was a game for Harry Latham, but the Blades could not have rated him very highly if the poor attendance was any guide.

1976–77: A County Cup semi-final meeting at the Lane attracted a rather poor attendance of only 6,985. Wednesday lost the game 2–0, thus ending their grip on this illustrious trophy.

1977–78 and 1978–79: No meetings took place on the field, which meant that the fans never got the opportunity to wage war on each other, apart from the odd skirmish if both clubs happened to play at home on the same day.

STEEL CITY RIVALS

THE SHEFFIELD DERBY: DIVISION THREE 1979-80

It was now the 1979–80 season and my season ticket had set me back a whopping great £21.50, which was a hell of a lot of beer vouchers in 1979! It was the first meeting of the Steel City clubs in the Third Division, and the last of the decade. Everyone, and I mean *everyone*, in Sheffield had been looking forward to this day for nearly 10 years, and the city just could not wait. This was the game we'd been waiting for since April 1971, when the Owls and Blades last met in the Sheffield derby.

United started the season like a house on fire, winning eight out of nine, to sit proudly at the top of the table. The diehards at the Lane were none too pleased after the powers that be ditched the traditional red and white stripes for what can only be described as a no-entry sign in reverse; probably it was telling them that there'd be no entry back to the Second Division.

The start of this long-awaited season kicked off, literally, with a visit to our near neighbours in Hull for a League Cup tie, and Wednesday started with another good performance, on and off the field, winning the game 2–1. Off the field – although that might not be strictly accurate – a pitch invasion by Wednesdayites, which led to them attacking the home end, caused the club to hit back at its rowdy element with the slogan 'Hooliganism is not Wednesdayism'. Most Owls fans took this on board, but omitted the word *not*!

The Owls progressed on aggregate to round two, while our sorry neighbours had been dumped on their arses by good old Doncaster Rovers. The first League game saw Big Jack take his charges to Barnsley, and Wednesday fans enjoyed another victory, this time by a 3–0 scoreline.

Once more, the ugly face of football hooliganism was on show after Wednesday's 3–0 home defeat to Blackburn Rovers. The rowdies in the North Stand had their cushions confiscated after littering the pitch with them following a dismal Owls performance. The average age of these hooligans must have been near the 60 mark, so probably our new slogan was directed at them.

The Owls were dismissed from the League Cup after a frightening visit to Maine Road, where, despite going ahead thanks to a Mark Smith penalty, two late goals were conceded to us out of the competition. The reception we got after the game was hostile to say the least, and Moss Side is not a place for the fainthearted. Mind you, we'd given them some stick at Hillsborough in the first leg, so it was only payback time.

By the end of September, United had added another 10 points to their tally, while Wednesday had just managed six. To add to this, we'd endured another night-time visit to Millwall, but this time, unlike 1976, when we'd travelled by minibus and got totally battered, we chose the safe option of the supporters' coach. The programme notes for this game told you not to arrive too early, and not to park your coach in the surrounding streets; only a driver with suicidal tendencies would plant his bus on the Old Kent Road. It also went on to tell you that you would be under police supervision on your arrival, and would be escorted into the ground, although it neglected to mention the bit about where you would come under a barrage of various missiles. What made matters worse was Mark Smith put Wednesday in front from the penalty spot, like he'd done at City, and we all know what awaited us after that one and we'd lost.

By half-time, we were behind, and for a few moments the missile throwing stopped, but when Hornsby stunned the home crowd it was tin-helmet time again. Then Wednesday legend Roger Wylde made matters even worse as the Owls went 3–2 in front, but Millwall rallied and the game ended 3–3. Now we had to get home in one piece, and run the gauntlet from the terrace to the coach. I cannot really remember if the coach returned to Sheffield with its windows intact, but one thing I do know is I'd just paid £3 for the privilege. In the 70s, following your team had its highs and lows on and off the field, and the start to the 79–80 season had seen yours truly suffer at Barnsley, City and now Millwall, while at Hull and Chesterfield the boot was on the other foot.

October was the month that saw both Wednesday and United visit our near neighbours Rotherham in successive weeks. The Blades visited first, and won 2–1. Crowd trouble led to a wall on the Tivoli End collapsing. When it was our turn seven days later, we too won by the same score, and again the wall came tumbling down. It has been rumoured over the years that Wednesdayites carried hammers and chisels to set about the wall, but I was on the Tivoli that day, and saw nothing untoward, except two men carrying a pneumatic drill.

By the end of the month, it was United who were top dogs, three points to the good of the Owls. Our friends from the dark side would gloat every time we ventured out to enjoy a night around town before heading for the legendary Limit. Things were lively in our city during this period with punk and the re-emergence of ska through such bands as Madness and the Specials. Sham 69 were still as popular as ever and fans of both clubs would frequent their concerts with little sign of trouble. As November rolled in, and good children across the UK indulged in ritual fleecing of pub-goers everywhere, under the guise of collecting for the one and only Mr Guy Fawkes, Wednesday were feeling the pressure and had slumped to sixth, while United had been knocked off top spot by Millwall. Suddenly, we were entering the month that an entire city had been waiting almost a decade for, and Boxing Day 1979 could not come quickly enough. We were still getting stick from our little red friends, but we had thick skins considering what we had endured over the previous few years.

This was also the period that introduced the InterCity Owl, and it beat Brian's battered old transit any day of the week. Our trip to Chester was a memorable one because, even though we only came back with a point, the antics of one Michael Payne would be remembered forever. I dedicate this section to Mick, who sadly died in 2004 just before our memorable day out in Cardiff. We had been playing cards most of the journey when Mick asked for the window of the carriage to be opened. We just thought he needed some fresh air because we'd been on the ale until the early hours, and no one thought anything of it. He proceeded to shuffle the cards but, instead of dealing them out, he threw the buggers out of the window! His explanation was that he'd had a bad run with the cards, and could not afford to lose any more money. He went on to explain that, if he'd just left the school, the temptation to return would be too great, so drastic action was needed and the only solution was to get rid of the damn things.

We went into the Boxing Day game seven points adrift of the Blades and the thought of defeat to the old enemy did not bear thinking about. The days leading up to the game were unbearable, and West Street was turning into a battleground most nights as Owl clashed with Blade.

That's something that never ever touched our crowd, and we were a very good mix. Don't get me wrong, at the times that we have crossed swords on the Shoreham, they are, for that moment in time, our bitterest rivals, but, once the game is over and we are out socialising, we stick together like glue.

I can only recall one occasion where we nearly came to blows with Blades on West Street when we were out for a quiet drink. We were all drinking in the West Street Hotel, and the Blades had made a good show. They entered the boozer and, knowing we were of the blue persuasion, wanted us to join them outside. They turned to our red mates and said, 'You're Blades, join us.'

This offer was soon rebuffed with the words, 'Not tonight we're not, we always fight together.'

With that, we poured out into the night.

Now, they had some very game lads, but so did we, and with our reds in tow it was a kind of stalemate. One of our lot made them an offer that he would have the mouthpiece that had put us in this situation, and they agreed. Once he'd been sorted out, they went their way, and we carried on as though nothing had happened.

The powers that be decreed that the long-awaited game would kick off at 11am, and with no public transport big Brian did the honours, and crammed us all in the Transit. The few Blades that had come along for the ride included our Mark, Malcolm and Shaun. On the day the attendance was 49,309, a record for a Third Division game, and the promised showing of the Shoreham boot boys did not materialise.

Chris and Pete had even got the legendary Hillsborough Kop idol Sammy out of hospital, where he was being treated, so he would not miss the game. The fact that it was also the 100th meeting in League and Cup between the city clubs added extra spice to an already eagerly awaited contest. United came as table-toppers, but it was the Owls who drew first blood when Mellor scored shortly before the break, and the half-time Bovril tasted like champagne. Further goals from Curran, King and Smith finished off the massacre. If anyone sees footage of the game, just look to the right of the goal when Smith puts the penalty in: one Blade jumps up and down in a right paddy and storms out of the ground; unconfirmed reports said he threw himself in the River Don.

When we poured out on to Penistone Road, it was a Blade-free zone; even our mates that batted for the other side never got that lift back to the boozer, and, while we partied, they must have found a dark room in some rundown boozer to drown their sorrows. While we were on a high, our bloody licensing laws meant that the boozers shut at three and did not reopen until five-thirty. That fact appears to have passed by those Blades who claim that they rampaged around the city centre seeking out Wednesdayites. The thought of town being a drink-free zone for three hours sent most Owls heading for their bustling locals, and we were no exception. The Frecheville never knew what last orders were and still doesn't to this day. Even when we went out Boxing Day night you could count the Blades on one hand, and those that did venture out were miserable fuckers. The Harrow at Gleadless was bouncing to the sound of 'High-Ho Sheffield Wednesday' and it was like we'd been given the freedom of the city.

Wednesday had been in the doldrums for the past decade and United had, for a few years, entertained the likes of Liverpool and Manchester United while we settled for Lincoln and Mansfield. As we moved into 1980, we'd already been dumped out of the FA Cup, but so had the Blades and it now looked as though both clubs could concentrate on promotion back to the Second Division.

Wednesday only managed two games in January because of the bad weather and found themselves six points off the top of the League, but with three games in hand. I was now into my third decade of supporting the Owls, and for most of that period we'd been on a downward spiral.

While we were freezing our nuts off at home, Big Jack took the boys to Torremolinos for a sunshine break, and it must have done the trick because on their return they hammered Colchester 3–0 on a snow-covered Hillsborough pitch. Also during this period Terry Curran, the ever-popular Owls star, set up his fan club, and for a quid you could get a TC badge, an autographed photograph and a certificate. I may have gone out and bought his record but the thought of joining his fan club was a definite no-no.

We were now on a roll. After the InterCity Owl brought hundreds of marauding Wednesdayites to Swindon, it was another good day at the office, both on and off the field, with a victory that pushed the Owls up to fourth in the table, just two points off the leaders Grimsby.

I was now on the top of the world, but, just as my football was on the up, my employment prospects had taken a dive and I was made redundant. With the Conservatives now in power, I reluctantly pissed off to Jersey, just as my football club were enjoying the best run of results I had ever witnessed. But the lads gave yours truly a good send-off when we travelled to Oxford, and won the game 2–0.

While I was settling into the island's way of life, like working hard all day and boozing every night, Wednesday had gone top of the League after gaining a well-deserved draw at Gillingham, and United were now five points adrift of Wednesday. It was now, finally, the Owls fans turn to gloat as, since 1971, the Blades had held top position in the city. Terry Curran and Mark Smith were selected in the PFA team to represent the division along with Alex Sabella of United, while Big Jack was named Manager of the Month for February.

Another good result against Reading set us up nicely for our visit to the Lane on 5 April. On the morning of the game, the boys were out on the beer bright and early and, after United put up a no-show at Hillsborough on Boxing Day, I knew that the Wednesdayites, and especially our crowd, would be giving the Shoreham a visit.

Wednesday travelled to the game in large numbers and, after the trouble-free Boxing Day game, this was to be a different matter. The Owls were once again camped on the Shoreham, and the fighting started long before the teams would make an appearance. United have always disputed the numbers that infiltrated their end on that day, and claim it was mostly dads with their kids, but, even if that was the case, which it most certainly was not, it was a damn sight more than they've ever had on the East Bank.

Wednesday were again on a roll and, under Big Jack, were homing in on a long-awaited promotion. The gate on the day was in excess of 45,000 and Wednesdayites were everywhere when the teams came out in brilliant sunshine. After John McPhail had given United the lead, it was left to Terry Curran to score a superb equaliser, and give the Owls a share of the spoils. What a goal that was by Curran and it's a pity that we only came away with a point, but in the end it was enough as Wednesday would go on to secure promotion back to the Second Division. The Blades would languish in the Third Division for only one more season before they eventually left it behind, but, instead of following us to the promised land, they went in the opposite direction and endured the humiliation of relegation to the bottom tier of English football.

At the end of the season we entertained the Blades at Hillsborough in the County Cup Final, but only 5,430 bothered to turn up, even though the Owls had just celebrated promotion. Andy McCulloch scored for Wednesday, but goals by Sabella and Wiggan won the trophy for the Blades, their 19th success in the competition, and how they must have celebrated.

THE EIGHTIES AND NINETIES

The first three months of the 1980s would see Sheffield become a city no longer on the move. On 1 January 1980, workers in the nationalised sectors of the steel industry across Britain walked out on a national strike. The strike was triggered by rumours of a massive wave of redundancies and plant closures on a scale never before seen in the United Kingdom. The British Steel Corporation (BSC) had been set up in 1967 by combining many of Britain's largest steel producers, but a strict code had to be followed. Only producers making over 475,000 liquid tons of steel were to be included, and in the Sheffield region this meant the English Steel Corporation and United Steel, while the other big Sheffield steel companies, such as Firth-Brown and Hadfields, remained in private hands. This would prove to be a major flashpoint during the steel strike of 1980. The BSC had been losing money hand over fist for many years, and drastic measures were needed to try to save the steel industry in Britain. Redundancies and plant closures had been creeping in since the mid-1970s, but they began to gather pace as the new decade dawned, and thousands of steelworkers from Lanarkshire to Kent, fearing for their jobs and communities, walked out in the first national steel strike for decades. In Sheffield, while the workers at BSC plants such as Tinsley Park, Stocksbridge, River Don and Templeborough walked the picket lines, their colleagues in the private sector at Hadfields, Firth-Brown, Brown Bayley and Osborn's worked on. The BSC workers, fearing that work was being shifted to the private steelmakers by BSC management, sought to bring the private sector to a halt too. This led to scenes of Sheffield steelworker facing off across the picket line against Sheffield steelworker. The trouble reached a peak outside Hadfields East Hecla plant on 14 February 1980, and Sheffield would never be quite the same again.

When the strike collapsed in April, and the steelworkers were defeated, it was not just the public sector that would feel the icy wind of rationalisation. Over the next couple of years, thousands of Sheffield steel jobs disappeared at both BSC and the private companies. Companies that had been giants of the steel and engineering industry, such as Hadfields, were closed down as a direct result of government policy. Others, such as Firth-Brown and BSC River Don, faced with the prospect of merge or die, merged, again with the loss of thousands of jobs. Almost overnight, whole tracts of land opened up in the old Sheffield industrial heartlands, and by 1984 the city was on its knees. For many, the only bright spot in this maelstrom of industrial chaos and decline was the football, and how they needed something to cheer them up.

We only had to wait until the beginning of the 1980–81 season to face the Blades in a meaningful competition, when the two clubs were drawn together in the League Cup. Within the space of four days, Wednesday were successful at Hillsborough, winning 2–0 thanks to Taylor and Johnson in front of a crowd of 23,989, and in the return leg at Bramall Lane a goal by Curran was enough, in a 1–1 draw, to see the Owls through to the second round at the expense of our bitter rivals. So, while Wednesday were now getting ready to face Newcastle, West Ham and Chelsea, United were in for a dog fight with the likes of Newport, Walsall and Chester.

The next encounter with the Blades came on 21 May 1982, and again it was the County Cup Final. Once again, Wednesday were put to the sword on the Bramall Lane field with Neville, Brazil and Burke doing the damage. These players were not household names down at Sheffield 2 because both clubs had now come to despise this competition and both fielded reserve teams.

With the County Cup now defunct, it was left to the good old Testimonial to wet the appetite of the lovers of the Sheffield derby, and the first one up was in honour of the United legend Cec Coldwell. A crowd of 9,512 turned up to see the sides fight out a 1–1 draw on 14 November 1983, and we would then have to wait until 1986 before the sides met again, also at Bramall Lane. This time there was as much action in and around the ground as there was on the pitch. Wednesday won the game 4–3.

Fans clashed before and after the game, and it was now becoming clear that meetings of the two teams, outside of the League and Cup, were only proving attractive to the hooligan elements. After the triumph of the Wednesday hooligans after the Testimonial for United's Tony Kenworthy, the next meeting of minds would be close at hand, but again it was only a Testimonial that brought the fans out. This time the benefit was in aid of Owls defender Mark Smith, and was played on 15 September 1986 at Hillsborough. Goals by Varadi (2) and Hirst cancelled the lone contribution from Philiskirk, and sent the majority of the 10,800 present home happy.

The final three encounters of the 80s saw Wednesday victorious on all three occasions. First, in a game at the Lane, in aid of the World Student Games, Wednesday won 3–0 in front of a crowd of 8,724 and then a very poor crowd of 2,999 attended a benefit game for the Blades' Colin Morris, and Wednesday again won 3–1. The final encounter was on 21 November 1989 when 30,464 paying customers saw the Steel City derby revived in the now defunct Zenith Data Systems Cup. The Owls came through 3–2 at Hillsborough after extra-time, thanks to Atkinson, Palmer and a Johnny Sheridan screamer.

After a disastrous relegation on the last day of the 1989–90 season, which coincided with the Blades passing the Owls as they came down, Wednesday would embark on one of their most successful periods for some time.

The 1990–91 season saw the Owls bounce back at the first time of asking, and also saw them bring home their first piece of silverware since 1935, when they beat Manchester United 1–0 in the League Cup Final at Wembley. After a triumphant return to the top flight, Wednesday got ready to do battle once more with the Blades, and this would be only the fifth League meeting in 20 years. The clubs had managed one benefit match at Hillsborough in August 1990, for Owls stalwart Laurie Madden, and a reasonable crowd of 15,040 watched the Owls win 3–0 thanks to Williams (2) and Shirtliff. Before the game, Madden had pissed off United Chairman Reg Brearley because Stocksbridge Engineering Steels had sponsored the aptly named Steel City Cup and provided the trophy, but poor old Reg was a bit miffed that Lawrie had not informed them that the teams were playing for a trophy. Bloody hell! It was *his* benefit match so what he did for it was of no concern to the board of Sheffield United.

A couple of seasons earlier, the two boards had got together and decided to play for the annual Cutlers Cup, but after the County Cup had died a painful death many supporters could not see the point. This did not stop Brearley, who went on to add that the so-called Steel City Cup held no interest for Sheffield United Football Club; well, it's just as well because they got spanked good and proper.

This was also the first game at Hillsborough since the fences had come down after the Hillsborough disaster, but the Leppings Lane terraces remained closed. There were 14 ejections from the ground for fighting which resulted in nine arrests, but on the whole it was a quiet affair, which was no surprise as the game was at Hillsborough!

The cost of policing at football was going through the roof and, after paying £74,000 the previous season, the powers that be were now looking for a staggering £389,000. The new rate was based on a constable being worth £20.41 an hour! Not a bad screw nowadays, never mind almost 20 years ago.

THE SHEFFIELD DERBY: DIVISION ONE 1991–92

As the 1991–92 season dawned, the inhabitants of Steel City were ready for the real thing. It had been over a decade without a serious meeting, and Sheffield had now become a battleground most weekends, as Owl and Blade fought running battles on the city streets.

OWL VERSUS BLADE

It was 16 November 1991 and I'd managed to get 20 tickets for the John Street Stand, and, with the game being played on the Sabbath, our drinking time would be limited. We set up camp in the West End on Glossop Road, and with the wife for company the prospect of getting involved in any confrontation was about zero.

Most of the crowd I was with that day were far too well on in years to get into the aggro side of our beautiful game. We took our seats after our drinking schedule had been curtailed somewhat, and straight away the natives were in our face. We had positioned ourselves at the far end of the stand nearest the away end so if trouble did flare up they could only come at us from one direction. Some of the lads had opted for the terrace below and were spat at, but no fists were raised. If that had been the South Stand at Hillsborough, they would have been swamped, but United just stood back and taunted them for the duration.

The game itself was a nightmare for all concerned and it was not a very good day to be a Wednesdayite. After Deane and Whitehouse had won it for the Blades, we had to grin and bear it the best we could, as all around it was a sea of jubilant Blades. The game could not end quickly enough for yours truly, but we stuck it out to the end and, even after the final whistle, as Blades fans poured into the stand off John Street looking for confrontation, the first face I saw was an old foe from the 70s. His reaction to seeing me was: 'Bloody hell, tha's put some weight on,' before we exchanged pleasantries, and I made my way out of his godforsaken hole.

Wednesday lost 2–0 and I'd suddenly lost my appetite for a beer; that and the fact I was still exiled in Tinsley, which was one hell of a trek home from the Birley Hotel. Mind you, money was in short supply during this period, so getting hammered to drown my sorrows was not an option.

The return game was scheduled for March 1992, and it was off to Hillsborough, hoping for revenge. The match was a lively one and, when United scored through Davison, some Unitedites on the Kop celebrated before heading for the pitch, but one unfortunate individual was pursued by a good friend of mine, who is sadly no longer with us. Neil, the big man, was trying to bury the Blade in the goalmouth while the game was restarting. It took about six coppers to restore order as the fans were grappling pitch-side. Neil was dragged away while still swinging at the Blade.

After that, the game was all downhill and further goals by Whitehouse and Davison, again, put the result beyond Wednesday's reach, even after King had scored for the Owls just after half-time.

THE SHEFFIELD DERBY: THE PREMIERSHIP 1992–93

The First Division had now become the Premier League and the first ever derby game in this new chapter of the book of English football was played at Bramall Lane on 8 November 1992, and again it was a Sunday kick-off. As in the previous seasons, we again made for the West End, and enjoyed a nice drink and talked about our exploits in Europe, which had sadly come to an end some four days earlier at the hands of Kaiserslautern. I'd paid £13.50 for my ticket – a bloody damned sight more than the couple of shillings I'd coughed up when I first witnessed the Owls take on the Blades back in 1963.

This time the boys who got covered in spit joined us in the seats. It had been a struggle this time to acquire our tickets, and at first I was given the knock-back because they were restricting the sale to so many per person. I jumped in the car, and headed for the Fairway because I knew that, with it being a working day, my old mate Shaun would be in there knocking back the odd pint. He thought I'd got a damn cheek asking him to get the boys together and curtail their drinking for an hour or so, because I wanted near on 30 tickets for his ground. Shaun was fanatical about his football team and hated Wednesday with a vengeance, but that did not stop him, in his younger days, jumping on the bandwagon and joining us on a good day out if the opposition at the Lane was a bit on the weak side. The boy knew how to pick his games because two trips were memorable to say the least. First, he accompanied us to Millwall in the 70s when we got torn to pieces, and my best mate had an encounter with some ammonia. Then, he was with us again when I managed to head butt a bottle after we'd been to Luton in the 80s; saying that, I owe him big time because he was the one who waded into them when I'd been dropped and was at the mercy of the flying boots.

Sadly, Shaun died in 2005, and at his funeral it was standing room only inside the church, while there were just as many people standing outside. Both clubs were well represented and many old faces from the 70s put in an appearance. It is at times like these that people who probably would not give one another the time of day when it came to supporting their favourite football team show respect to a terrace veteran who has been taken from us. Shaun was a legend and is sadly missed. He was a very good friend to me, but it did not stop him trying to kick my head in every time Wednesday visited the Lane.

With the help of the Fairway Five, I had achieved my objective and managed to get practically the same seats as the previous year.

While Wednesday and United were ready to get to grips with one another, one Wednesday old boy was having the time of his life. Tony Toms, who was the larger-than-life coach under the stewardships of both Ashurst and Charlton, was given the role of protecting Madonna from the British media while she was in the country filming the infamous documentary *In Bed with Madonna*. I bet the players from that era break out into a sweat just when someone mentions his name. I can remember when he had them camping on the moors, and we got a credible draw against the sheep – happy days.

Wednesday had come a long way since those dark days, and we were in a buoyant mood after just visiting Europe. The game itself was much better than the previous encounter, if you were a Wednesdayite that is. Littlejohn had put the Blades in front on the 61st minute, and time was running out for the Owls. Warhurst had replaced Sheridan and this seemed to breathe new life into Wednesday. It came as no surprise, and was richly deserved, when David Hirst smashed in the equaliser in the 84th minute to cheers and relief all around.

THE SHEFFIELD DERBY: THE FA CUP SEMI-FINAL

After we'd gained our first ever Sheffield derby League points since 1980, both Wednesday and United were progressing nicely in the FA Cup. Wednesday had enjoyed victories at Cambridge United, while both Sunderland and Southend were beaten at Hillsborough.

United, on the other hand, had triumphed at Burnley, after being held at the Lane. In addition, Hartlepool and Manchester United visited S2, and they too were dumped out of the trophy.

In the quarter-finals, United played at Blackburn Rovers on 6 March, while two days later Wednesday faced a tricky tie at the Baseball Ground with Derby County. Both games finished level and, in the draw for the semis, the two Sheffield clubs were pitched against one another, provided they could overcome their opponents in the replays.

On 16 March, Sheffield United booked their place in the semis by defeating Rovers on penalties. Twenty-four hours later, Wednesday beat Derby 1–0 to set up the first ever FA Cup semi between the city clubs.

The FA Cup semi was at first scheduled for Elland Road, but, following pressure from the Sheffield public, it was switched to Wembley. I'd managed to get myself a coach from Diamond Travel, and the scene was set to transport a mixed bag of supporters from the Tinsley area. We ran the bus from the Fox and Duck, but, because of the wrangling over the match location, I'd only got a couple of weeks to get ready.

The usual crowd, with whom I would also be going to the League Cup Final weekend, had been sorted and we were using Bagshaws Luxury Coaches. Bagshaws had served us so well over the years, but I was never one to miss an opportunity to make a couple of bob in the process.

I even toyed with the idea of charging Unitedites a couple of quid more than their blue and white neighbours, but it was just a thought! In next to no time, the bus was full and, if I could have got my hands on another bus at the right price, I could have filled it, but the costs had spiralled out of control and I was just glad to get the news, on 3 April, that the game would be played in London after all.

The city was a buzz for 14 days and the media were working overtime. I'd made sure that I'd got the weekend off, and thankfully for me not many people I worked with did the football.

On the day of the game, outside the Fox and Duck, the atmosphere was electric, and, even though I had so much to organise, the thought of defeat in this Steel City derby was unthinkable. Myself, my wife Christine and my younger brother David were laden with goodies to sell on our way home. Samantha, my daughter, had been dispatched to Lincolnshire to stay with Christine's mum and dad, as she was not quite old enough to sample the delights of a football away day, but before she left she had handed her mother her two prized possessions to bring us luck – they were two black spiders that she called Viv Anderson and Carlton Palmer. Now before any of you out there get a bit politically correct, it is not a race thing; it's in honour of two great players who have served our club well in over 350 appearances between them.

I busied myself collecting the fares, and the rivalry on the bus was top dollar. We'd not even reached Leicester Forest and one or two were feeling the strain on the old voice box. The banter was good but controlled and, with the bus sorted and a nice little drink in my pocket, it was time to put my William Hill hat on and distribute the match-day odds. Everyone to a man, woman and child had a punt and, with a very good mix on board, it was odds-on that the bookie would win the day.

We were making good time and, although the kick-off was unbelievably early, I was hoping for a good hour in the boozer. I'd decided on the outskirts of London with a direct rail link to Wembley, as we all know what the Wembley car park was like, and the thought of sitting in that for a couple of hours was not appealing.

I'd totted up my takings and was confident of making another nice little drink out of it. I must have been busy because, before I knew it, we were at our destination and headed for the nearest public house. The 1pm kick-off was a bit out of order, but you can understand why. It was bad enough when those pissed-up Jocks descended on the twin towers, let alone 70,000-odd thirsty Sheffielders.

Everything was going to plan as we boarded the train and headed for Wembley Way; Wednesday and United together and no trouble so far. The stadium looked magnificent and the amount of balloons that were floating about was an awesome sight, as the teams came out side by side, like gladiators, ready to do battle.

When the game kicked off, the atmosphere was something I'd never witnessed before in my life, and in front of the Sky TV cameras Sheffield was putting on one hell of a show. The game was only a couple of minutes old when Wednesday were awarded a free-kick and Chris Waddle smashed it into the roof of the net from a good 25 yards or more. We went crazy and all around the jubilation was paramount.

We were winning in the greatest ever Steel City derby and the Blades were stunned. Wednesday continued to dominate the game, and the shots that peppered the United goal were mounting by the minute. United's 'in-your-face' style was not suited to the wide expanses of Wembley Stadium and our class in midfield was awe inspiring, with Waddle and Sheridan pulling the strings, and Harkes and Wilson tackling like terriers. Palmer was a rock as usual and I felt it would be only a matter of time before we netted our second. As the game edged towards half-time, with Wednesday well in control, United broke away, and, in one of their attacks that you could number on one hand, Alan Cork stunned the Wednesday faithful by equalising.

I could not believe that they had managed to withstand all that pressure and administer such a sucker-punch. I felt deflated but knew we were still well in control of this game.

The second half got under way and it was more of the same, with Wednesday pressing for that elusive second goal, and again the United goal was leading a charmed life. On the hour, David Hirst replaced Warhurst and in the remaining half-hour Wednesday's corner count went into double figures and shots on and around the Blades goal neared 30, compared to a measly five United corners and about 10 efforts that hardly troubled Chris Woods.

The referee then blew his whistle and it was extra-time. The only good thing about playing an extra 30 minutes was I'd not have to pay out on the football, even though some lucky sod had wagered £2 at very generous odds of 22/1 that Waddle would score the opener, but overall I'd still made another nice little drink out of it.

The first period had drawn a blank and, with little over 15 minutes to play and the scores still level, the prospect of a trip to

Old Trafford on the following Wednesday was all I needed, with a trip back to Wembley for the League Cup Final against Arsenal planned in two weeks' time. The Owls were soon on the offensive, and won another corner. The ball was swung over, and Mark Bright seemed to be in the air for an age as he rose unchallenged to head past Kelly. The United end fell silent while the blue and white half were falling about everywhere, hugging, kissing, shouting, swearing and the steam of delight had just been released from this pressure cooker of a game.

We were now only 10 minutes away from not only another trip to the twin towers, but also victory in the greatest ever Steel City encounter was ours for the taking.

As the minutes ticked away, Unitedites tried to rally their troops, but it was having little effect, as Wednesday stroked the ball around like World Champions. We kept looking at the referee and praying that he would blow any minute and end this drama. The minutes had now become seconds and with every tick my heart was pounding, my mouth as dry as the Sahara Desert.

Then it was all over and we had been victorious.

I wanted time to stand still and soak up every precious moment, but I was gagging for a pint. My boys had done me proud, and, in the words of one famous Norwegian commentator, David Bassett, your boys took one hell of a beating.

No colours were needed to tell the difference between Owl and Blade. The Blades were the ones whose facepaint had run under the floods of tears and the older ones had faces like thunder. Wednesdayites, on the other hand, had won the lottery twice over. First, we had beaten our fiercest rivals and, second, we had to endure another tedious trip down Wembley Way.

Back at base camp, Wednesdayites were drinking to their heroes, while the Blades were going at it to erase this day from their memory. With the off-licence raided, we were on our way home, and the bus was like nothing I'd ever witnessed in my life. Kids with red-painted faces looked like Christmas had been cancelled, while the blue side was in full swing and loving every minute.

For one mega-second, I started to feel sorry for them, but gave myself a good smack in the mouth, and proceeded to pin up posters that I had acquired from work which had been slightly doctored. One was of United's Brian Deane saying, 'Fuck this I'm off to Leeds', and another had Wednesday's Paul Warhurst proclaiming, 'United were worse than Spora Luxembourg', which at times they were.

The day had been a major success for the city of Sheffield. It is no mean feat transporting 73,000 people some 190 miles to the capital. Hundreds of coaches, and four soccer specials made the journey. Cars on the M1 were bumper to bumper all the way home, and, as we returned home from the pub in the early hours, I knew I'd witnessed something unique in the history of Sheffield football and that this day was unlikely to ever be repeated.

THE SHEFFIELD DERBY: PREMIERSHIP 1992–93

After such a good day out at Wembley, we were now back in the real world, and the game at Hillsborough on 21 April 1993 was one hell of a confrontation on and off the field. Owls and Blades clashed on Penistone Road, and bottles and bricks were exchanged at an alarming rate. The police were having trouble getting to grips with the situation and several arrests were made.

On the field, United were well up for it, and they were intent on dishing out some retribution for their humiliation some 18 days earlier. Ryan Jones was the first Wednesday player to feel the pain when he was stretchered off after only seven minutes, to be replaced by Graham Hyde. United players were acting like thugs, and it put Wednesday off their game. Deane scored on the stroke of the half-time interval to put the Blades a goal up. Wednesday finally got their act together when Warhurst equalised, but the game sank to an all-time low when Glyn Hodges elbowed John Harkes, sparking a free-for-all, and the referee had no option but to send off the Welshman.

The game then petered out, and most of the paying public could not wait for the final whistle. United hadn't come to play the game as it should be played, but to set their stall out like some Sunday pub team who were only content to seek confrontation.

Then again, I'd probably have been more than a little pissed off if I'd had my arse spanked in front of 73,000 Sheffielders, plus the many millions more that had witnessed the semi on Sky. United have always been, and always will be, bad losers and can never accept that sometimes defeat has to be taken in a dignified manner.

THE SHEFFIELD DERBY: PREMIERSHIP 1993–94

Wednesday had not had the best of starts to the season, and had only managed one home victory in the League before we readied ourselves for our trip into bandit country. The boys had managed to obtain 40 tickets for their South Stand, and the boys who got their mitts on them ranged from the old-school boot boys of the 70s to the lads that were enjoying the thrill of the chase like we did all those years ago. We met early doors and headed for the Railway Club, which sits behind Queens Road, to enjoy our pre-match tipple. The place was rammed, with a good mixture of red and blue, and the atmosphere was jovial.

With kick-off approaching, we made our way to the ground and headed for the South Stand. I envisaged no trouble at all, even though we were in with the enemy, because, on scanning the faces that made up our group as we trudged along Shoreham Street, even with one or two of us being well past our sell-by dates, the rest were as game as they come.

Once inside the ground, we were at the rear of the stand nearest the Kop, and the supporters around us were none too pleased that Wednesday had taken up residence in their humble abode, but we were only out for the beer and the football, and anyway our near neighbours were not what you would call hooligans. We knew that the Blades would have parked themselves up nearest to the visiting supporters, so purchasing the tickets in that area would have resulted in us being shown the door by South Yorkshire's finest upholders of the law, and anyway, as I said, we'd only come for the football.

The game started well and it was evenly balanced as we approached half-time. Wednesday were doing well but I hated derbies as there was far too much at stake to really enjoy the game. As soon as the referee blew his whistle for half-time, we made our way on to the concourse and headed for the toilets. I knew, if it was going to kick off, this would be the moment and we watched each other's backs while we took a leak.

The Blades by now knew we were amongst them, but the place was rammed with coppers, and these Wednesday lads would not back away. I am just telling it how I saw it, and anyone who was there, without the need to name names, knew that our little bunch of happy souls would have given as good as they got.

We'd enjoyed our day out, and Wednesday had got a useful point. We headed into town to get cabs to take us back to the pleasant surroundings of Sheffield 12. Bloody hell, we had just spent over six hours in and around Bramall Lane, so we needed a good drink and some fresh air.

For the next few hours, we drank in the Royal Oak and Noah's Ark at Intake, and the Birley Hotel. Then we decided to go and have a drink in the Sportsman at Hackenthorpe, and on entering the premises it was mainly the red boys who were having a drink. One of the Blades was an old acquaintance from my town and Limit days, and we used to travel extensively following Sham 69. While we were deep in conversation, one of our lot, Neil, came in brandishing a baseball bat. He was a bloody awesome sight without a tool, so the half-dozen or so Blades quickly vacated to the Blue Bell next door.

Now, it's one thing having a good flare-up at the football and – call me an old dinosaur if you will – but that's where I believe it should belong. Mind you, the boys today have not got wide-open terraces and mobs of a few hundred aside going hell for leather, so I suppose they have to take it into and on to the streets.

As everyone moved outside and the road quickly filled, I turned round to see a youthful-looking lad depositing pool balls into his sock. I thought to myself, He's too young to have seen the classic film *Scum*, in which Ray Winstone's character Carling does the same thing. He told me that he was not scared of the baseball bat-carrying Owl, and he was getting himself psyched up before making his way out of the door to do battle. I told him he'd need more than a few pool balls to shift the man mountain Neil, and I suggested one of two things; first, he removed the balls and we had a game or, second, he sought the services of an elephant gun.

The boy sensibly chose the first option and, while it was a bit of a stand-off on Main Street, we were knocking the balls about. That was about it because the resulting sirens filled the night air and most of the boys went their separate ways, while myself and the young lad finished our game of pool. Blades drifted back into the Sportsman and I felt uneasy as I finished the game, but the sight of my old pal coming back through the door put my mind at rest, and we concluded our conversation before finishing the evening off in the Frecheville Hotel.

Neil, like Shaun, has sadly passed away and he is truly missed by his friends and family. The man got us out of many a scrape on our travels watching the Owls, none more so than when we visited Stamford Bridge for our League Cup semi-final. Unfortunately, after his death, a few Blades posted disparaging comments about him on various websites, and it was those fuckers that wouldn't have said boo to him when he was alive, but I suppose it's easy to mock the dead from behind a computer screen. In all fairness, though, it was only one or two, and the real Blades, who knew him, showed the proper respect.

While we were doing well in the League, our poor neighbours were struggling, and fighting a losing battle to hold on to their Premiership status. I was thinking to myself, Wouldn't it be a shame if that lot were relegated? I concluded that it would be brilliant.

Anyway, we'd played them six times already in the 90s, and that was enough. I just hated their ground and it put me into deep depression every time I went near the place. Fortunately for me, the game on 22 January 1994 was to be our last encounter of the decade. Goals by Pearce, Bright and Watson sent them on their way and, even though Whitehouse grabbed a consolation, United were doomed, and finished up plying their trade in the second tier of English football.

INTO THE MILLENNIUM

THE SHEFFIELD DERBY: WORTHINGTON CUP 2000-01

Well, at long last, the Sheffield derby was back on the menu but first up was this little taster when 32,283 flocked to Hillsborough to witness Wednesday get the better of things thanks to Ekoku, who netted twice in our 2–1 victory. Paul Jewell was by now in the manager's chair at Hillsborough, but Wednesday had not adapted to life in the Nationwide and victory over the Blades was scant consolation for our very poor League form.

THE SHEFFIELD DERBY: NATIONWIDE LEAGUE 2000-01

We had not played the Blades in a League game since 1994, the reason being that they unfortunately dropped out of the Premiership soon after we'd turned them over at Hillsborough in January of that year. But what had happened to Wednesday from that day and why were we gearing ourselves up for the resumption of the Sheffield derby? At the end of that 1993–94 season, the Owls had finished in a respectable seventh position and also managed to reach the semi-final of the League Cup, where we had suffered at the hands of some grumpy Manchester United supporters who mistook our celebrations for a dig at Munich, and we had to run the gauntlet after the game, but revenge was sweet when they visited Hillsborough.

Trevor Francis was in charge, but players like Nilsson, Palmer, Worthington and King were allowed to leave and they were not replaced with players of the same quality. It was also reported that there was unrest in the dressing room, although this was denied by the club. Things got so bad that Nottingham Forest inflicted our heaviest home defeat when we were turned over 7–1. With the club staring relegation in the face, Wednesday managed an end-of-season victory to stay up against the odds.

The start of the 1994–95 saw Francis depart to be replaced by David Pleat, but again the Owls flirted with relegation, and stayed up by just a two-point margin. Our fortunes took an upturn the following season when we finished in the top seven, but Pleat never saw out the following season, and was sacked after a 6–1 defeat at Old Trafford. Next through the door was Danny Wilson, but this former crowd favourite was sacked in March 2000, despite finishing 12th in his first season.

As we entered the new millennium, Sheffield had changed beyond recognition, some say for the worse. The town centre was crammed full of so many plastic pubs it was frightening. Many of you reading by now must be thinking that I'm a raving alcoholic because all I've done is talk drinking and football, but to me they go hand in glove. Match day is all about meeting your mates in the pub, and having a few beers before cheering on your favourite team. My team at the moment was in freefall and after the glory days of the 90s we were back treading the boards with our near neighbours. Long gone were those trips to Wembley and Europe, but at least we had experienced them, unlike our second-rate cousins from Sheffield 2.

As we headed for Christmas 2000, Sheffield city centre, with all its plastic boozers that had no character, and even West Street, which had been the focal point of the football-loving public over the past 25 years, had lost some of its sparkle. I know times change and we must move on, but give me the likes of the Saddle, West Street Hotel and Limit any day.

Would I go back to the boot-boy days of the 60s and 70s when Wednesday and United mobs would clash in their hundreds around the ground and town centre? Even during that period, I

Above: Owls and Blades together before the greatest Steel City derby ever, but it would all end in tears for the Blades thanks to Waddle and Bright.

Below: Ian Hendon celebrates his only memorable moment as an Owl after cancelling out Bobby Ford's opener at Bramall Lane in December 2000.

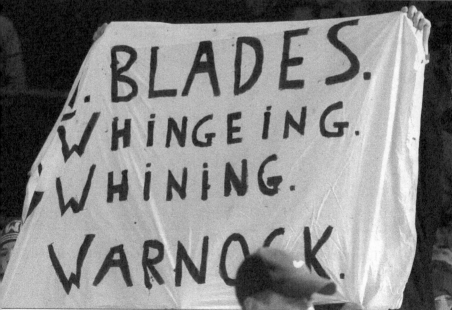

Above: In the mid-1990s, the famous East Bank became all-seater, but even then on derby day no Blades could be found in there.

Below: Owls showing their contempt for the most reviled man in Sheffield 6, and half of Sheffield 2 as well.

Above: Terry Curran, the legend, after slotting in number two. In the background one United player seems to be throwing up ... sick as a pig maybe?

Below: The 26th of December 1979 would mark a watershed in the history of the two clubs, as a decade of on-field dominance for United came crashing to a halt. The prime architect was a gentleman by the name of Terry Curran (see above). Mark Smith rounds off the scoring with number four in a 4–0 thrashing of the Blunts in what became known as the Boxing Day Massacre.

Above: 'We've got Carlton Palmer, he smokes marijuana' was the cry from the East Bank in the early 1990s, and here the Owls legend takes great delight in letting the Blunts know how he feels after stroking an equaliser at 'Ugly Downtown Bramall Sty' in October 1993.

Below: The Park and Arbourthorne boys were fully paid-up members of the EBRA, and from 1967 to 1987 derby day would often find them, among other Owls mobs, camped on the Shoreham. In contrast, no meaningful mob of Blades ever set foot on the East Bank.

never saw as many coppers as I see today. I wonder how today's Robocop would have faired back then with only a truncheon for company.

I had wondered what the atmosphere would be like after the Sheffield derby had been put on hold for six years. Well, I was not disappointed, and the youth of the city had not let me down. Well before kick-off, the police, who numbered an incredible 300, had their work cut out. Two very large mobs of Wednesday and Unitedites confronted one another around our old happy hunting ground that was West Street. The police were using horses, dogs and CS gas to keep the warring factions apart as over 150 Wednesday fans alighted from a tram on West Street, and tried to get at a similar number of Blades that were holed up in the Walkabout. The police managed to keep a lid on it by barricading United in the boozer while driving Wednesday away from the area. A splinter group of Wednesday moved down Carver Street while the Blades were redecorating the Walkabout. The CCTV man was working overtime gathering evidence – and aren't you glad this tool was not around in the 70s? For a good five hours after the game had finished, the use of mobile communication was ringing red hot as gangs roamed the city streets looking for confrontation. The police arrested well over 30 fans, but most were released without charge the following morning.

In so far as the game went, it was the first time I'd actually got a ticket for the Wednesday end and, as I scanned the programme, I thought, Oh how the mighty have fallen. What you wouldn't give for a Waddle, Hirst, Palmer or Sheridan and how the Blades longed for a Deane, Whitehouse, Hodges or Bradshaw.

The first half was evenly balanced, but after the break United went in front thanks to Bobby Ford. I feared the worst until Hendon blasted in to even things up. Wednesdayites danced on the pitch, and one or two had their collars felt, but who could blame them for celebrating?

By now, though, it was Wednesday who were struggling at the wrong end of the table and the thought of falling through the Second Division trap door was unthinkable.

When United turned up at Hillsborough on 1 April, another manager, Paul Jewell, had been shown the door. Peter Shreeves had been put in charge, but the Owls were in a sorry state, and United triumphed, thanks to Asaba and D'Jaffo.

THE SHEFFIELD DERBY: NATIONWIDE LEAGUE 2001–02

After holding on to our League status, we went into this derby game in front of the Sky cameras, and were looking for a change in fortunes. The game was to be played on a Sunday, and, with the venue being Hillsborough, crowd disturbances were minimal. Shreeves was still in charge, but we were too close to the bottom of the League for the game to be enjoyable. The attendance was a promising 29,281, and this was despite it being shown on TV. The game itself finished goalless, only the second time that no goals had been scored in a derby game at Hillsborough, the first being 1971.

By the time the Owls had played at the Lane later in the season, a number of things had happened. We had a new manager, Terry Yorath, and we'd just taken 5,000 fans to Blackburn for the League Cup semi-final. Sadly, another trip to the Final was not to be, but I think the behaviour of some of the officers on duty, who were dressed like something from the film *Robocop*, was out of order against the Wednesdayites that were housed in the lower terracing. After the game, I saw many Wednesday fans sporting cuts and bruises.

Back at the Lane, the game also finished goalless, and this was only the second time the derby score at the Lane was 0–0, the first being in 1938. Again, Wednesday just avoided relegation, and the writing was on the wall that we would again be up against it when the new season started in a few months' time.

THE SHEFFIELD DERBY: NATIONWIDE LEAGUE 2002–03

The 2002–03 season dawned, and Terry Yorath was still at the helm. It was Hillsborough that was first up, and again it was a Sunday and again the cameras were rolling. Despite being outplayed for long periods, Wednesday won the day, thanks to Owusu and Kuqi.

STEEL CITY RIVALS

The return game at the Lane was incredibly played on a Friday evening as the cameras had insisted on it. We met early doors and enjoyed a nice drink, while the boys who were carrying on the old tradition of trying to kick the shit out of one another were not letting the old-timers down, as we reminisced about years gone by; 25 years had now passed us by since we met in the famous Claymore to plan our all-out assault on the Shoreham back in 1975. We engrossed ourselves in conversation about the lack of character that our city centre now had; long gone were the Claymore, Blue Bell, Golden Ball, The Daizy and the Limit, while outside the sirens were screeching like cockerels, and every now and then designer-clad youths would enter our arena and gaze over these 40-plus-somethings who were immersed in their own little world. Not a word was spoken, but the glare from our ageing eyes was enough to send them on their way. The talk was of when we strutted around this area in all our glory and the Blades knew that this was our turf and rarely ventured off London Road. Maybe one or two of them who still like to get involved are reliving their youth because this area was out of bounds to our red and white neighbours back then.

While we enjoyed the Dog and the Grapes, West Street was as lively as ever and arrests were being made on both sides. Probably it was payback time for all that heavy-handed policing which had occurred after the game at Hillsborough when the local constabulary besieged the Sportsman pub, near Bramall Lane, and, according to the landlady, overreacted to those drinking inside the establishment. Custodial sentences were meted out to those involved. Had this incident not been football related, it would probably not have received the publicity it garnered, unlike when two gangs of youths went at one another with enough weaponry to start World War III on the streets of Tinsley and no one was arrested, never mind jailed. It just goes to prove that the football supporter is public enemy number one, but, there again, they are an easy target.

We'd enjoyed our pre-match gargle and went out on to the mean streets of Sheffield to make our way towards the hell-hole they call the Lane. Sirens still cried out in agony, and gangs of youths were on every street corner, but never gave our motley crew a second glance. We eventually made the ground, having opted for the Wednesday end instead of mixing with our second-rate cousins, and we'd only just taken our seats when a couple of flares were heading in our direction, fired by some cowardly Blade who prefers to do his fighting behind a barrel of a flaregun. A couple of young girls were hit, and I was thinking that could have been my daughter. This really incensed our crowd, but times had changed and the cowards were out of reach. In the good old days of the terracing, Wednesday would have been on to the pitch and in amongst them, but now they were safe behind rows of stewards and police. After that, the game was immaterial, probably due to the fact that we got turned over 3–1 with Kabba, Brown and Allison doing the damage while Quinn grabbed our consolation.

Trouble flared after the game and for the first time in many years I felt like getting involved, but the prospect of another charge sheet quickly put me off. A grand total of 26 arrests had been made out of a crowd of 28,179. Fans clashed with police all over the city and they must have worked late into the night to keep the rival factions apart, but what the hell did they expect allowing the game to be played on a Friday night?

By season's end, Wednesday had yet another manager at the helm, in the shape of Chris Turner, and to make matters worse we were relegated back to the old Third Division, while United made the bloody play-offs where they would face Wolves in the final.

The boys decided to watch the game in the Birley and it was crammed full to bursting with the red and white bastards all decked out in their finest gear. Some lads just could not bear to watch it, and sat drinking in the car park until God answered our prayers and Wolves scored and scored again. The boys were dancing for joy as the little porkies sat there with faces like thunder. Wolves tore United to pieces and, as the score increased to 3–0, the boys decided the game needed a brilliant finale. On cue, at the final whistle, a good half-a-dozen champagne corks popped and the red and white rabble were drowned in the finest champagne money can buy. It was

Threshers premier and at £2.99 a bottle it was money well spent. Some of them emerged like drowned rats, but this was our moment and it was priceless.

THE SHEFFIELD DERBY: THE CHAMPIONSHIP 2005–06

Wednesday had returned triumphantly from their brief stay in the Third Division, under yet another new man at the helm, Paul Sturrock, and the Owls faithful were confident that victory could be ours at the Lane when we met on 3 December. Sadly, it was not to be and we lost the game 1–0 when the traitor Quinn became the first player ever to score for both sides in the Sheffield derby. My daughter Samantha had attended her first game at the Lane, and strolled through the streets of Sheffield 2 in the blue and white. She wore her colours with pride, and took the flak that came her way from the foul-mouthed Blades who found her and her best friend Becky an easy target. At least she was not assaulted like that poor woman and her two kids who the Blades manhandled, but I suppose it was to be expected down there, as some of the United fans had now started to get a reputation for attacking regular fans. The Blades were now flying high in the table, while the Owls were finding it difficult to adjust to life back in the Championship.

After all the matches we'd played against our fiercest rivals over the past 100 years, this looked like being our last for some time because the Blades were a whisker away from a return to the Premiership, and our hopes of joining them were about zero because of the board's lack of ambition. The only way that the Sheffield derbies would continue was if the Blades made a swift return to the Championship.

For the second meeting of the season, we decided to make a day of it and were out early doors, and in town for opening time. There must have been a good 100 drinking in the Dog and Partridge on Trippet Lane, and the lads who were still bang at it were ready to do battle with the Blades, just like our boys had done in previous decades, but we were only here for the beer, and had no intention of indulging in any fisticuffs. I saw many lads who I had rarely seen over the past decade and, as we busied ourselves with the drink and the chat, the younger element went off in search of confrontation. These days were getting rarer and we were growing older none too gracefully. A meeting of minds on a similar wavelength to ours is still as strong as ever, but we always keep hearing the same old chestnut that football hooligans are not true supporters. I'll tell you this, our little lot drinking in the Dog that day, between them, had mustered about 500 years' service in the cause of Sheffield Wednesday.

After the humiliation of suffering another defeat, we drowned our sorrows around Hillsborough while the young guns headed off for a prearranged meet with the Blades. We were still going strong late into the evening, and safely tucked up in the Birley, but to say some of the lads were in a foul mood was an understatement, and one or two Blades overstepped the mark when it came to taking the piss. You allow your close friends their moment of glory, but when others step out of line it's lights-out time. Drink, obviously, plays a factor in the football violence, but it's the hurt you feel, especially when losing against your sworn enemy, that makes people throw punches in the honour of your club.

THE SHEFFIELD DERBY: THE CONCLUSION

What is so special about putting one over on your city rivals? Words cannot express the sheer delight of winning a Steel City derby and having the bragging rights for weeks to come. In this city, you are either Wednesday or United, and anyone who says they want both clubs to do well are in the very tiny majority. I was lucky because my father was a Wednesdayite, but there are many different reasons for choosing your allegiance. It could be that you live in an area that is close to either Hillsborough or Bramall Lane. And, if your parents aren't into football, you may go with your mates from school. But, whatever the reason, by the time you start your schooling, you're either Wednesday or United.

During my schooling, in the Wednesday stronghold of Shirecliffe, you could count the Blades on one hand and they suffered constant abuse. The fights were endless, especially during the run-up to derby day, and, if Wednesday were beaten, which they were on five occasions during my early school years, many a Blade would be thrown down the banking or have their head shoved down the toilet. Even on the occasions that Wednesday won, the Blades were still given a torrid time because we totally disliked them, and, if any Unitedite dared to bring his scarf to school... well, it would keep us warm in the playground because we'd set fire to the damn thing. I had a good dozen close friends in primary and junior school, and all bar one were Wednesdayites.

By 1968, United had been relegated, and my father had remarried and we'd moved to the Birley Estate. At least we were a family again because my birth mother had pissed off early doors, leaving my father to bring up me and our Mark with the help of my grandmother; rumour had it that she ran off with a Blade, but this was never confirmed. Mind you, it must have had a damaging effect on our kid because he went over to the dark side. What is it with younger siblings? Why do they go against the grain? Me, Bob, Wayne and Andy all supported the Owls while Mark, Malcolm, Shaun and David went the other way. At Birley School, it was about 50/50, so the bog-drowning ritual was not really on the curriculum, and anyway, by 1970, we had joined the Blades in the Second Division.

By the time I had finished my education and stepped out into the real world where you had to earn a living, the Sheffield derby was off the menu. Wednesday and United would only clash now and again, usually in nothing friendlies, or United's favourite competition, the County Cup, but the hatred was still there, week in week out.

It was not until 1974 that I put my boot into the hooligan arena, and I'd missed the fun at Woodward's testimonial the previous May. The 1974–75 season was when the Red Army was rampaging around the Second Division, and we never managed to entertain the Blades. On my first sortie into enemy territory, we took the Shoreham in the County Cup Final, and we would have run-ins with their mob if ever we ventured through Pond Street while they were about, but this was very rare because Wednesday ruled the roost in the city.

OWL VERSUS BLADE

On 13 December 1975, a couple of months after we'd been on the Shoreham, I got my first kicking at the hands of the Shoreham Army. We had been at home to Wigan in the second round of the FA Cup while Manchester United were at the Lane. A crowd of 31,741 had been at the Lane, while our attendance was only 12,436. In our haste to get back to our local hostelry, we jumped aboard the soccer special back into town, and must have been the first Wednesdayites in Pond Street where we were met by a good mob of Unitedites. Punches were thrown, and we were on the back foot. There were that many of them that they were fighting each other to get at us. We managed to get in between the bus and the shelter, and it was impossible for them to swamp us. The eight of us were cut and bloodied and my legs were bruised for weeks, but we had survived, and when we finally boarded the Hackenthorpe flyer we eyed their mob and picked out some familiar faces.

It would take us all season but we exacted revenge on some of our assailants, and, boy, did it taste sweet when it was our turn to put the boot in.

The following season, we had Stockport County on 20 November, while the Blades were at home to Orient. Their gate was a very poor 14,745 while the Wednesday faithful numbered 13,886. This time it looked as though all of the East Bank Republican Army (EBRA) was marching towards Pond Street, but the Blades were nowhere to be seen. Probably they'd all had to go home for their tea, but the city was ours and we boozed well into the night.

The following season, the two clubs were again at home on the same Saturday. Even though our crowd was a very poor 11,571 for the visit of Bury and United had 13,177 for their game against Bristol Rovers, it was, again, an early tea for the Shoreham Republican Army (SRA). What was up with them? It would only take them five minutes to make Pond Street their own, while it was a nice steady walk for us. Mind you, they may have picked off those arriving by soccer special, like they did to us, and then pissed off before the EBRA made it into town; again it was another Blade-free zone and, again, the town was ours.

During this period, Wednesday dominated the local hooligan

scene, and the town centre and West Street, and we made the Limit our own. We lived on West Street seven days a week and, with our crowd being a good mix of red and blue, football violence was left to Saturday afternoons and any midweek games.

My confrontations with the Blades have been limited, but I hate their club so much it hurts. I want them to be playing in the lowest division possible, or to not exist at all.

Some people seem to love our games against them, but it would not bother me if we never played them again. I have seen some crazy things in my time, but nothing beats the emotion that is stirred when Wednesday and United meet. Through the 80s and 90s, the rivalry bordered on life threatening, and nothing was sacred; your home, your workplace, even a night out with non-footballing mates could leave you vulnerable. Even taking the missus for a nice drink in town left you wide open to this new breed of football hooligan. I am not condemning it because it also happened in our day, and some say it is bullying, but I believe it's being in the wrong place at the wrong time when you are on the receiving end, and the right place at the right time when it comes to dishing it out. Anyone can pick a fight when the odds are heavily stacked in your favour, and it is very rare that you get all the top guns of both camps in the same place at the same time.

Sheffield has always been a rough place and derby day is no different. United would never come to Hillsborough Corner mob-handed, unless they were well wrapped up by the police, and nor would Wednesday stroll down London Road. I have been luckier than most because, while I was enjoying myself on the hooligan front, the lads that were very close to me were of the highest calibre and, even though we took one or two kickings along the way, we came out the other end relatively unscathed except for the odd fractured skull. Today, I still enjoy the football and the odd beer and the company of more mates than I could possible mention. I still get myself in the odd scrape, but, thanks to my youthful minders who seem to have one eye on the opposition, and one on the old man, I get by.

I wish sometimes I could take the easy option and settle back in the old armchair, but, as my wife says, I'm the only 51-year-old who still thinks he's 21. At present, I'm not having a very good time of it because those bastards are lording it in the Premiership, and every time you think they are on the slide they come up with another victory. But, you never know, come May, the champagne corks could be popping again in the Birley, if they suffer relegation humiliation.

SWAMPING THE SHOREHAM

The previous chapters have given a brief overview of the Steel City derbies, and how they have played out since the first meeting between the two professional Sheffield clubs. Paul Allen will narrate much of what follows, but a huge thank you must go from me and Paul to all the lads who took time to contribute.

The following chapters focus on the history of the violent rivalry that exists between the two sets of supporters. We look at some of the major flashpoints over the last 40 years, and at how the Wednesday and United mobs evolved. At no time do we ever seek to condone violence, but we attempt to explain what has gone on, and how the combatants, both active and retired, see the way forward. Many will disagree with what we have to say, but I am not trying to bullshit anyone, and the way it is written is the way it is seen from the viewpoint of the person telling the story – perception is everything, but also nothing at all.

Before we look at the history of football violence in the Steel City, I would like to share a little piece of information with the readers, and especially those readers who are neither Owl nor Blade, as it may help to explain some of the language that follows.

THE PIGS

The use of the term 'pigs' by each of the Sheffield teams' fans to describe the other is a very contentious issue in the city, and has been the source of much debate, claim and counterclaim down the years. Almost all Wednesday supporters agree on why they call United the pigs, and it is because the Blades' red-and-white-striped shirt resembles a strip of bacon. In the olden days, the story goes that Wednesday supporters would not eat bacon on match days, because it reminded them of their hated enemies. This story goes back countless years, and can be confirmed simply by asking around. It is unclear when the fans started to refer to the United team and fans by the moniker 'pigs', but it probably started during the 1960s or 70s. All I know for certain is that, ever since I have followed Sheffield football, it has been the term used by both sides, so it certainly predates my time.

Of course, United fans also claim they invented the term, and have called Wednesday pigs since time immemorial. Now, all I can say about that is our Blade cousins claim to have invented almost *everything* to do with Sheffield football, but I won't go into this claim in any depth. I will simply allow the reader to view evidence and make up his or her own mind. The old United hooligan element was called the Shoreham Republican Army (SRA), and their Wednesday counterparts were the East Bank Republican Army (EBRA). SRA old boys claim the SRA came first, and was copied by Wednesday. Furthermore, I have even heard it claimed that the East Bank at Hillsborough was only called that in response to United fans calling their home end the Shoreham, shortened from the Shoreham Street End, as the terrace is situated on Shoreham Street. Blades claim that Wednesday fans used to call what is now known as the East Bank the Penistone Road End, as it is situated on Penistone Road. They insist that Wednesday fans only shortened the name to copy United fans, but, if this is the case, then why did Wednesday fans not call the Hillsborough Kop the Penistone? I could continue with the list of things they claim to have done first, but it bores me fucking rigid, so I will get back to the origin of the use of the word 'pigs'.

Almost all Wednesday fans agree on why they call United the pigs, but United fans cannot come up with a definitive answer why they use the term. In Gary Armstrong's book *Knowing The Score*, a number of reasons are given, including the one about Wednesday fans being filthy animals; if they stuck to that explanation I could possibly appreciate the reasoning for the insult, although, naturally, not for one moment do I accept that Wednesday fans are filthy animals.

Sadly, though, our porky pals from Sheffield 2 have come up with numerous other reasons why they call their infinitely wiser cousins from Hillsborough this name, and methinks that they do protest too much. One of the best, and most absurd, tales I have heard from the dark side relates to the location of the Hillsborough ground. United fans claim that the land Wednesday purchased for their new home in 1899, from local silversmith James Dixon, was actually the site of a pig farm. Now, quite why a silversmith would own a pig farm is open to debate, but anyway no local surveys done in the area from around that time show any evidence of this being true. If anything, the agricultural land purchased from the Duke of Norfolk in 1855, on beautiful downtown Bramall Lane, is far more likely to have been used for pork production, but let's not go there, eh?

Over the past few years, this story has become something of an urban legend in the murky streets surrounding Bramall Lane, but anyone with half a brain knows it is pure bollocks. Until recently, I thought even Blades themselves realised it was just a story, like the Bogey Man or the Easter Bunny, and just perpetuated it to piss off their blue and white neighbours. Imagine my surprise, while researching this book, when I discovered that many Unitedites actually believe the fable! No doubt, in a few years, it will have been certified by the porky-pie tellers of S2 as absolutely, completely and utterly true, and history will once more have been rewritten. Well, if that is going to be the case, I am off to mug the Easter Bunny next April, so that those little piggies living down the Lane have no eggs to gorge themselves on. What should we expect though? After all, as the old saying goes, you can't educate pork.

THE 60S AND 70S

As mentioned earlier, it is likely that violence between Wednesday and United fans goes back as far as the history of both teams, and records do show that fan violence existed back in the 19th century. And, as the grounds, prior to Wednesday moving to Hillsborough, were a mere stone's throw from each other, is it impossible that supporters of the two clubs would have clashed in pubs around the area? Sheffield folk are tough, hard-nosed people and are not keen on taking shit. The city also has a history of violent behaviour and drunkenness, so my inclination leads me to believe that football violence between rival Wednesday and United fans in Sheffield is not a recent phenomenon. Of course, we can only guess at who the main faces were in the boot-boy gangs of the late-19th and early 20th century, but I am pretty sure the Blades will claim that it was them, and, furthermore, that their predecessors helped repel the invading Viking hordes, and even took it to them in Denmark! There is little documented evidence of fan clashes involving the fans of the two clubs, though – apart from the incidents at Bramall Lane in 1891, mentioned earlier – until the 1960s, and from there it has, at times, seemed as though the Owls and Blades have constantly been at each other's throats.

As I was only born in the late 60s, and did not come on to the football-hooliganism scene until 1985, I must allow others to share their experiences. I first hand back over to Tony, as he relates a trip to Bramall Lane in 1967:

BRAMALL LANE, 1967

A popular meeting place during the 1960s was the Heart Beat Club on Queens Road where you could dance the night away to the reggae-orientated beat that was ska. Many skins in attendance would be tooled up with pieces of lead piping and steel combs, and these weapons would be used to good effect in the forthcoming Sheffield derby at Bramall Lane on 2 September 1967.

Wednesdayites travelled in good numbers and gathered missiles from the area that was being revamped around the Midland Station. There had already been sporadic outbreaks of violence in the city centre and this was some four hours before kick-off. Shoppers in town had been forced to run for cover as Owl and Blade got to grips with one another.

The Wednesday mob was now marching along Shoreham Street and they were armed to the teeth. On the corner of John Street an almighty roar went up and the rival factions clashed. Fans were getting downed under a hail of missiles as Wednesday made an effort to invade the Shoreham.

Wednesday got on to the Kop and the fighting was intense around the turnstiles. The police were finding it difficult at first to regain control, and, as the fighting continued on the terracing, ambulances were rushing the growing number of casualties to hospital; house bricks, bottles and anything else that fans could find was used in anger.

The police for a time restored order and an appeal by John Harris and Alan Brown, the respective managers, fell on deaf ears. Wednesday were on the Shoreham and that's where they were staying.

The violence that day was, I am told by an old timer, 'Eric', who did not want to appear in this book, in response to United fans coming on the Wednesday Kop the previous season. The game at Hillsborough in 1966 has gone down in S2 folklore as the 'eggs' game. United fans that day got on to the East Bank early and pelted Wednesday, and United, latecomers with eggs. That was as far as it went, though, because the Blades made no attempt to take the Hillsborough Kop, and contented themselves with holding the high ground at the top of the steep terracing. After the events of 1966 and 1967, the Wednesday cry was 'you threw eggs and we threw bottles'. And the seeds of a violent rivalry had been sown.

Over the next 15 years, the Wednesday hooligans would make incursions on to the Shoreham at every opportunity, making life extremely difficult for United supporters. A chance for the Blades to even the score somewhat would present itself at the end of the 1969–70.

Jon, an old campaigner of the 1970s, now recalls a time the Blades had a perfect opportunity to take the East Bank, but blew it.

OWL VERSUS BLADE

GERRY YOUNG TESTIMONIAL, 1970

This game could not have come at a more depressing time for Owls fans, only three days previous, on a very cold and wet Wednesday night; the Owls had been relegated from the top flight after a disastrous performance against Manchester City. The City side did everything they could to help us win the game but score a couple of own goals, and we lost 2–1. This result meant that Wednesday now faced the prospect of Second Division football.

By Saturday, the weather had hardly improved and the mood of the Wednesday followers was as damp, but we had to rally the troops in honour of Gerry Young who would serve the club for 20 years and make 344 appearances. The opponents were our fiercest city rivals and they were rumoured to be coming in the thousands to gloat at our demise. Gerry would always be remembered for that slip which let in Mike Trebilcock for the winning goal in the FA Cup Final of 1966, but he deserved his testimonial for being such a great servant to the Owls, a trait that is so sadly lacking in the modern game.

This was some 20 years before the onset of the mobile phone, and word soon spread that the Shoreham boot boys were on their way. I was nearing my 12th birthday, so I was hardly a fully paid-up member of the EBRA. I was there with several of my pals and we swore that we would defend our sacred ground from those lowlife invaders. We were in the ground at 2.15 and it was virtually empty with just a few people scattered here and there on the vast open terrace. There was, as yet, no sign of either mob, but, at about 2.30, people were running up to the top of the Kop and peering down on the turnstiles. We joined them and to our dismay saw about 500 Blades mobbed up and it did not take them long to get through, and once they'd got their act together they marched up to the back of the Kop in force, singing and chanting. Wednesday at this time only numbered about 100, so we moved away sharply, expecting the Shoreham boys to sweep them away and take the middle of the East Bank. They had entered from behind the old scoreboard, and the East Bank was theirs for the taking, but incredibly they went to the highest peak and continued the singing and chanting.

As we neared kick-off, the crowd had climbed to a gate of 12,120 and the East Bank boys had now swelled to about 250, but other Blades, seeing that they for once had a mob on our Kop, joined and increased their numbers to near on 1,000. We were readying ourselves for the onslaught, but it never happened. About 100 got to the side of the Owls with only a couple of coppers to keep order, but all they did was sing about our fall from grace.

The game passed without any major incidents and now my school friends and I were back in the middle, strutting out our chests and gloating at the way we had seen off superior numbers and, boy, could we not wait to get to school Monday morning.

Again, it seemed that United had missed an opportunity to exact some revenge on the Wednesday hordes by taking their end, and one really does have to ask the question why around 1,000 Blades did not have the strength of character to sweep aside their hated rivals.

Over the next few seasons, the decline of the on-field performance from S6 and the relative success of the Blades meant the League matches between the clubs dried up, and so, for the hooligan elements, the rivalry needed to continue through County Cup and Testimonial games. Two such matches occurred during 1972 and 1973, which were benefit games for United heroes Len Badger and Alan Woodward, and on both occasions Wednesdayites swarmed the Shoreham in their thousands.

I was not around back then, but talking to old boys of the era you get the feeling that Wednesday certainly held the Shoreham boot boys in contempt. Another opportunity would roll around in August of 1974 for the United mob to regain some pride, and do what Wednesday seemed to do at will, which was take their hated rivals' Kop. Jon, again, takes up the story.

OWL VERSUS BLADE

COUNTY CUP FINAL, 1974–75

This competition has been spoken about on numerous occasions in relation to the 1970s. Primarily because it was one of the few opportunities that Owls had a chance to get to grips with their local rivals. This particular game was actually held over from the previous season. Twice the game had been called off due to bad weather. Now the two clubs had agreed to play the fixture on the first Saturday in August, and use it as a pre-season warm-up game. Not that Wednesday ever warmed up properly that season as the following April we were relegated to Division Three, while the Blades were mixing it with the big boys in Division One.

As usual, the days leading up to the game gave the chance for rival fans to throw predictions around as to what the outcome would be. More interesting was the talk of what could happen on the terraces; Blades, as always, talked of invading the East Bank en masse and wiping the floor with Wednesday's mob. Owls fans bid them all the best in their efforts.

On the day itself, the weather was definitely not summer-like. Intermittent showers and grey skies gave a more traditional football-season feel to proceedings. I travelled by bus with around 10 other lads from Chapeltown, and the bus dropped us off across the road from the Kop on Penistone Road.

At this time, the East Bank was a huge open terrace with a steep gangway running up the back, with the entrance to the terracing emerging to the right-hand side of the old scoreboard. Alternatively, you could enter the terrace by going left and walking under the tunnel formed by the floor of the Ozzie Owl club (Wednesday supporters' bar), which was on the south side of the ground, and come on to the Kop by the corner flag in front of the South Stand.

As the bus pulled away, we all looked up towards the back of the Kop. Around 100 young Owls had gathered on the gangway and were using this as a vantage point to spot any intrusion by Blades. The age range of these lads was in the

13–17 bracket; the older Owls would be mainly drinking in the Ozzie Owl club.

Rumour had spread that an altercation on Penistone Road had resulted in an Owls follower receiving a minor stab wound to his leg. Everyone expected a Blade incursion, and at around 2.30 the wait was over. Our numbers had swollen to around 250, almost all young lads like me. Many were just there to observe what they thought would be an afternoon's entertainment.

The first Blade foray involved six older lads aged around 23–25. They looked the part, all bigger than any of the Owls now gathered, and all of them were well intoxicated. They dressed in the standard clothing of the day; all wore sheepskin coats, flared trousers of varying colours, Doc Marten boots and all were adorned with Blades scarves tied around their heads. The leader of them had long straggly ginger hair and was fronting the younger Wednesday lads, who in turn were reluctant to attack the bigger lad, but they were not backing off either. The six Blades put a few yards between themselves and the Owls and turned to face them. After a few moments of mutual abuse, Ginger Blade, and one of his mates, moved menacingly towards the Wednesday mob. At this point, two Wednesday lads known to me challenged them. Both were from the Chapeltown area, around 17–18 years old, and very game. Within seconds, two brawls had started, with all four combatants going at it enthusiastically. In one scrap, the Ginger Blade was getting slightly on top, and his Owl opponent was backed up against the wall. In the other, the Owl (I'll call him Shiner for reference) was getting the upper hand. The Blade was a bigger lad but Shiner was throwing fast accurate punches and the Blade was somewhat pissed. Shiner had him reeling, and soon had him on the floor punching him at will. Although Ginger Blade was winning the other scrap, another of his mates decided to join in. This in effect caused Ginger's downfall as other Owls, incensed by this bullying, steamed in to help the Owl. Soon, around 30 young Owls were booting the Blades all over the place. Eventually, the police did arrive and the Blades were ushered away while the Owls were encouraged by the police to take their places on the Kop.

As all this was going off, the Blades main mob had arrived en masse, and around 300 were queuing up at the turnstiles, marshalled by the police. The older Wednesday lads were also beginning to arrive in numbers. Inside the turnstiles, the Blades were reluctant to come up the back of the Kop and were shepherded by the police to the left and under the tunnel. They came on to the Kop behind a heavy escort and were escorted up the left-hand side towards their usual standing point at the very highest peak of the East Bank. However, Wednesday had anticipated this and had occupied that spot. By now, it was quite clear that Owls were out in good numbers. I believe we had around 1,200 in our mob that afternoon and the Blades mob of around 400 in total had to be content with a position halfway down as far to the left as possible and surrounded by ranks of police.

All through the game, Owls attempted to breach the police lines, but were frustrated. Wednesday fans took to taunting their higher-League rivals and belittling their attempts to invade our Kop. Despite repeated attempts to get at the Blades, it became clear we would have to wait until the end of the game to get at them. The game was a scrappy affair, which ended 0–0. The resulting penalty shoot-out saw Wednesday emerge victorious 5–3. Now the fun started.

As the police kept a close watch on the main Wednesday mob, menacing behind and to the side of the Unitedites, the police tried to usher the Blades out by the same way they had entered. As their mob made the left turn to walk back under the Ozzie Owl tunnel, they suddenly turned and rushed back on to the Kop. Some jumped the perimeter wall and ended up on the pitch. Under the tunnel, a mob of Owls had lain in wait and attacked as the Blades emerged from the terracing, running them back into the ground. The police were now resorting to frantic baton charges to keep the Owls hordes back, but the Blades were now well and truly cornered. More and more sought the safety of the pitch. Eventually, all Blades were taken off the Kop via the perimeter wall and exited through the South Stand.

The Wednesday mobs were themselves now exiting on to Penistone Road to confront Blades outside. The Blades had been encouraged by the police to make for Leppings Lane. This was advice that the majority of them accepted, but this was the 1970s, and the police did not give the type of escort seen today. Many of the Blades headed back towards town in ones and twos, or small groups. Foolishly, some 200 walked through Hillsborough Park and they were quickly spotted. Hundreds of Owls swamped the Park through two entrances, and the retreating Blades ran towards the far side where they would eventually emerge just outside Hillsborough Shopping Centre. Numerous unfortunate Blades were caught and beaten. Some made a spirited stand, and, even today, they have my respect for having a go against the odds. Most that stood suffered the indignity of being thrown into the boating lake. I believe around two dozen at least suffered this fate.

This to me was the day that Wednesday confirmed their superiority off the pitch over United. These events would be supported by our taking of the United Kop on various occasions over the next four years. Blades will argue that they stood their ground on our Kop, that we couldn't budge them and that Wednesday had far superior numbers.

The counter to those arguments is that they only stood due to a massive police presence, and I can guarantee that few Blades that day watched the game. The vast majority spent the entire match apprehensively watching for the Owls breaking through the police lines. As for numbers, that is a matter for the Blades. They were the top side in Sheffield at the time and had put up a few good shows off the pitch against the likes of Newcastle and Leeds, but had failed to turn up when it mattered – against their most feared and hated rivals.

Wednesday taunted the Blades that day with the chant 'You'll never take the East Bank'. Never was a taunt so truly made.

The following season, the County Cup would once more give the Wednesday gangs an opportunity to flex their muscle against their cross-town rivals. This time the game was at Bramall Lane, and once again it was camp day on the Shoreham. Tony picks up the story.

COUNTY CUP FINAL, 1975–76

The year was now 1975–76, and we had slumped into the Third Division, which meant that, while we were off to Aldershot and Mansfield, United were at Manchester and Arsenal. We got the chance early on in the season to give the Lane a visit, and now I was ready to join the ranks of the EBRA for my very first battle on the Shoreham.

This game was played three days after Millwall visited Hillsborough, and the East Bank boys had got to grips with the F-Troop on the Kop. Although the Cockneys were heavily outnumbered, they were game as they come, and put up some stiff resistance before being expelled from the vast open terrace.

After the game, word spread that we were going to have a pop at the Blades in the County Cup Final, and the meet was planned for around six in the Claymore. When we arrived it was crammed with Wednesdayites and everyone was on a high, but we were not boisterous because we didn't want the police on our case. We spent the next hour just having an enjoyable drink before moving out on to Arundel Gate and heading in the direction of the Lane.

We moved off the beaten track and took the back streets to our destination. You could have heard a pin drop as our group, which numbered around 100, snaked its way towards St Mary's Church. We were now a few hundred yards from John Street, and I don't know who started it, but a 'UNITED' chant went up and we all joined in. The police thought we were Blades and ushered us towards the Shoreham, and for good measure we hurled abuse at passing Wednesdayites. It did the trick and even some gullible Blades joined us. It took a few minutes for us all to gain access to the ground, and even the Unitedites had not got a clue who we were until we showed our true colours, and walloped them. We ran up the staircase and charged across the Shoreham like screaming banshees, and most of the Blades ran away except for the usual suspects, who stood their ground, but we were too strong and forced them out of the middle and the Shoreham was ours. Other Wednesdayites joined us and we must have inspired our team because we won the game 2–1 and lifted the Cup.

We had done what United never achieved and that was take their end. There was the odd scuffle during the game, but the damage had been done, and, when we poured out on to Shoreham Street and headed back to the Claymore, anybody watching would have thought we'd won the League, Cup and General Election for good measure.

We finished off what had been an enjoyable evening in the legendary Crazy Daizy, and bopped away to the sounds of Roxy Music and Dr Feelgood. Our Blade mates joined us and we all had a good drink well into the early hours.

The fighting was over for another day, and Wednesday once again had shown their superior firepower when it came to a meeting between the Owls and Blades.

Few would dispute that the 70s had belonged to Wednesday off the field, but things change and, by the beginning of the 80s, a turning of the tide was imminent, but, before moving on to that, I will give Jon the opportunity to wrap up a very eventful decade for the Steel City hooligans.

OWLS V BLADES – AN OVERVIEW OF THE 1970s

For the majority of the 1970s, United were the top dogs on the pitch. They enjoyed five years or so in the top flight before their decline began in 1976.

For Wednesdayites, it was a depressing era as far as football was concerned. Relegated from the top flight in 1970, the downward spiral continued, resulting in a last-match victory over Southend in 1976 to avoid relegation to the old Fourth Division.

Off the pitch, things were very different in Sheffield. Despite obviously attracting bigger crowds, United's hooligan element nearly always came badly unstuck when meeting their Wednesday counterparts. Our away followings during 1971–79 usually left people shaking their heads in amazement. We didn't always take thousands to every away match, as has been falsely claimed, but the followings were not in proportion to the home attendances. We had to accept that United held sway football-wise during this era, but we never missed an opportunity to raise Wednesday's profile against them off the pitch. We had to rely on non-competitive matches (if that's possible in a local derby), such as pre-season friendlies, Testimonials and, of course, the Sheffield County Cup.

Several times, we played at Bramall Lane against them and simply swamped their Shoreham End Kop, running them ragged. Various excuses were offered, but the most bizarre came after a Testimonial for one of their most talented and much loved players, Alan Woodward, in 1974. Wednesday had 3,000 on the Shoreham that night and United's pitiful mob of 400 had been routed. They later claimed that their entire mob went to the City Hall for a Slade concert rather than pay respects to one of their favourite sons, and defend their end against their most hated enemy.

To me, the United mob were a strange breed. I went to Bramall Lane several times during the 1970s and witnessed them put up sterling efforts against the likes of Arsenal and Leeds. I also witnessed them destroy a 600-strong Newcastle mob in 1973, battering them down the Kop during the second half. This was after the Geordies had wrecked numerous pubs in Sheffield city centre, but for some reason they rarely put up much resistance against us. On one occasion, at another Testimonial in 1973, we didn't take the Shoreham, but even at that game Wednesday pushed the Blades mob at least 20 yards across the back of the Kop. A funny incident that night came when a small mob of Owls, around 20-strong, led by a big black lad called Colin, sneaked into the middle of the Blades mob. Once settled in, they started to chant Wednesday songs. The gap that formed around them was huge. United wouldn't go near them. The police moved in and surrounded the Owls and forced them back out, and over to the rest of the Wednesday mob. As they did, the Blades started chanting, 'We've got you on the run.' As a much-missed Wednesday lad from that era once stated, 'You couldn't make it up with them fuckers.'

It was largely due to United's inadequacy against Wednesday that a few of their new breed began to get very pissed off with their own mob. This small group of around 40 lads had fronted the Blades mob at a game in 1977.

As Wednesday went into them, the main body of Blades ran as usual, leaving this 40 to take the full brunt of the attack. To their credit, they were very game and had a go, but, as some of them now admit, they were thankful for the police for getting them out when they did. This mob started to stand away from the main Blades mob at home matches and do their own thing. Relying on each other and hoping other Blades would start to show more bottle, these new kids on the block led from the front and became well known and respected in Sheffield over the next four years. But, despite their willingness to stand against Wednesday, it wasn't enough.

Proof of this came in the 1979–80 season. The teams met in competitive action for the first time in eight years. Although it was in the Third Division, over 49,000 were at Hillsborough on Boxing Day and almost 46,000 at the return match on Easter Saturday. Both games were all-ticket, but getting them for the opposition end wasn't a problem. Nevertheless, United made no show at all on Wednesday's East Bank, while, in the return match, Wednesday had a mob of around 1,500 on their end. I disagree with those who claim we had 5,000 on that day. We may have had more fans on there, but they were by no means all lads. We mobbed up to the left-hand side of the Kop, which by now had section fences, making an attack across the top impossible. Incredibly, the Blades launched an attack from below – suicidal in my opinion, such was the size of the slope. Wednesday's mob simply surged forward and fell on them. It was the Blades' usual suspects but they were given a definite silver medal that afternoon. When the police eventually gained control, it was interesting to note that the Wednesday fans were stood as close to the dividing fence as possible, while the Blades backed off several feet away. This match summed it up for me as to who ran Sheffield at the time.

After the game, the police pushed us away from the ground and up Shoreham Street away from town. At the junction of Queens Road, they left us alone and 1,500 Owls charged down Queens Road towards Pond Street bus station. The two roads converge near to the Howard pub. As we reached this point, we were joined by hundreds more Owls who had been on the Bramall Lane End. We waited for the Blades to show, but the wait was in vain. Eventually, police on horses and with dogs began to scatter us.

A group of 300 or so made their way round past the train station and headed towards town. It was then that the Blades' main lads were spotted outside the Penny Black pub. As usual, it was their group of 40–50. Wednesday charged up towards them as police raced to get between the groups. Unable to reach each other, the two groups hurled missiles at one another. The police suffered the most from this, but meted out swift retribution, courtesy of their trusted truncheons.

On reflection, it is easy to summarise that Wednesday were the top boys in the 1970s. It wasn't until 1978 that United began to get their act together against us, but it would be almost another decade before they turned the tide. I always respected their lads who began showing up around that time. They were a small group of willing and game lads, and the type anyone would be happy to have on their side, but, in the final analysis, they simply couldn't live with Wednesday at the time.

THE TURNING OF THE TIDE

In *Flying With The Owls Crime Squad* (*FWTOCS*) it was noted that, by the beginning of the 1980s, United had started to develop a mob that was capable of challenging the Wednesday supremacy in the Steel City. Both Jon, in the previous chapter, and the much missed Stevie Steve, from *FWTOCS*, had noted the emerging mob during the 1979–81 period, and, throughout the early years of the 80s, this grouping began to make their presence felt. This was also the dawning of the Casual era, but it was slow to take off at Hillsborough. I can recall being perplexed by the new clothing styles, and, even as late as 1983, when I went on holiday to Mallorca and met some proper Millwall blokes, I was still wearing my stretch jeans. Many of the old faces of the 1970s dismissed the new 'trendies' and I believe that this attitude ultimately played a part in the disintegration of the powerful force that had been the EBRA.

During the early years of the decade, United trawled the lower reaches of the League, after suffering relegation to Division Four at the end of the 1980–81 season — a day forever written in Owls hearts as 'Thanks-Givens Day', which was christened as such in gratitude to old campaigner and Blade of the time Don Givens. Givens missed a late penalty in the final game of the season against Walsall, which doomed the Blades to a 1–0 defeat, and pushed their sorry backsides out the Division Three trapdoor. The upshot, from a United point of view, or rather a United hooligan point of view, was that their upcoming mob got a chance to gel as they travelled to clubs such as Crewe, Rochdale and Hereford. The lower standard of policing in such places allowed the Blades followers to swamp these clubs, much as Wednesday had done when they first dropped into the Third Division. Getting a result off the pitch every week breeds confidence, and the United thugs started to transfer this confidence to the streets of Sheffield.

Across the city, the Wednesday hooligan element was finding it tough going dealing with increased, rather than decreased, police scrutiny, and it would be a violent backlash against the police that lead to Owls fans rioting at Oldham on 6 September 1980. The club faced major sanctions after the trouble, and if anything the policing got more hostile. For many of the old East Bank boot boys, the fun had been taken out of their Saturday afternoons, and also the team was winning for the first time in more than a decade.

Tougher ticketing restrictions in the higher divisions also took a toll on the Wednesday mob. The EBRA had never really been a unified single force, but instead had found its strength in being numerous small mobs that came together on a Saturday. On any given match day, there could be small mobs from all around Sheffield and South Yorkshire; they came from Beighton, Chapeltown, Mexborough, Stocksbridge, Parson Cross, Doncaster, Darnall, Rotherham and all points in between. Suddenly they could no longer just come together in distant towns because games became all-ticket, and the police forces, used to dealing with the likes of Chelsea, West Ham and Leeds United, were more than ready for them.

Even Hillsborough became a difficult nut to crack. In the old days, the Wednesday firms used to take to the Leppings Lane End, where away fans were housed, because hardly anyone ever dared bring a mob on to the East Bank, but those days too were coming to an end. Far larger away support was coming to Hillsborough, and the police were becoming ever more vigilant on the turnstiles, so it became difficult for Wednesday lads to infiltrate the away support in large numbers, and increasing success on the field only helped to marginalise the Owls thugs.

Suddenly, the 12–15,000 crowds were 25–27,000, and more families were coming to S6 to get on the bandwagon. The dawn of the Casual was the final straw for many of the old EBRA campaigners, and most simply hung up their scarves and walked away from the violence.

This scene was repeated across the country in the late 1970s and early 1980s, and, while some of the big mobs of that era managed to adapt and buy into the culture of the new football firm, others did not, and Wednesday were one of those that began to go into decline. I don't proclaim to be an expert on why the Owls mob went into decline the way it did, and the reasons laid out are just my own personal recollections from the time. Others may have different ideas, but, whatever the reasons were, it was clear that the Blades were gaining ground. They had some good old campaigners from years gone by, and into that they mixed some game young lads, many of whom had grown up together, and who had looked on while the EBRA put their older comrades to the sword throughout the 1970s. Combined with the complacency which had also set in across at Hillsborough, the scene was set for a radical shake-up.

By 1985, the gap between the two mobs in the Steel City was barely distinguishable, although it has to be said that they rarely clashed in those days outside of a match between the two clubs. The two mobs could co-exist in relative peace within the same city-centre pub on occasion, but by and large the Wednesday boys stuck to West Street, while United patrolled London Road, and never the twain shall meet.

Things were changing, however, and West Street throughout the 1980s would increasingly become a battleground, as the weekend calm of the previous decade became a distant memory. The thoroughfare, which heads out of the city centre to the north-west, and was a popular haunt for Sheffield's growing student population due to its large number of pubs, had until around 1980 been a relative Blade stronghold, but an incident in the Wicker area of Sheffield during that year would lead to a chain of events which saw Wednesday make it their favoured drinking spot. Again, I hand over to Jon to relate what happened.

There are probably people who would be better at giving a blow-by-blow account of the Owls/Blades confrontations in town during the 1979–81 era than I am, simply because I was not out week in week out like a lot of others were. For around two years, I entered this arena roughly about once or twice per month. The main reason for this is that, unlike many of my fellow Wednesday brethren, I was not a great lover of punk and certainly not a fan at all of the mod revival or ska music scene of 1979 onwards. This, after all, was the main reason Wednesday started meeting in town as a firm in the first place. Inevitably, most Friday and Saturday nights would end up in the Limit club on West Street, and so West Street became the main drinking area, due to its large number of pubs.

We weren't restricted to just this area, though. Often we would meet up in the Marples in Fitzalan Square or the Claymore, which was just around the corner and was a Wednesday stronghold. It may be coincidental that around this time a mob of United lads started coming into town on a regular basis. It seems inevitable now that paths would cross and fights ensue, and this proved to be the case. My recollections are that United had a tight little firm of around 50 tops. Wednesday could muster around twice this number. This doesn't mean these were always the numbers that were out, nor does it mean that fights happened every time we ran into each other. I have been out when Wednesday have had only six or eight lads out and Blades have had a similar number. The numbers involved fluctuated. For the record, the Blades had some game handy lads, make no mistake. Their problem was that Wednesday's game hard lads were more numerical and harder. Don't run away with the idea that Wednesday's success was all about numbers. I have witnessed fights where Blades had the numerical advantage and still got done or run. By and large, the fact is Wednesday ran the show, simple as that. Of course, Blades had some results, that is always going to be the case, but by and large Sheffield belonged to Wednesday during this era.

In his book *Knowing The Score*, author and Blades fan Gary

Armstrong gives the impression that the Blades mob at this time just decided to leave West Street to Wednesday and preferred to drink on London Road. Nothing sinister, just decided. The reality was slightly different. For some reason, unknown to me, hostilities seemed to escalate around September 1980. Almost every time the two groups ran into each other a battle would commence. More and more, the Owls began to exert their authority, as Blades would be put on the back foot. Wednesday now began to actively go looking for Blades. For a time, Blades would still come on to West Street, but were becoming more wary and would not be seen unless they had what they considered to be sufficient numbers to make a show. They were now being spotted meeting in the Attercliffe area, around three miles out of town. Often, they would move on to the Wicker, a street around 150 yards long and full of pubs. This was on the edge of the city centre. From there, they would judge their strength and decide accordingly. Wednesday began meeting up more frequently in the Claymore and Marples before venturing up to West Street.

I was on the receiving end of one Blade success at this time. It was early December 1980. Around 70 Owls were gathered in the Claymore. After a couple of beers, eight of us decided to walk round the corner to the Marples for a game of pool. The Marples is famous in Sheffield for taking a direct hit from a Luftwaffe bomb in 1940, killing scores of people. It was rebuilt as a three-storey pub. The top floor was mainly live music, the ground floor housed the main bar and the basement (now in 2007 a bookmakers shop) was the pool room. It only had one table though! We had been in around 10 minutes when 30 Blades walked in, and, without any sort of stand-off, steamed into us. For around five minutes, the eight of us took a decidedly second best before they made their way off. Too late the alarm was raised, and, as the main body of Owls came round from the Claymore, the Blades had vanished.

The rest of the night was spent in a fruitless hunt. I wasn't involved in the hunt as my shoulder, although not dislocated, was badly bruised and my ankle twisted. Not to mention a thick lip! Unbeknown to us, the Blades were holed up in the Dove and Rainbow, a pub on a back street near to Sheffield Newspapers main building.

I can recall little of the next month or two, probably due to the fact that one incident occupies my thoughts. This is the incident I regard as responsible for Wednesday finally ridding West Street of the Blades and bringing to an end the battles of the previous two years. It was one Thursday evening in late February 1981 at around 5.30, long before the advent of all-day opening for pubs, and one of Wednesday's main faces, Tommo, had called in to one of the Wicker's numerous pubs. If memory serves me well, it was the Bull and Oak. He was alone and the pub was empty. As Tommo enjoyed a pint and a read of the local evening paper, 10 Blades walked in. Later, Tommo reported that three were young lads, three were known faces, but not main actors, and the other four were arguably the Blades top boys of the time. There was no protocol or code of conduct observed, the Blades proceeded to boot Tommo around the pub. He covered up as well as expected, but still took a good kicking. Full credit must go to the landlord, a man of the old school, who waded in and stopped him from more serious damage. Tommo took a taxi home and cleaned himself up. He spent the next 24 hours calling his numerous Owls mates to meet up for revenge.

Two days later, Wednesday beat Swansea 2–0 at Hillsborough, and after the game 100 Owls headed for town. We all gathered in the Marples and Tommo was like a cat on hot bricks, hardly touching a drop of beer. We had to wait for the Blades to arrive home from their away game. Occasionally, lads would go for a walk and look around. No Blades were spotted at all that night.

The following Friday, Tommo was again fired up as around 90 Owls met in the Claymore. This time, lads in cars went scouting; London Road, Wicker and Attercliffe were all searched to no avail. Eventually, a car with three Owls in spotted some known Blades entering the West Street Hotel, and while one of the Darnall lads, Greeny, kept watch the others drove back to report. These were the days before CCTV, mobile phones or large groups of sinister OB to watch your every move.

We left the Claymore, and headed up town. Tommo always seemed to be 30 yards in front of everyone else. This could have been dangerous, and everyone hurried to get up West Street and keep together. Wednesday's inability to do this in later years would prove disastrous, but not tonight. As we approached the pub, Greeny reported that around 40 Blades were inside. They had clearly made a decision to bring it on. As everyone got close by, we crossed over to the same side of the road to avoid being spotted. As expected, Tommo ran to the pub and, with five others, including Motley, a big game skinhead from High Green, steamed into the West Street Hotel. The Blades responded, but were drawn out. Only around 10 of them got outside before they realised just exactly what they faced. As these few tried to retreat, they were swamped. Tommo was battering any Blade that moved. Although supposedly a tight-knit firm, this did not stop the Blades still inside from slamming the pub doors shut and barricading themselves in as their few colleagues outside bore the brunt of the onslaught. The unfortunate lads outside were totally written off, but notably no weapons were used. Wednesday now tried to batter the pub doors down. I can still see Tommo now, like a mad wasp almost climbing the walls as he sought his revenge.

After what must have been an age, the first sirens were heard. No one budged. The Blades were trapped inside the pub as more police began to arrive. Eventually, we just stood chanting 'Wednesday Wednesday' and 'You'll never take the East Bank' to the Blades inside. As the police pushed us up West Street and we went into the Mailcoach pub, the Blades were given an escort out of the West Street Hotel and down into town, taking their injured with them.

It would be several years before Blades began venturing

along West Street again. A new era would unfold with different lads. My West Street days became few and far between after that night, but not as few as the Blades. Again, I reiterate, they had some very game handy lads, but were no match for Wednesday in the final count.

Me? I was no top lad either, just a young proud Owl, one of many at that time who had a bit of bottle and enjoyed being part of Sheffield's finest.

After that night, there developed a period of relative calm on the city streets, but it just needed one spark to ignite it, and that would come in the autumn of 1986. I will not go into the details again as the story has been told before in books by Gary Armstrong, Steve Cowens and myself. Suffice to say, though, that this one incident is probably to blame for starting a spiral of violence which has left scores of lads, from both sides, injured and/or incarcerated after around 20 years of almost constant duelling between the two factions, and maybe it really is time to say enough.

Before that night on London Road, the two mobs had clashed head-on yet again in a Testimonial for a United old boy, Tony Kenworthy. The match at the Lane in May 1986 saw two new-look firms meet in violent confrontation, but, while the faces had changed, the result did not and, in a major clash, ironically near the Peace Gardens, after the game, the 'new' Blades were given a rude awakening, in much the same way as the next generation of Owls would be in the clash at Aunt Sally's some 17 years later.

After the 'Battle of the Peace Gardens', the two mobs seemed to go in differing directions. I was a member of the newly formed Owls Crime Squad (OCS) that swept much of what was put in front of them up to the end of the 1986–87 season, but after that we struggled, while our arch-rivals, by now known as the Blades Business Crew (BBC), went from strength to strength. They began showing at places such as Leeds and Middlesbrough, and not just showing, but also more than holding their own. In contrast, we seemed to seek refuge in the Rose after every game, and only dribs and drabs would bother heading for town on Saturday night.

Now, the business of which mob rules town is an issue which still raises its head. In 1985–87 – and probably before, although I wasn't around – the Wednesday mob would meet on Friday and Saturday nights in town before heading up Division Street and on to West Street, where we would inevitably end up in the much missed Saddle for last orders, before entering the legendary Limit club. During this time, we rarely ever saw Blades, well, not in a confrontational way. Many of them would go to the Limit, but they never went in mobbed up, but went for the music and a laugh. I often spent nights in there chatting with odd Blades, and there was rarely any trouble with them.

It seemed to be from about the summer of 1987 that things turned nasty. Our turnouts in town usually numbered only in the twenties most weeks and, of that, a few of them were old-school Blades who were on friendly terms with some of our old faces. Seemingly overnight, we would be confronted by larger and larger groups of increasingly aggressive Blades, and it really started to come on top most weekends. Looking back, we could have thrown more bodies at the situation, and made life difficult for them, but we didn't and, to be honest, a lot of lads just stopped coming into town regularly. As the problem escalated, many of our older lads remained cocooned in a dismissive 'they're wank so we're not bothered' mode, but they failed to see the problem until it was much too late. Most of the time, the Wednesday lads in town became simply the Stocksbridge lads, including a few lads from Hillsborough and Ecclesfield, and a few others, mainly from the Intake and Gleadless areas.

Unless Wednesday had a big game on, this was the last line of defence, and many weeks we would be simply overrun. However, unlike the Blades who meekly surrendered West Street in 1980, we kept returning to our trenches, week in week out, and on some occasions even took the fight down London Road. Matt, one of the main Stocksbridge OCS lads of the time, remembers the era very well.

When I was asked to contribute a section to this book I wanted to write a piece not just slagging the opposition, as most people do, saying we are the best 'Never been run, never been done!'

I wanted to be honest and say every firm has its day and over the years Wednesday and United have both come unstuck, and not just against each other. Anyone who disagrees has either never been there or lives in a dream world.

On both sides over the years, emotions have run high, and through my generation nothing has changed. I was there week in week out from the mid-1980s to the mid-90s, and until recently was still on the scene, although not a regular.

It was tough from 1988 to 1992 when Wednesday's firm was virtually non-existent, but, all the same, every week, the usual faces turned up knowing we were going to be outnumbered, but not always outclassed. During those days, it was the usual routine, six to eight of us drinking and two on the door ready for when *they* turned up. Every now and again, we would run clandestine attacks on the Domino, or venture further up London Road. It was in this period you certainly realised who the game lads were and who the enemy was; it was close combat for both sides, and absolutely no hiding behind police lines shouting 'OCS'.

Major offs were few and far between, but this football violence was every Saturday night, and all too often Fridays, midweek and even as you were doing your weekly shop. It certainly became personal.

Many times, the confrontations involved 20 of them on 10 of us, and then 20 of us on 10 of them. It was very seldom that the sides were matched evenly, and the balance would tip each week, or even on the night the tide could turn one way or another. The BBC would catch us early on and then we would return the favour later that night, or the OCS would do them early, and they would get some of ours outside a club. Anyone who is in a city that has two firms knows exactly what I mean. The BBC is claiming to have run Sheffield. All I can say is it must have been a different Sheffield to the one I was running around in!

On one occasion, five or six of us were walking down West Street to the Limit (our club) on a Saturday night. A favourite trick of the BBC was to wait outside and pick off stragglers that were making their way in. We spotted about 25 Berties waiting outside near the doorway in a couple of groups. After a quick chat, it was decided by all that this was our club, and we were going in. Each of us had served our time on the scene and trusted each other with our backs, even at these odds. First, we walked straight through one of the groups and nothing started. It was just the usual mutters of 'These are them! They're here!' Once we got to the club door, we all turned and stood there. The Blunts were full of it, they outnumbered us four to one, and were sure we would not start anything. A mixed-race lad, called V, reeled up to us first. He was spouting, 'We're on your manor now, what the fuck you gonna to do about it?'

Without thought, the cosh was out and he was whacked on the forehead. His eyes rolled and knees buckled, but he was not down. It took another hit to put him completely out of the picture. As he went down, all hell broke loose in the doorway. Mayhem followed and it went toe-to-toe for about two minutes before we were dragged into the club and the doors closed. The bouncers picked up the cosh and gave it to the girl in the cloakroom. She hung it on a hanger and told us to pick it up when we were leaving, which we did. It sounds surreal, but that is the type of club that the Limit was, anything went. Luckily, the lad who T (our lad) dropped against the wall didn't press charges, and all credit to him; he knew why he was there and took it on the chin – or forehead, depending on how you look at it.

On another night, United had been running amok on West Street early in the evening, so we decided we would return the favour. A group of around 20 of us decided we would take it to them. We got tooled up and walked down to London Road to hit the Palais nightclub (their club). A few of their lads were on the door, and we were straight into them without a sound, but they quickly retreated inside. After grouping, they attempted to storm out of the exits, but were beaten back inside, although a handful managed to get out. They were game and put up a fight, but they were taking a beating. One was thrown through the window of a Chinese takeaway, which caused them to retreat again. On the third attempt, more of them made it out and we gave it them big time. Never been run, never been done?! We had just given it them in their own back yard.

Little did we know the old bill had been sat across the street watching! Soon it was the usual long journey to the charge office, another year in court and, luckily, a six-month suspended. I don't know how we used to get away with it back in those days. The arresting officer that saw the incident told the court he witnessed us striking several lads over the head repeatedly with a tyre iron, pieces of wood and coshes... none of us did time!

Over the years (nearly 25 of them on the football scene), I've learned a lot of lessons and gained some good friends – on both sides, believe it or not. Like a good few retired and reformed followers of the game, I've now left the UK and moved to a sunnier climate. When people ask me why I did it and would I change anything if I had the chance, I'd have to say, 'Bollocks! I loved every minute of it.'

Matt's story can be echoed by many of us that were there at the time, and I can freely admit that United were a bigger, more organised and probably nastier firm, but those who like to believe we never did anything during this time are definitely wearing rose- or red-and-white-coloured spectacles. It took an immense amount of bollocks to put yourself on the firing line, week in week out, and I mean that for the lads on both sides. The youngsters today do not have a clue, and the petty scuffles in pub doorways that lads nowadays rave about are nothing like the violence that erupted every weekend during the 1988–92 period. It was never easy but, let's face it, anyone thinking they can live the life of a football hooligan should never expect an easy ride, well, at least not in Sheffield during these turbulent years. As Matt says, it was rarely major offs between both big firms, it was nasty in-your-face stuff where no one could hide.

★ ★ ★

By 1989, it was clear to everyone involved in the hooligan scene in the Steel City that the tide had turned red. Violence on the day of a pre-season friendly in August of that year was some of the worst I have ever seen. Before the game, an ill-conceived unco-ordinated attempt to attack the Blades uphill led to us getting swamped, as 200-plus BBC launched themselves out of the Wheatsheaf pub, and down into us as we exited the Earl of Arundel. We numbered 70 lads that day, but were gutted to take a second prize, and how many firms can say that when outnumbered three to one?

During the game, we plotted up in the Dog and Partridge pub on Trippet Lane, which was adjacent to West Street, and was a spot where we often headed if the police were applying the heat. For some reason, the South Yorkshire bobbies never seemed to realise where we had gone when we sloped off down to the D&P or Grapes! After the game, a lightning attack was staged on far superior numbers of BBC at Silks, and some honour was restored. After all these years, I still cannot recall too many times when we unleashed assaults of the ferocity shown at Silks; maybe if we had, things would have been different heading into the 1990s.

Away from the match day, though, the tit-for-tat stuff seemed to continue unabated around this time, and there was rarely any telling where and when it could strike. Lads were attacked while out shopping, riding a bus and even while playing football. Many of the firm members from both sides played for local Sunday-league teams, and all you needed to do was find out where your enemy's team would be playing and show up ready for action. Numerous attacks on the football fields of Sheffield parks resulted, and all too often innocents would be brought into the fray. To round out this chapter, I want to go back to Matt, as he recalls one of the Sunday-morning battles, and the reasons behind it.

This tells about the events of a late summer's evening in 1991, and, like I said earlier, back then emotions were running high and the scene was getting very personal. All kinds of shit was happening, house and work calls were being made and daytime beatings; it wasn't pleasant.

One of our younger lads had been done by a group of the Berties while he was walking his dog across Hurfield School fields. Apparently, some of them trained there for their Sunday-football team. The phone calls went round and the word was passed that we would meet the following week at the Arbourthorne Hotel for a revenge attack.

Everyone who needed to be was there. Myself, Fingers, Shane and One-Eye had travelled 15 miles from Stocksbridge for this. There were no hangers-on and everyone was buzzing. The scouts were sent out while we had a pint, and they came back reporting that there were more of them than the previous week. The Berties by now knew we were coming, but that didn't faze anyone.

The shout went up and we left the pub. It was only a short walk to the fields and we split into two groups, one straight on and one round the side of the school. The lads who lived local didn't want to be identified for fear of repercussions and more house calls, so they donned black balaclavas. Twenty of us walking through the council estate tooled up to fuck, and some wearing balaclavas, it looked like a bad day in County Armagh! It really was no wonder that the OB got there so fast.

As we entered the fields, they saw us, about 10 of them were shouting and running for their bags. You could see who was there, and it was their lads who had turned out, but they weren't there for the training. They were pulling out cricket bats and golf clubs, but we were no mugs either. Up went our scarves and out came the hammers, machetes and bats. The pace quickened to a jog until we were only yards apart, and the stand-off lasted maybe five seconds until the adrenalin-rushing shout of 'Come On!' filled the air. Black T was first in, as he steamed through and smashed his bat into a fella's mouth; the lad's teeth went flying everywhere! Then we were all into them. Everything was being swung and people were going down hurt. It was toe-to-toe for maybe a minute or so, then they were off. Their bottle had gone and the chase began. Not even a turn and a shout of 'Stand United' was uttered. We had done them big time and they knew it. The all-too-regular shout of 'bizzies' followed and everyone scattered.

Some of our lot returned later to collect the Blunts' bags and belongings that they had left in such a hurry. They torched them in the school car park. And, even though this time we did have the numbers advantage, it was still a good day for the OCS.

The constant violence had become a way of life by the time the mid-1990s rolled around, and for many there was no way out of it. I would soon be off for sunnier climes, and my days of week-in week-out involvement with the struggle for supremacy would be over, but it was certainly with mixed emotions that I turned my back on the Steel City. On the one hand, I was getting older, and needed to put down some firm roots, but on the other I knew I was going to miss the lifestyle, even if we were on the back foot far too often. Those who have never been involved will struggle to understand why we did what we did, but at the time you don't even think about it, and it's a question of honour, pride and respect. Whether it is misplaced is not my call to make, but all of the lads from this era, whether Owl or Blade, who played by the rules demand respect, and those who did not play by the rules deserve fuck all!

REQUIEM FOR THE STEEL CITY

Split from the Flock

An echoing sound is 'Son, fight your corner'
But push came to shove and I need a blood donor
I'm laid on me back and leaking like mad
The worrying thing he weren't their top lad
It's a youth with a tool who should be at school
But he's just wrote me off and I'm laid in a pool
There's a glimmer of hope and I've just seen the light
The fucker's a blue one
It's that bag of shite
I'm trying to get up to sort me sen out
But a worn-out Doc Marten gives me a clout
I'm more worried now than I was on me own
There's a man in me side and it's worse than a thorn
He ant got a brain just a key in his back
And while I'm ont' floor he shows me no slack
He thinks I'm a number and a bit of a twat
And probably deserved to get hit with a bat
From pillar to post, I've now made the van
This is the start of my three-year ban
With no questions asked, I'm sat in the dock
Another good lad that's been split from the flock
For most of my life I've followed with pride
The two sides of football that turned with the tide.

Douglas Naylor

By the early 1990s, the OCS was a shadow of its former incarnations. The youth movement had apparently dried up, and the 40 or so regular participants were all in their late twenties or early thirties, and it seemed only a matter of time before Sheffield Wednesday no longer had a hooligan firm. But, incredibly, as the new millennium approached, the firm was once more on the rise, and by 2000 they were starting to pull numbers that those of us who endured the torrid years could only dream of. The BBC claims that Wednesday didn't dare show in town were bullshit at best. By the turn of the century, this was being exposed as pure mythology, and it wasn't just in town that the thugs fought their never-ending war. Clashes between gangs of OCS and BBC were also occurring in the suburbs.

Tony takes up the story of one such clash which occurred in 1999 as both sets of supporters were out in force to watch England take on their old enemy Scotland.

I had travelled up from Tinsley to join the boys in the Birley Hotel for the Euro 2000 qualifier between England and Scotland at Hampden Park on 13 November 1999. On entering the boozer, the place was rammed as usual and the landlord was dodging about looking a little more flustered than usual. I mentioned to the lads that there were some unusual faces sat grouped together. The boys told me that these chaps were fully paid-up members of the Owls Crime Squad, or OCS for short.

I acknowledged the ones I knew from Hillsborough with the customary nod, and I settled back to see the beer flow and England turn over the old enemy. As the day wore on, and with the advent of the mobile phone, it became apparent that verbal abuse was being thrown through the airwaves between the boys in the Birley and their bitterest rivals the Blades Business Crew, who were apparently holed up in a boozer not too many miles away, doing the same thing that we had been doing for the past five hours, which was enjoying the two great pleasures of male bonding: boozing and watching the football.

The landlord was now in full panic mode and the word spread that the BBC were on the way. As our lot settled back, the ranks of the OCS were assembled ready for confrontation. I weighed up this new breed of football hooligan who had been forced to take their war to the streets because the infamous terracing had been snatched away from them. They reminded me closely of our old boys, who had assembled beneath the steps of the Shoreham some 25 years previous, as they geared themselves up to face the immortal enemy, only this time the bovver boot, silk scarf and jean jacket had been replaced with enough designer gear to pay off my mortgage. Bloody hell and they were about to rip each other to shreds dressed to the nines.

Then it happened. A van had parked itself some few hundred yards from the boozer, and four youths had disembarked and made for the pub's open doors. Their actions were commendable, and at first only a handful of Owls went outside. In the ensuing confrontation one lad was struck across the face with a metal object, and another Owl was swinging his belt at the retreating Blades. Now the four were up against it, and one fell to the floor under a barrage of fists and boots, which left him in a bad way. A regular punter from the boozer went to his aid and the man mountain stood over his prone body like a guardian angel.

The Blades' actions were futile and it became apparent that these boys had come on a suicide mission. Things cooled for a while, but I could not fathom out why the rest of their boys had not followed the gang of four. The lad who was injured wore a very bad gash across his forehead, and he looked in a very bad way but the boys helped him the best they could until the ambulance arrived.

The landlord now started bolting the doors and it was locked up in no time, but most of the Wednesdayites had vacated the premises for the boozer across the road, so we settled back to drink some more and reflect on the dismal start Wednesday had brought to Sheffield 6, while outside the sirens were wailing and riot vans were strewn across Birley Moor Road. At last, reinforcements had come to the aid of the gallant, but suicidal four. The moment was lost, however, as many of the Wednesdayites had drifted away, but there were still enough present to make a charge into the car park of the Sherwood. As is always the case, though, it was now the riot police that had the best firm on show, and, while our 40-somethings watched the drama unfold from behind the windows of the Birley, the landlord was frantically trying to redraw the curtains in case flying debris was heading his way.

Numerous arrests were made that day and many more got stitched up – literally – but these would have been small in comparison if United had mobbed up and accompanied their mates and took it to the Owls straight away rather than waiting another hour, when the place was swarming with riot vans. I heard later that the fighting had gone on all the way up Mansfield Road to the Ball Inn, well over a mile away.

Who am I to talk though? We had it laid on a plate in my day; all we had to do was walk through the turnstiles to get it on with our rivals from Sheffield 2, but nowadays the lads go to great lengths to confront one another and it's not getting any easier. Football violence was now a completely new ball game and I was glad it was over for me.

I made my way home late in the evening, and still the riot police had fans cuffed and ready to be transported to the nick, as I enjoyed the comfort of the Hackenthorpe flyer to transport me into town.

As I was wending my way home I remembered another confrontation that happened at the very same spot some 20 years previous. The exact time and date was etched firmly in the minds of the two combatants that stood gamely in the face of the ensuing enemy.

It was 2 May 1981 and the time was 5.30, they knew this because the Birley was about to reopen its doors. These two boys waved their blue and white scarves frantically at the passing cars and coaches that were full to bursting with tearful grown men, their eyes damp with the frustration of relegation. Yes, God had answered our prayers and Sheffield United had been shipped off to the depth of the Fourth Division. How the lads were lapping it up, and two fingers, or was it four, were shown with such vigour. Unfortunately, one vanload of surly-faced Blades took exception to the joyful youthful Owls and gave chase. The boys were off like a shot with the grown men hotly in pursuit bellowing the immortal words: 'Come here, you little bastards!'

The chase was soon over and the Wednesday boys hid while the coast was clear. They'd had their fun at the expense of our very sad neighbours, and spent the rest of the evening showing Don Givens the art in penalty taking, the sad bastard.

They say that football comes back to bite you where it hurts, and it did this to one of those same youngsters on 14 May 2000. We too were relegated, but only out of the Premiership and the boy took it badly.

After the home game with Leicester City, he walked into the club shop and bought himself a replica Wednesday shirt that was worn so proudly by the likes of Terry Curran and Mark Smith, and then he was off like a shot to the Blade heartland of Mosborough before settling himself nicely in the Queens for a pint. The landlord was none too pleased that this lone Owl was knocking back the ale dressed in all his blue and white regalia, and asked him nicely to remove it because he didn't want any trouble, but the boy was not for reforming, and he was asked to leave. He then headed for the Vine and walked in, still sporting our famous colours. The place was full of Blades, who looked uneasy, as our boy stood his ground looking like a million dollars.

The place had seen one or two skirmishes between Owl and Blade but this time Wednesday was given a wide berth. Eventually, he left the place totally unscathed, happy in the fact that he'd come looking for confrontation to ease the pain of his beloved club's relegation, but none was forthcoming.

Shortly before my visit over the Christmas period of 2000, the two firms would clash on derby day. For a broader view, I refer to the NCIS report of the evening's events.

> There was serious disorder in Sheffield city centre after this fixture. At 5.30pm, a group of 250 United supporters appeared at a public house in the city centre. At the same time, over 200 Wednesday supporters left Hillsborough and boarded the supertram to the city centre. The rival groups made their way to West Street. Police formed a cordon across the road when the Wednesday group alighted from the supertram and the pub containing the United group was surrounded by police in an attempt to prevent confrontation and serious disorder. Batons and CS incapacitants were used when the United group did a starburst from the pub and the Wednesday group charged the police line. The United group caused damage to the pub. Both groups were dispersed, but fighting broke out in different parts of the centre. The two main groups were gradually fragmented following police searches and in excess of 30 arrests were made.

Lee, an old friend of mine, describes how he saw the violence that night.

> We had been in Hillsborough when we got the call through that the Blunts were on West Street. Within minutes, we were all out on the platform waiting for the tram into town, and I would say we were easily 150-strong, if not more. On the ride in, we heard that the pigs had holed themselves up in the Walkabout, so we got off the tram at the bottom end of West Street. Fuck me, when we arrived, it looked like a scene out of some science-fiction film with the number of bastard robocops around. Within minutes, we heard a roar go up, and saw the pigs battling with the old bill at the pub doors, so some of ours charged the police too, meaning they now had it on two fronts. These coppers were tooled up to fuck, though, and soon the CS gas was choking us up. They tried forcing us further up West

Street, but about 30 of us slipped them, and got down to Division Street, which, with hindsight, was not a good move as the pigs had got out of the Walkabout and were also trying to get down Division Street. As soon as they saw us, they were into us, but we did put up a good effort before being overwhelmed and legging it. It would probably have been different if our entire firm had got down there, but they didn't, so credit to the Blades for taking the result. It does make you wonder why the police let 30 or so slip away, right into the spot where they knew the Blunts were, but that's the way it is I suppose.

I returned to visit Sheffield in 2002, and travelled to Grimsby and Stoke during that visit. On both occasions, we came straight back into town, even though the Blades claim Wednesday were scared to come into the city centre. After the Grimsby trip, I saw their bullshit up close and personal, as they kept phoning Owls lads, saying, 'Come to this pub,' and so on. The first call said they were at the Cavendish at the top of West Street, which was handy as the Owls were in the Harley, a mere 100 yards up the road. The 40 or so Wednesday lads, including myself, immediately went for a look, and, surprise, surprise, no Blades. Five minutes later, and it's 'We're at the Devonshire Cat'; again, no sign of them. The next call claimed it was the Dickens that they were now holed up in, and again it was pure bollocks. The Blunts making these calls must have been pissing in their little rubber pants, but to me it just showed how far they had fallen. The BBC faces from the late 1980s never pulled stunts like that. The lads back then, on both sides, got on with it without the need for childish games.

Eventually, the 20 of us that were left fucked off to Hillsborough, after trawling town on a fruitless search. Imagine our collective surprise when, just as we entered the Freemasons Arms, one of the lads' phones went, and it was the Blades with another pile of pigshit. All I can say is that lads who indulge in games like that are pure mugs, end of chat.

The following week, we came back from Stoke with about 70 in hand. Some Blades, old heads, came down for a chat at the Yorkshire

Grey, but admitted they had nothing out. So much for running town, eh?

Over the next few years, the Owls turnouts got larger, but so did the police turnouts, and trouble was largely averted by a massive presence of the boys in blue. There were some clashes, and one that occurred after Wednesday had played Rotherham in February 2002 began to make the young OCS – or ITI as they were now calling themselves – believe that the tide was starting to turn. The two firms clashed at the Brown Bear pub in Sheffield city centre, and the BBC were forced to flee to the Bankers Draft. The Blades claim that they regrouped and came back at Wednesday after emerging from the pub, but Owls in attendance that day maintain that the Wednesday they had on their toes were stragglers just arriving in town, and not part of the mob at the Brown Bear.

Alex, a participant in the evening's events, picks up the story.

We had headed into town after being unsuccessful in our attempts to get at Rotherham, due to the OB wrapping them in cotton wool. About 50 Wednesday headed into town knowing there were Blades about, and within a few minutes the lads were nicely installed in the Brown Bear. All of a sudden the shout went up that the pigs were down the road. A handful of the 50 were out of the pub and down the road, as about 30 mobbed-up Blades came round the corner from the Mulberry Tavern.

T was leading a very strung-out line of Wednesday, with a traffic cone in hand, and he went straight into them, at which point the rest of the Owls were making good headway down the road and into the Blades. They pretty much bottled it straight away, and legged it; with a few of theirs taking a hiding, and the Wednesday lads chased them straight into the Bankers Draft. A few Wednesday went over and started banging on the door, but they did not come out. At which point, sirens could be heard behind the Brown Bear mob, so we made headway back to the pub – duly surrounded by OB for most of the night. What's the point of being caught slap bang next to the pub, having just chased the running bastards into an area that is surrounded by cameras?

A few minutes later, a tram pulled up outside of the Bankers Draft carrying about a dozen Wednesday fans from the match, and these lads, not all firm, I might add, were then duly scattered by the pissed-off BBC lads in the Bankers. The Brown Bear mob did not get run, did not fuck off and stood long enough outside the Bankers for them to come out but they didn't. All the BBC in the Bankers did was surprise a completely unaware tram full of Wednesday, albeit carrying a couple of known faces; one of whom got badly done I seem to recall.

About a year later, a mob of Blades were back-pedalled at TP Woods bar in town. This incident was caught on CCTV, which eventually made its way into the outside world, and made a mockery of the BBC claims that 100 OCS had attacked 10 BBC. The video shows about eight Owls walking past the pub, and up to 20 BBC rushing out to attack them, not realising another 40 or so Wednesday lads were coming up Surrey Street. The Blades ran back inside the pub, and only came out again when the police arrived.

Buoyed up by success, the young Owls became a little complacent and, after the last game of the 2002–03 season, a mob of about 60 OCS came seriously unstuck against about 35 BBC at Aunt Sally's bar on Glossop Road. It was certainly a rude awakening, but the BBC needs to remember a night at the Peace Gardens some 17 years prior, when an up-and-coming mob was brutally put in their place by a smaller, tighter, fiercer unit.

I now hand over to Dale, to give a summary of the last few years in the never-ending struggle for dominance in the Steel City.

What can I say about Sheffield United, or rather their lads, the famous BBC? Well, I can say that they have had a good firm, of that there is no doubt, but I can also say that they have now become masters of believing their own bullshit. I'm really not in the mood to rubbish them, and try and say I am right and they are wrong, but it's certainly nice these days to read websites and see that other firms are now catching on to their myth of invincibility bollocks, and that's exactly what it is... bollocks.

I had a good chuckle reading their piece in *Hooligans 2*. They have enough in the locker for Wednesday, whether it be five on five, 10 on 10, blah blah blah! Funny really, because I could relate numerous small-scale spats that went our way and numerous that went theirs, but I'm honest, and I fully believe many of theirs are not. It also says in that book that they turned big numbers out for the match at Hillsborough in 2006. Really? Where the fuck were they then? I never saw them, and neither did anyone else. Maybe they were still hiding up Handsworth. I have been to numerous Sheffield derbies at Hillsborough, and can say that the only time they have ever been, and looked serious, was for the League Cup game in, I think, 2000–2001; every other time they have either not shown at all, or shown with half the South Yorkshire old bill in tow. On the other hand, games at Bramall Lane have been quite hairy at times, and the days of our showing up there taking the piss are definitely consigned to the history books. I remember one particular match there, a night game, about five years ago where they had some seriously tasty lads about, and we were lucky to come out unscathed. Last season's visit to the Lane was nothing like that night, and I would say we had the better of a number of little flare-ups, but again it's nothing like it used to be.

Away from the matches, they claim to run town. Again I have to laugh! If running town involves sitting in a boozer with the beady eye of the law on you all night, then, fair play, they run town. The days of the 1970s and 80s when large mobs could just show up on each other's manor unannounced are over, and the police run town. Anyone who thinks different is deluding themselves, and that includes both sides. The last proper ruck between the two firms came over three years ago at Aunt Sally's up Glossop Road. The Blunts took the honours that night when about 35–40 of them turned over about 60 Wednesday, but the result was not as clear-cut as many BBC like to claim. We dithered that night and paid the price, but in our defence many of our lads could not get out the pub and were being held back by police in riot gear. I saw numerous lads with head injuries from being clattered by those baton-wielding officers, and many of them never saw a Blunt, but that was poor planning on our part, and good planning on the part of the Blades. The result was theirs, but they love to forget the numerous incidents that season where they took seconds, and it's about time they confront their bullshit.

A prime example of their lies came in early 2006. We had played Burnley at home, and I have no idea who they played, but that doesn't matter because they never travel. Anyway, a leading Chelsea face was in Sheffield promoting his new book. Wednesday were about in town all night, with the police spying, and about eight of us, including the said Chelsea lad, decided to head down to the Casbah. Upon reaching the bar, we found about half-a-dozen BBC milling about, and these were the old guard, the so-called invincibles. A bit of a do arose, and one of their leading faces wound up sparked out. The others, who were seriously shitting it by now, were told to fuck off, and they did. Nothing really to write home about, it was just a little scuffle between a dozen or so lads, but imagine my surprise the next day to hear that our six to seven Wednesday and one Chelsea was actually *25* Chelsea! That was the story that these pigs put about to try and save face, and it is far from the first time they have made stuff up to make themselves look better than they are. Fuck me, gents, everyone can come off worst now and then. Just fucking live with it. These lads were game, but unfortunately bit off more than they could chew. There's no shame in that, at least they had a go, and didn't just leg it like so many, so why not just admit the truth? Why completely exaggerate the situation? Maybe it helps them sleep at night, who knows?

Another of the favoured myths they peddle is the one about Wednesday being afraid to drink in town. Well, lads, that always make me laugh. I have drunk in town for over 25 years, and not once have I, or any other Wednesday lads I know, said, 'Oh I'm not going into town because those naughty BBC might be about.' It's just fucking ludicrous, and completely false, but, hey, it makes them sound good, and I bet they actually believe it too. In the last five years or so, the majority of the big firm turnouts in town have been Wednesday, and they know it, but, yet again, let's not let the truth get in the way of the lies peddled by the Bertie bullshit crew.

I see that just recently a story about when we came back from QPR has raised its head, but we only hear the piggy version. Here is another version that the S2 bullshit crew don't like to admit. We had taken a big firm down to London for a match with QPR, and on return headed into town. The pigs had been home to some nondescript team, and when we landed in town we easily saw off the red and white chav scum we encountered. In fact, they shit themselves so much that they called some of their old hitters, who were drinking down London Road, to come rescue them. The facts are these, about eight or nine of them ventured up, and they were their main faces, but, despite the fact that we had over 100 lads on Cambridge Street, they chose to attack the Yorkshire Grey, about 100 yards away, where about 15 of our young stragglers were drinking. All they did was bounce about and smash a couple of windows, in full view, I might add, of the police. Big fucking deal, you might say, and so would I, but just recently they have been putting this tale into print, and using it as evidence of Wednesday's cowardice, but I tend to think it's just evidence of their stupidity, and the curfews that these dimwits received were about the lightest sentence they could have been handed.

At the end of the day, both firms have some very handy lads, but nowadays it's not enough. The police have cameras, dogs, helicopters and a harsh justice system on their side. The clashes of the past will now forever remain there, and, if you want to have a decent ruck, you best be prepared to pay the consequences if you get that tug.

OWL VERSUS BLADE

The hairy night that Dale talks of came in the 2001–02 season when a badly organised Owls mob struggled to make a reasonable show in S2. The recriminations that followed the poor show that night reverberated around the Owls hooligan element, and there was a great deal of finger pointing. The consensus was that this should never happen again, and for the following season a number of different meets were planned.

Ade takes up the story of what the Blades called another 'Wendy no-show'.

This was the night match when we lost 3–1, after Alan Quinn scored for us, before fucking off to join the piggies. I met Mick, Kev, Tommy, etc. down on Hillsborough Corner at about four-ish. There were already a few in Legends, but the window makes it a bit open so we went over to the Masons. There was already quite the motley crew in there, about 40–50 in total and all older lads. We had spent an hour or so having a gargle when in come South Yorkshire's very own cyber-men and they were all padded up like the Refrigerator of Chicago Bears fame. Nice of them to come out and close the bar! What gives them the right? No bollocks whatsoever.

We were then escorted to the tramstop opposite the Deep End boozer. Within a couple of minutes, a tram from Malin Bridge turned up, and the few passengers that were already on it were taken off and we were put on. Well, the police escort they gave us to the university was worthy of the Krays and Ronnie Biggs. From the university, we were taken to the Varsity, where, upon our arrival, we were met by a good 300 Wednesday lads already there, and this, I think, makes it a good turnout by anyone's standards. Thinking back, it's probably the worst place they could have put us, with the one door to the front and all glass fronted, but the old bill had all those inside well sewn up now, and the outside was surrounded by half-a-dozen vans, horses, dog-vans and plenty of foot soldiers, meaning there was absolutely no way we were going anywhere.

A group tried to make an exit, but those at the front were just manhandled and pushed back.

Seeing this, I had a bit of a brainwave. Syd and I decide to go out via the beer garden. The big gate was closed, so we scaled it, only to pop our heads over the top to be greeted by a good 20 more riot police. The gate opened for Syd to be Section 60'd and, just as he was going to do me, my missus (perfect timing) rang my mobile. 'No, he won't let us out; you'll have to wait for me… blah blah blah,' I mumbled down the phone to her, but just loud enough for the robocops to hear, and it worked a treat. We were off, two-handed!

By about 20 minutes to kick-off, we had got to the roundabout at the bottom of Ecclesall Road, but had seen not a sausage (pork). Onward we pressed, and reached the bottom of London Road, and had still seen nothing. Then, as we were going towards MFI, I noticed a dozen or so, on the corner of Bramall Lane, at the railings next to the road, and what's more they'd seen us and knew who we were.

'Call their bluff here, Syd, and do a right down this side street,' I told my mate.

We got a good 20 yards up when they came around the corner, just as two police vans came the opposite way, and it was game over as we were escorted to the turnstiles.

The game itself started reasonably well when Quinny popped one in to put us in front, and we all steamed up the steps into the stand to celebrate, but that was it for the night. We all know what happened next, and we don't need to print that; it's not worthy.

With five minutes to go, we decide to make an exit as I am totally fucked off and fed up of calls and texts off work pigs and colleagues. Gloating bastards!

We walked up the Moor, getting stopped twice off the SYP. 'Where you going? etc,' and the usual shit.

'Hillsborough, mate, to drown our sorrows,' was my matter-of-fact response.

We hopped on the tram and all looked well, till we got to the

Varsity, and it seemed like all hell let loose. Some black lads were at it with, I assume, some young Owls lads, and there were bicycles, bins and the lot flying about.

We tried to get off, but the doors were well shut. These black lads were like fucking yo-yos, and they put up a right show, but so did the Wednesday youth. It was even numbers and a good three or four minutes it went on.

For us, though, that was it, night over, as old bill turned up and the tram set off.

Back on the Corner, the drinks flowed, but the taste wasn't the same as a couple of hours earlier. It just doesn't taste the same when you lose to them bastards, does it?

At the end of the night, it was a result to forget, but once again a massive turnout by Wednesday, although that's always unrecognised with the grunters.

WEDNESDAY NEVER TURN OUT FOR THE BLUNTS, DO THEY?

Sadly for Owls followers, the club was relegated at the end of the 2002–03 season, and would spend the next two years treading the boards in the First Division (old Third Division), and so the Steel City derby was put on ice. By the time the Owls returned, the red half of the city were getting ready to celebrate a return to the top flight of English football.

At the end of the 2005–06 season, United were promoted to the Premiership, while Wednesday continued to languish on the second rung of English football. The derby games of that season could be the last for a while. Wednesday, by most blue and white accounts, took a good firm to Bramall Lane, but once again United failed to show at Hillsborough, and Owls fans fought with police at half-time. Tom, a young Owl, rounds off the contributions with a look at the last Steel City derbies for the time being.

We had arranged to meet up in Hillsborough early doors (about 10am, I think). Anyway, three of us from our end of the city went up on the tram, hoping to get a full English and a few pots of tea down us before the boozer opened. As we got on

Hillsborough Corner, it became apparent that the police had told the boozers to shut, so we ended up with the 10 or so early birds sat in a café on Hillsborough Corner. As we ate up, the Ball opened so we went in.

The meet was set at 10am and, come 11am, there was only about 30 lads out. There appears to be a tradition at Wednesday (especially with the older lot) that dictates, if a meet is set for a certain time, then you can be certain no cunt will turn up until an hour-and-a-half later.

As the lads started rolling in, word was going round that the Berties had heard we were mobbing up with Chelsea (yawn), that we were going to stay in our main boozer all day (yawn) and the usual bollocks they come out with. I am convinced that one of them sits there in the week thinking of shit to pass through the ranks about us, absolutely certain of it.

We left the ball about 12-ish if I remember rightly, and 50 of us started to make our way to meet 30 or so Wednesday already in town. We got off before town and tried to get into a quiet boozer unnoticed, which included some comical attempts at hiding behind corners from the chopper and vans. We nearly made it but, as we got 100 yards from the chosen boozer, suddenly riot vans and more coppers than we had lads appeared. We got put into the Swim Inn with the rest of our mob, now numbering around 120.

As more and more of ours turned up, we got a mob together that must have been 200-plus, although admittedly I would only have trusted 70 of them to stand and be counted if it came on top.

Word went round that the BBC were in Handsworth (now, lads, we get slated for going up Crookes – no pig fans in town and all that – so how is you lot meeting in Handsworth any different?), but we were being escorted to the ground. Even the ones who didn't have tickets! We went down in one big escort, passing a few dressers on the way (who looked piss poor) and to be honest it was a doddle until we got to the ground.

Now all credit to United, the walk down Bramall Lane was

intimidating because 40 or so of us without tickets knew we would have to walk back through all this lot.

We got to the petrol station and there were a few well-known faces – including some who claim to have retired now – with a mob of Everton. What the fuck has Everton got to do with a Sheffield derby? Did the BBC not feel safe without them? Perhaps this is why there were (untrue) rumours going round that we were mobbing up with Chelsea.

Anyway, it was restricted to verbals as there was more coppers than I've ever seen, and, as we got took to the away end, a police officer came up and asked why we had not joined the queues to get in the ground. We informed him that we said we didn't have tickets when we were in the Swim Inn, and obviously the situation hadn't changed. In my opinion, it seemed that the slimy bastard was trying to set us up muttering something along the lines of 'Oh, well, you'll have to fuck off back to town then through this lot' (pointing towards the BBC stood outside the Cricketers).

I have to admit thinking we were going to get it, especially when they opened a fire door and let half the 40 lads in for nothing, which left 20 youths with the prospect of walking past their rivals' main boozer on derby day. One youth went into the middle of the road and shouted, 'Come on, Wednesday, if we're going, we're fucking going together.'

Someone ought to give that lad a medal, because it saved us from a right hiding. As we started walking back (with no coppers), it took us 10–20 yards before the first lad popped up, saying, 'Come on, lads, I'm B** S****.' I was later informed that he used to be a face in the 70s for the Blades, but, at the time, us 20 youths didn't have a clue who he was. Things were edgy for a second, and we could see their main boozer emptying. Just as I was wondering how long it would take an ambulance to get me to the local hospital, something caught my eye. It was a mob of around 15–20 old-school Wednesday, some of the main boys from the 70s and 80s. I could almost hear the music for the cavalry charge as these older lads who had slipped the escort came to our aid. Old BS took an almighty slap, which left him sparked out, and the roar went up. Buoyed by the fact it was now more even, we all started bouncing like frogs and getting ready to have a pop at anything BBC. This alerted the coppers, who rushed over in numbers to nip the trouble in the bud. Our inexperience looked like counting against us, but everything came good in the end.

We went back to our main boozer (which was shut) and so had to make do with listening to the match on the radio in another boozer in Hillsborough. As far as I know there wasn't much to write home about after; a mob of our youth terrorised their young lads at the Pump Tavern and things got a bit tense at St Mary's roundabout, but I wasn't at either so I can't comment with any certainty.

To round up the day's events, we had been largely wrapped up, but had been to their ground and come away unscathed.

Later that season, at the return match, they brought 12 youths (I kid you not) and half of them left a few lads to stand and get a clip at Hillsborough Park. If I was one of those who stood, I'd seriously have a think about how good my 'mates' are.

Tony, long since retired from his old hooligan days, now rounds out the book with his view of the return game at Hillsborough.

The old days were special to us and now it would be near on impossible to re-enact the night that we snaked through town on our way to the Shoreham; it would never happen because of all the CCTV cameras and helicopter hovering overhead. The lads I was with decided to give Hillsborough Corner a miss and instead park up in the Cask and Cutler so we could drink without fighting to get served. We'd had a good drink and now it was time to head for Hillsborough, and as we waited for the next tram our attention turned to the game and could this be our day. The Blades were on the verge of the Premiership, and how they were lording it on the radio and the internet, but we thought they can have their five minutes of fame because the whole country knows which one of the two city clubs is steeped in history and they don't play in red and white.

When the tram arrived, it was rammed with Blades who were giving it the 'we hate Wednesday' bit. The journey to the Burgoyne was uncomfortable, to say the least, and they knew that the six of us were Wednesdayites. Years gone by, we would have thrown a few but the tram contained children and, though our blood was boiling, we kept a lid on it. I can still taste the spittle today from one young chap who was giving it the 'Wednesday hate' bit with such venom he was blow-drying my hair. We managed to sink a couple in the Burgoyne after we'd alighted from our five minutes in hell.

The atmosphere was bordering on hatred and I have not witnessed that from a crowd at Hillsborough since Manchester United copped for one after they had intimidated Wednesday fans leaving Old Trafford during our League Cup semi in 1994.

With kick-off time approaching, the crowd fell silent and paid a moving tribute to the two Wednesdayites who had sadly lost their lives on their way back from Coventry. This was applauded from all around us, and it is in times like these that Sheffield comes together as one and mourns the passing of any supporter, be it red or blue.

As the players trooped off at half-time, with the Owls struggling, those Wednesdayites congregated under the North Stand vented their anger at the heavy police presence and trouble inevitably broke out. Missiles were thrown at the officers, and there was hand-to-hand fighting. Wednesdayites were going mental and lashing out at the heavily armed police who looked like some Eastern Bloc militia. Numerous arrests were made before the police restored order and everyone settled back for the second half.

Wednesday were sadly outplayed and, even though we rallied slightly, the day belonged to the Blades on the field. But off it Wednesdayites were targeting anyone in red and white and scuffles were breaking out all over the place. The police were hard pressed to keep a lid on it, and if ever such a code of conduct existed between hooligans it was certainly thrown out of the window this day.

The total number of fans arrested during the game numbered 22, of which three were charged with racially abusing the United striker Ade Akinbiyi, but it didn't say if they were Wednesday or Unitedites. The others were charged for such offences as threatening behaviour, criminal damage and breaking the Public Order Act. The police had warned that anyone using abusive language or gestures would be arrested. Bloody hell, then why was the arrest rate so low? Most of the crowd had been abusive to one another all day. In reality, there should have been near on 30,000 banged up. Don't the powers that be realise football is a passionate game?

Over the past six or seven years, the number of major clashes between the two firms has decreased dramatically, and the police are well on top, but the rivalry persists, and both firms nowadays could turn out big numbers, but also the price to pay has increased. Banning orders, in many cases just for being seen in the presence of 'prominents', have bitten deep into almost every football firm in the United Kingdom, and the Steel City mobs are no different. Jail sentences are now the norm for anyone caught being involved in football-related disturbances, but deterrents cannot ultimately change behaviour, they can only push it underground, where it will fester, awaiting a chance to grow undetected. To eliminate a problem successfully, one needs to expose and destroy the root, but no one, it seems, has the imagination or know-how to do that. They think waving a big stick can stop it; it can't, it can only make it more wary, and force it to evolve into something far more dangerous, but, hey, what do I know?

I want to end by taking a quick look at how the fans of the city relate to football by class. Many, many United supporters claim that United are the club of Sheffield and, more, that they are the working man's club. Now, for most of my working life in Sheffield, I worked in the steel and engineering sectors, for centuries the backbone of the Steel City, and by far and away the bulk of people I worked with were Wednesday supporters. In fact, I would even go so far as to say that the Blades were only the third team of the steelworker, as I met just as many Rotherham fans down the Don Valley in those dark satanic mills. Of course, my years in the works were spent when Wednesday were the dominant force on the football fields of Sheffield, and now the red half (?) of the city can claim that title, so maybe all the quiet chaps have dusted their red and white scarves off now. But one thing I am confident of is that, as history has shown, the red and white dominance is only fleeting, a mere blip on the radar, and the blue and white will return to their rightful place as the number-one team in Sheffield, just as Hallam FC will never truly unseat Sheffield FC. I said in *Flying With The Owls Crime Squad* that I don't hate Sheffield United, and I don't, but I don't particularly like them either.

Up the Owls.

SAD, BITTER AND TWISTED BLADES

Since the completion of the first edition of this book (originally called *Divide of the Steel City*) in April 2007, life in this great city has been very good – if you happen to support the blue and white half, that is. And yes, those lovely champagne corks did pop at such an alarming rate in the Birley Hotel thanks to West Ham United, and especially that lovely little Argentinean – the one and only master, the man who was granted the freedom of Sheffield 6, Mister Carlos Tevez. You see, he single-handedly stopped the Hammers from getting relegated and brought those sad and bitter Blades back to earth with an almighty bump, to the delight of the vast majority of the good folk of Sheffield.

And did the bastards moan! United's chairman, McCabe, and his cohorts (including Sean Bean) marched on Parliament and tried to get the government to relegate West Ham and have poor old Carlos deported as an undesirable. (Well, that was the rumour that was circulating around Sheffield 6. Some might say they were just disputing his eligibility to play for the Hammers under present transfer rules.)

They went under the banner of Campaign For Fairness and had a signed petition of well over 50 Members of Parliament. Sadly, this didn't include staunch Unitedite Richard Caborn, who probably thought there was no point lingering around in the top division and getting thrashed every week. Anyway, the bastards got the knock-back because the tribunal, in their wisdom, concluded that the

Blades had been shite all season and rightly showed in favour of West Ham United and good old Carlos. It wasn't their fault the sad Blades couldn't grab a single point on the last day of the season and found themselves stuck firmly in the bottom three – if you finish in that position you are relegated, nothing more, nothing less, so get on with it!

You got sick and tired of the scumbags moaning. One good thing did come out of their relegation though, which was that Sheffield's most hated, Neil Warnock, moved on and was replaced by England legend Bryan Robson. What they were going to do with this man in charge was incredible; they would bounce straight back at the first attempt and show those in the Premier League that you cannot mess about with Sharpe.

While they were getting relegated we'd enjoyed a decent season, finishing ninth and only two wins short of making the play-offs. Had we not had such a bad start to the season, which saw Paul Sturrock replaced by Brian Laws, we may have made the top six.

But Unitedites hate Wednesday more than they love their own team. I mean, wouldn't you get the face on if all your mates got together and obtained a piece of land for playing sport but kept you in the dark? Well, that's what happened when the local cricket teams purchased the land where their ground stands today.

It was not long after when they wormed their way in, and in a sad way took up squatters' rights. Wednesday moved out after 20 years and bought their own ground at Olive Grove, while United were still squatting at the Lane. Even years later, when the Football League didn't want the Blades in the first division and reluctantly let them play in the second, it pissed off the Unitedites who blamed Wednesday for turning everyone against them.

Even today the sad clowns keep the tradition alive. Have you seen the photo of that bastard wearing one of our shirts? You'd never get a Wednesdayite to put on one of theirs, and he tops it off with a pig's head – when everyone in the world knows that their ground is the birthplace of the little pigs.

They also have amongst them an idiot who forks out a few hundred quid on a flag and, instead of putting his favourite football team's name on it, he writes WE HATE WEDNESDAY. But you can't blame him for such hatred, it must do your head in when your team keeps kicking you in the bollocks so many times. I've got mates my age who have followed the Blades for the amount of time that I've been supporting the Owls and what have they got to show for it, compared to my good self? Fuck all. They haven't seen their team win a trophy at Wembley or a Play Off final, or been to an FA Cup final (even though we did lose that one to Arsenal), or win the semi-final of that very same competition. (Remember 1993, you mugs! That's when we were travelling around Europe with good old Woodcock Travel!)

They seem to get onto the verge of something good and then their board just offload all their decent players and replace them with any old Wednesday rejects. To make matters worse, when they thought they'd come up in the world and got themselves a World Cup hosting stadium, just like Hillsborough, the good people at the Football Association kicked them right smack in the bollocks and opted for the pleasant surroundings of Sheffield 6 yet again.

Poor old United. They must think the powers that be really hate them, what with missing out on European football in the sixties and getting relegated by them in Soho Square. Then, lo and behold, those same masters of the English game give Sheffield Wednesday the nod and inform us that we are to host the World Cup in 2018, if this country is successful in obtaining enough votes to return the competition to these shores.

No wonder they fucking hate us, after we've done all that while those sad bastards have achieved sod all! Mind you, with their board's vision for the future, the Johnstones Paint Trophy could be on the horizon – unless they reintroduce the County Cup.

When you come to think of it, being a Blade certainly leaves you sad, bitter and twisted.

CITY FULL OF HATRED

We'd not had a Sheffield derby for nearly two years, but that didn't stop the hatred that was felt between the rival supporters whenever their paths crossed. You could not have a quiet drink in town on a non-match day if you were known to support one team or another, because your rivals would be in your face.

This happened to me because of my association with this book. It was in July, the fucking cricket season, and about 10 of us had decided to have a night in town to celebrate my 25th wedding anniversary. While the good wife was having another hen night with all her mates, I was trying to retrace my steps on my stag night all those years ago. We'd done about half a dozen of the old Sheffield boozers; on entering number seven, it was rammed with young lads enjoying the delights of what our fine city has to offer.

I was then informed by a dodgy-looking elderly gentleman in their company that me (as the writer of this book) and my Wednesday mates were not welcome in this drinking establishment. On informing him that some of the lads in my company followed the same football team as him, he replied, 'What's fucking Blades doing drinking with Wednesdayites?' We decided to drink up and leave because trouble was the last thing on our minds, we were enjoying ourselves too much and the beer was flowing. On leaving the premises, our newfound friends decided to follow us; we were outnumbered about four to one, mind you, though verbals were exchanged and little else. I think they were a bit wary of those present or they probably would have steamed straight in.

To me it was a non-event, but had I been in the company of friends they thought they could take on, the outcome could have been very different. It bears out the frustration of the lads today – that they cannot have what we had all those years ago, when rivals set about each other on match days and only on the very rare occasion while out socialising.

The flashpoints occur when Wednesday or United have been visiting a near-neighbour, arrive back in the city en masse and then go seeking out one another. The police do their best to keep the rivals apart, and on the whole they do keep a lid on it. But on the odd occasion that they are allowed to meet then it's fireworks, boozers are targeted and weapons of any description are used, with the knife making a comeback.

Stabbings are rare when the two teams meet, but with knife crime on the increase I feel that a fatality is waiting to happen. Hooligans through the ages have used knives (none more so than the Scousers), and I may be wrong, but I cannot recall many uses of the knife when Owl meets Blade.

But still, it's not getting any better and the hatred felt towards one another seems to get more intense year by year. Our next instalment comes on the 18th of April 2010. It kicks off on the Sabbath at 1pm, so there's not much chance of a beer before the game unless you find somebody who's doing a lock-in. But with the match finishing around 3pm, that gives everyone another nine hours to get to grips with one another. What with the venue being Hillsborough and us giving them a good allocation, trouble is definitely on the menu.

Police will probably close the boozers in and around the ground, so people will probably head back to their locals. I've got a feeling that we'll head into town to enjoy a nice quiet drink and this time, hopefully, we will be left alone to enjoy our victory – unlike 2008.

HELLO, HELLO, WEDNESDAY ARE BACK!

THE SHEFFIELD DERBY, CHAMPIONSHIP 2007-08

We had to wait until January 2008 for our first crack of the season at our near-neighbours. When United were enjoying another visit to the illustrious surroundings of Sheffield 6, we had Brian Laws as our manager while they had the under-pressure Bryan Robson. The run-up to the game was just as hostile as it had always been, we were taking the piss about them mumping over good old Carlos and their manager.

Wednesday, on the other hand, were not pulling up many trees, but unlike our second-rate cousins we'd enjoyed trips to cup finals and to Europe. On the morning of the game the lads met bright and early as usual, and we enjoyed our pre-match tipple in and around Hillsborough.

There were 30,178 in attendance as the teams took to the field and the stadium was rocking. Then, to the delight of the majority in attendance, Akpo Sodje scored in front of the Leppings Lane end just like good old Terry Curran had done nearly 30 years previous. This time though, no Blade left in a strop and threw himself in the River Don. 'You're going to get the sack in the morning!' we shouted at Robson, while Laws was swinging a blue and white scarf around to the delight of those positioned in the South Stand.

Half-time saw missiles rain down on those Unitedites within throwing distance of the North Stand. The second period brought more Wednesday pressure and, on the odd occasion that United had a shot, our keeper Grant was in outstanding form. Then, with only 15 minutes remaining, Wednesday had Brian Laws sprinting the length of the South Stand in celebration of Marcus Tudgay's goal. I was wishing he'd keep on running round to the Leppings Lane end and do a Terry Curran.

The ground then erupted into 'There's Only One Bryan Robson!' and those traitors Bromby and Geary were getting torrents of abuse, especially with the little leprechaun playing in front of the North.

On the final whistle we all poured out onto Leppings Lane, giving it large to the humpbacked Blades; kids were making their red and white face paint run with a torrent of tears; the odd scuffle broke out but nothing major – the South Yorkshire riot police saw to that.

Why does your post-match pint always taste better when you've done your old enemy? It's at times like these that all the heartache you've suffered over the years is worth it. We'd had our fill of Hillsborough and decided to head to town and enjoy a quiet drink off the beaten track; we knew from experience that West Street would be a hot spot for confrontation.

The old-fashioned boozer just off West Street was our first port of call, which hadn't seen the sad transformation of so many of its counterparts. When we'd had our fill in there we bypassed West Street and headed for Cambridge Street, choosing a Wetherspoon's for its cheap beer; it was reasonably quiet for a Saturday evening, the beer was flowing and everyone was enjoying the fact that we'd done the Blades.

We were also keeping a close eye on the door. It was known to kick off whenever the two sides met, and United would have the face on because of the result. Three lads made their way into the bar but it was okay, they were Wednesdayites; then, all of a sudden, a very large group of Blades followed them in. They totally outnumbered the Owls and those three came under a barrage of punches and kicks.

Even though it was not us they were targeting, our lads nearest the situation felt they had to intervene. You cannot just stand by and watch fellow supporters take a kicking. One Blade was put on his arse in no time and a standoff occurred; while this was happening, the South Yorkshire Police made an appearance and separated the rival factions.

I could not believe it, we'd been minding our own business and it still came on top like that. It was hardly a full-scale riot though, thanks to the installation of more cameras than *You've Been Framed*. If that had happened 20 years previous, everyone in the boozer would have been limping for weeks! We'd have had a good old-fashioned punch-up with the Blades and enjoyed every minute of it, but times have changed and the slap on the wrist and the £50 fine are long gone.

The Blades moved off into the night while we finished our beer and moved further down the street to the next public house. It was then, as we were trying to leave, that our group was issued with a Section 27 of the Violent Crime Reduction Act; this really pissed me off, I fancied having one of those 60s that the youngsters get, but the copper was having none of it. He took down all my details and, after transferring them to his notebook, abruptly slapped the piece of paper in my hand. We'd been minding our own business once again, and confrontation had not been on the menu for us. But once we'd become involved this meant that we had to leave the city centre forthwith and not return for 24 hours; once the paperwork was completed for all of us, we were ushered to the front of the taxi queue. Those waiting to go home must have thought we were some kind of celebrities as the coppers filled one taxi after another; in no time we were wending our way back to suburbia. The funny thing was that we'd picked that area of the town because we believed it would be on the quiet side.

The one good thing to come out of these two incidents was that I knew that I had some very good mates who put their friendship before their football club. I have a good mix of mates who support both clubs and, when threatened, will take on anyone, blue or red, just like they did back in the days when I was enjoying my misspent youth.

The return game in April saw United give the worst ticket allocation to the Owls in the history of the game – 2,500 was the measly number on offer. United also allowed their supporters to take up residence above the visiting supporters; this was asking for trouble. Wednesdayites had also purchased tickets for the home areas, but not in the numbers like we'd done in years gone by. Before the game had started there was a minute's applause for the footballing legend of our great city, Derek Dooley, who had served both clubs as a player, manager and director.

But that was as good as it got. Missiles rained down on the Wednesdayites from the first minute, bottles containing beer and urine, plus coins and anything that was throwable. A crowd of 31,760 enjoyed a close encounter and, with half-time fast approaching, Wednesday did their travelling fans no favour when Adam Bolder put the Owls one to the good. More piss and crap rained down on those situated on the away end while fighting broke out on the Shoreham, and it took the good old riot police wielding their big sticks to restore order.

Just after the interval Wednesday went two up thanks to Bolder again; there was more piss and fighting on the Shoreham but the Wednesdayites couldn't give a shit. We were winning at this shithole and it felt good.

Unfortunately, a Woods own goal and a cracker from Beattie got the bastards out of jail. Well, at least we hadn't been beaten on our short trip across the city, and with United well down the league we knew we'd have another crack at it next season.

So Robson was then replaced by Blackwell, a clone of the departed and much hated Neil Warnock. United were once again lording it; this season was to be their return to the big time. All through the summer months they were strutting around the city while Wednesday were still singing the praises of one Carlos Tevez, and they hated it.

THE SHEFFIELD DERBY: THE CHAMPIONSHIP 2008-2009

It was October 2008 before the teams were due to do battle again, with Hillsborough being the chosen venue this time. Our team and fans were ready for payback time for their fellow supporters being covered in piss and spittle at the Lane the previous April. It raised the temperature before the game and a supertram carrying Unitedites was showered with bottles and glasses as it reached Hillsborough Corner. Once again, Wednesday had given the Blades a decent allocation. Some of the lads, me included, had opted for the boozer to watch the game; the draw of this fixture had lost its sparkle for those of us well past our sell-by date, our experience the previous season had brought it home that even having a quiet drink post-match could land you in trouble. One of the lads had been arrested weeks after our run-in with the Blades in Wetherspoon's and had been charged with threatening behaviour, the SYP had decided to prosecute and a court date was set, which resulted in a not guilty verdict. It was all a waste of tax payers' money. Mind you, the lads who went as witnesses got a good drink out of it.

While a good crowd of 30,441 were in attendance, with the vast majority being of a blue persuasion, the travelling Blades were having a rough ride. Across the city we were enjoying our pre-match tipple in our local boozer and the banter was being thrown back and forth. Up to now, thankfully, that was all that was being thrown.

When the game eventually kicked off, I was wishing I'd opted for Sheffield 6 instead of 12. It was not the same, and this was the first home derby fixture I'd missed in over 45 years. After nearly half an hour the game got tasty, with that animal Killgallon nearly beheading McAllister. This led to the referee rightly brandishing the red card, while Blackwell was doing a nice impression of his predecessor Warnock with his insane rants and arm gestures. Hillsborough had exploded into life and so had the boozer.

Minutes later, a mix-up with Kenny and Morgan saw the ball fall to the feet of Watson who was some 30 yards away from goal. He lofted a shot that seemed to take forever to head in the direction of the Blades goal; it was like time stood still while we watched and held our breath as it sailed sweetly to nestle in the back of the net. Sheffield 6 and 12 went crazy while we watched replay upon replay of our finest moment of the day so far. I glanced towards my beer and, thankfully, not a drop had been spilled. Kenny and Morgan were still having a rant to whose fault it was and I'll bet you a million dollars they were blaming poor old Carlos Tevez!

By half-time, with the teams leaving the field, there was barely time to get your breath back; people were heading outside for a quick fag and a breath of fresh air. Across the road at the Sherwood, you could see the kids' face-paint starting to run already. Come the start of the second half I was back in the seat that had saved me a good £25, this one in the boozer being free while my usual one at Hillsborough knocked me back about 12 pints of lager.

The game had another sending off, but this time Johnson had already left the field when he received another yellow for kicking a water bottle into the crowd after being substituted. Blackwell wanted the referee to reduce the Owls to 10 men and felt it was all a ploy by the FA to get back at United because of their threats of legal action over the Tevez affair. Wednesday also had a penalty saved and, as the clock was ticking down, we were waiting for the usual kick in the bollocks that our beloved team gives us now and again when we throw it all away in the last moments of a game.

My eyes were glued to the referee (I even took 'em off my pint for a few minutes) and I was willing him to blow the fucking whistle. Did he not know what this meant to the blue half of the city's weekend and their work on Monday morning? He'd earned his money and there was no need to prolong this game any further. He was now starting to piss me off and if looks could kill he'd have been a goner. Then he raised his whistle towards his lips, took one last breath and blew it for the final time.

The boozer erupted and one or two mardy Blades threw a couple of punches, but this was Wednesday's moment. We'd sent Blackwell's boys home empty-handed. We partied well into the evening and those face-painted kids from the Sherwood were off home for an early tea and bed; their day was over so there was no point in prolonging the agony. Tomorrow was another day, but mind you they'd got school on Monday morning and more grief to follow.

Wednesday had now been undefeated in the last three meetings. As far as the two sides were concerned, they were now getting the upper hand.

We were to meet again in February 2009, when United were pushing for promotion to the promised land while Wednesday were struggling at the other end of the table. Once again our allocation was piss-poor, while Unitedites had crawled out of their hovels in their thousands to jump onto their bandwagon. For once their attendances were on the up.

This time the first few rows of the Bramall Lane upper were cordoned off, which would hopefully stop the piss being thrown. I was away for this fixture so it was left to my daughter Samantha to fly the flag for our family, while myself and Christine relived the 70s at Butlins – the era when the working class people of this country both watched and played the game, not some overseas mercenaries who cared little for the club they were playing for (except Carlos Tevez, that is).

But fuck me! We couldn't even get the bloody radio to work in deepest Skegness, with the game starting at noon (curtailing the boys' pre-match pint). No matter where we placed the radio, we buggers could not get a signal. We were less than 100 miles from home and Radio Sheffield was out of reach. Then, at five past 12, the phone was ringing; it was Samantha, informing us that good old Tommy Spurr had put the Owls 1-0 to the good. We were going mental and passers-by must have thought we were on drugs, but we were having a good old fix of Sheffield Wednesday! The phone rang again and this time we were like heroin addicts coming down from a high, when we were told that Lupoli had brought the game level.

I'd witnessed some Sheffield derbies in my time: the 3-0 victory in '64 and the 2-0 loss the same year. But then I missed our victory in '65 because I'd been caught nicking in Woolworths pre-Christmas, and as a punishment I was grounded; because of hooliganism I was not allowed to witness our victory in '68. When we lost 3-2 in 1970 I was parading around Bramall Lane in a white coat with a tray around my shoulders, ripping off Sheffield United FC, and in 1979 I was present at the Boxing Day Massacre. But for me that's as good as it got.

Just after half past 12 the phone rang once more and this time you could hear the crowd going mental, Marcus Tudgay had screamed in a scorcher and by all accounts it nearly rivalled Terry Curran's all those years ago. As the game approached half-time the suspense was killing me. I felt like jumping in the car and heading back towards Sheffield to pick up a radio signal. Christine informed me that this was out of the question because, in the excitement, I'd consumed half a bottle of vodka and was well over the limit. This was the worst place ever to witness the Sheffield Derby, but as the second half got underway we managed to get Five-Live on the radio.

I had one eye on the phone and one ear on the radio as the minutes ticked by. We were now 30 minutes away from our first double since 1914; the phone was still silent and nobody on the radio was one bit interested in what was happening in Sheffield 2. This was now getting unbearable. Yet again we were minutes away from victory, just like we were the previous season, but this time I'd got no referee to look at – just a phone and a poxy radio.

Five-Live had now started to take an interest, with the words, 'Now let's go over to Bramall Lane for the latest update,' (he should really have been saying, 'We are just popping over to that shithole in Sheffield'). Silence was golden as I checked that we'd not had a missed call on the phone. Then it was all over, with the presenter on the radio telling us that Sheffield Wednesday had achieved the first double in 95 years. The phone rang, we put it on 'speaker' and listened to the Wednesdayites going mental.

Samantha was crying with joy, she'd done something her mum and dad had never achieved and that was seeing her team win at the Lane. You could feel the atmosphere oozing out of the phone, as she told us that her and our family friend Greg were heading for the more pleasant surroundings of Sheffield 6.

Eventually, when they'd managed to get to The Rawson at Hillsborough Corner, she asked for vodka and lemonade and the barman told her they were only serving doubles. She'd never seen the place so lively; every boozer was doing a roaring trade and it was still early, what with the stupid kick-off time that the police had insisted on.

The Owls finished the season in 12th place, which was a vast improvement on the previous season when we were 16th. That was about as good as it got for the Owls – but then, could it really get any better?

United finally made the play-offs and reached the final, where they would meet Burnley – who just happened to play in claret and blue. So it was now time to exact revenge for the wrong they felt they had been done by the Tevez affair, and to regain what they saw as their rightful place amongst the elite of our beautiful game.

Mind you, I wasn't complaining. Myself and my good mate Renwar had a nice little earner transporting them to the final.

I was asked on numerous occasions by my passengers if I was going into the game, but I said no, I told them I'd be watching it in some little ale shop that did a nice dinner and had the match on. After I'd dropped them off at Stanmore I met up with my mate behind a pub called The Man in the Moon and it was full to bursting with the bastards. It put me right off my food. Anyway, we moved off with about seven buses in convoy and found a nice quiet pub up the road that had been converted into a curry house. What a result – somewhere with free parking, the match on the big screen and a chicken tandoori.

The day could not have been better scripted if I'd wrote it myself: Burnley won 1-0 and yet again Unitedites had been let down badly by their team. I thought I'd do the decent thing and replenish the cool box with a lager and pop for the kids; I was just hoping the face-paint didn't run all over my seats. The journey home was the quietest my bus had ever witnessed and I kept my joy under my hat for the time being anyway.

I'd made it all the way back to Leicester before I was rumbled. When one kid enquired why I didn't like football, I just told him I didn't go as much as I did during the previous 40 odd years, but I was still a supporter. 'Who's tha support then?' he asked. 'Sheffield Wednesday,' was my proud answer. He was a little taken aback before his mates told him to shut it; I'd looked after them all day with my planning, getting them a decent breakfast on the way down without paying a king's ransom at some service station, getting them to the boozer bang on opening time and having a cool beer waiting on their return.

It was not my fault Blackwell and his boys had yet again kicked them in the bollocks, and kept the Steel City Derby on the football menu for the following season. We loved the rest of the summer, secure in the knowledge that, after them bigging it up all year, they were still in the second tier of English football.

THE SHEFFIELD DERBY: THE CHAMPIONSHIP 2009-2010

This was the season we'd been told that our neighbours would be leaving us for good; they'd got more money than us, better players than us and it was only a matter of time before they'd be back enjoying the delights of Old Trafford and Stamford Bridge. We had to wait until the 18th of September 2009 before the first derby game was played at the Lane; again, only a couple of thousand tickets were heading our way.

The authorities in their wisdom had once again gone for a Friday-evening fixture. Do they never learn from past experiences? I'd even given the boozer a miss and plumped for a seat in front of the telly with a few mates. (I must be getting too old even to watch it in the alehouse.) This had the worst derby attendance for a few years, only 29,210; Wednesday had sold all their paltry tickets, so it looked like some Blades were going back under their stones after the disappointment of the previous season.

The game was soon underway and, before I'd taken the top off my second lager, we were 2-0 down thanks to Ward and Henderson. It was all one-way traffic and in one incident Ward was badly injured. The travelling Owls support were wrongly accused of unleashing a rain of coins in his direction, but I reckon they felt sorry for the little bastard and, knowing his wage would be on the low side, decided to have a whip-round for him!

To make matters worse, Buxton put one through his own goal to make the half-time score 3-0, just one short of a massacre. It was not good viewing, to say the least, and I'm glad we'd opted out of the boozer because it would have been a powder-keg atmosphere.

A minute into the second half, Tudgay pulled one back. For the time being, the massacre was off the menu and I felt a little better now. Wednesday started to rally and, with 65 minutes on the clock, Esajas sent in a scorcher of a free kick that gave the keeper no chance. It was now 3-2 and it was all Wednesday, but could we buggers get that third? With time running out, defeat was staring us in the face for the first time since 2006.

The fight-back was not to be and Blackwell won his first Sheffield derby. Brian Laws had won three and drawn one, so he'd had the most success since Alan Brown but fell short of the record set by Arthur Dickinson, who mustered 18 victories. (Mind you, he was manager for 29 years.)

After the game, Wednesdayites knew what reception awaited them on the mean streets of Sheffield 2. As our meagre contingent made their way out of the ground, many of the lads held back and congregated under the top tier of Bramall Lane. After, as the media put it, the 'proper supporters' had left, the lads made their move and went en masse through the police and Unitedites that congregated in their usual position on the Lane, right outside the BP garage. The Wednesdayites had them on their toes before turning to face those coming from the Cricketers; once those had been routed it was back towards St Mary's Gate.

It just goes to show that if you have the quality and you are as one, you are untouchable. But we know that there will be no credit given by those street urchins of Lowlife City.

THE FUTURE'S BRIGHT, THE FUTURE'S BLUE AND WHITE

So what lies ahead for my football club? Well, I cannot see us gracing the Premier League in the near future, but who cares? Have you seen the amount of debt some of these mega-clubs are in? It's frightening, and our 27 million deficit is chicken feed in comparison.

The only thing that matters is that our bitterest rivals fall flat on their faces and go into freefall. We lived the dream during the early 90s and I enjoyed every minute of it, but their board is just like ours – it won't flash the cash.

We now play our final game on Sunday 2nd May, with a winner-takes-all encounter with Crystal Palace after they failed to beat West Brom on Monday evening. The game sold out by the following day, with a crowd of about 38,000 expected. I could have waited a couple more days to finish this book, but the writing would have been too painful. The ordinary man in the street does not understand the pain you go through when relegation raises its ugly head.

I may have witnessed my last Steel City showdown for some time, but I just have a feeling that the boys roared on by the Wednesday faithful can do something that Ken Knighton did in 1974, when we cheered him off the field, or in our encounter with Southend in 1976, when the loser finished up in the old Fourth Division. Once again, Wednesdayites turned up in their thousands and, thanks to Eric Potts and Wednesday legend Michael Prendergast, the Owls made the great escape – unlike United and the legendary Don Givens some years later, you losers!

Wednesday fans seem to pull together when they are most needed, and none more so than on Sunday 18th April 2010, with our latest clash and fight for survival in the derby.

Mind you, times have changed and watching your club is a dear do, but that is what football is all about today – money, money and even more money. In years gone by nobody gave a damn who the chairman was, you were more interested in the league table, who your next opponents were and whether you had enough dosh for a mid-week visit to Exeter City.

One thing that has never changed, in all the years I've attended football, is your hatred of your near-neighbours. This does not include my friends, to me friendship is bigger than football – though I've seen very close friends come to blows in honour of their football team, especially if it's in the city of Sheffield.

The future of our great club now lies in the hands of the future generations that will grace our fine stadium in years to come; we need to attract them before they get tempted over to the dark side.

Our family is fortunate enough to be full to bursting with Wednesdayites; my father James first took me to Hillsborough in 1963, but he had graced our fine stadium for the very first time back in 1939, also at the age of eight. Our opponents on that day were Sheffield United, who we thrashed 4-1 in a pre-season friendly before a modest gate of 14,917.

Later that same season, along with my father another 48,982 saw Fallon put the Blades to the sword; this was in the second division and we finished third, but United got promoted. The following season, Wednesday and my father were getting ready for another crack at the second division title; after losing to the Blades pre-season, we then went on to lose our opening game at Luton before we sorted out Barnsley 3-1.

But at 11am on the morning of our home fixture with Plymouth, war was declared on those bastard Germans. (Mind you, we still played the game and lost 1-0.) Those Krauts took away the next seven seasons of league football for my father, until the league restarted in 1946-47 and we nearly got ourselves relegated to the third tier of English football. Mind you, he did enjoy himself when we beat Everton in the FA Cup with a crowd of 62,250 witnessing a 2-1 victory.

In 1949-50 Wednesday regained their first division status, but, while they were achieving this (with a win at Hillsborough over the newly relegated Sheffield United), the unluckiest football supporter in Sheffield, my dear old dad, was fighting the communists in the Burmese jungle. Can you imagine how he felt? Those Germans had deprived him of the Sheffield Derby for over seven years and then, when it's back on the menu, he's doing his national service in some stinking jungle. Mind you, it must have seemed like a trip to the Lane with all those creepy crawlies about.

Then, after doing his bit for king and country, he's demobbed in 1952 and comes home to see the Owls having a rough time of it before being relegated in 1955. He'd also got married and that's when I came along to join this Wednesday world, during the 1955-56 season. I must have brought my team good luck because we changed places with the Blades when they were relegated.

I then took over the reins in the family until my brother David joined the ranks in 1968; my other brother, Mark, had unfortunately opted for the dark side. During most of my childhood the Owls played their football in the top flight and we reached one FA Cup Final; it was the 70s that saw my beloved club go into decline when, for the first time in our history, crowds dipped below 10,000.

Our fight-back started in the 80s. By the time I entered the marriage club with Christine in 1983, we were one step away from the top flight; this was achieved two months before our first anniversary, so you can say we'd achieved the double. By 1988 our daughter Samantha was born, and she too came into this world with her football club enjoying life at the top – just like her granddad, mother and uncle. (I, on the other hand, had to settle for Second Division football, even though we finished the season as champions.)

Samantha was to make her Hillsborough debut at the age of three, becoming the youngest ever member of our family to enjoy the delights of Sheffield 6. My sister Donna was never interested in football until she had two boys of her own – the oldest, James, was press-ganged into going along on a couple of occasions, but unfortunately for us has not joined the Wednesday faithful just yet.

Thomas, on the other hand, loves his trips to Hillsborough and gets Auntie Christine to teach him all the Wednesday songs. Our David has got three lads and the eldest two, Liam and Harry, have also enjoyed what Sheffield 6 has to offer, while the youngest, Jack, has yet to make his Hillsborough debut.

This is as good a time as any to introduce the kids to the electric atmosphere of the Sheffield Derby. For one, it is at Hillsborough so it will be safe as can be, and it's an early 1pm kick-off on Sunday the 18th of April 2010.

The kids are the future of our beautiful game, but up until now clubs (including ours) have been pricing them out of the market. Now the powers that be at Hillsborough, in their wisdom, have introduced free season tickets for the under-eights, it costs the under-13s only £50 and the under-18s get their football for £100.

Our family has been going through the gates of Hillsborough for the past 70 years and I think it's just about nailed on that, come 2080, a member of this family will be keeping this tradition alive. Because, as we all know, the future's very bright if your club plays in those blue and white stripes!

BLADE VERSUS OWL
STEEL CITY
RIVALS

STEEL CITY RIVALS

BLADE VERSUS OWL

STEVE COWENS

JOHN BLAKE

Published by John Blake Publishing Ltd,
3 Bramber Court, 2 Bramber Road,
London W14 9PB, England

www.johnblakepublishing.co.uk

www.facebook.com/Johnblakepub ❏
twitter.com/johnblakepub ❏

First published in paperback by Pennant Books in 2010
This edition published in 2012

ISBN: 978-1-85782-817-7

British Library Cataloguing-in-Publication Data:

A catalogue record for this book is available from the British Library.

Design by www.envydesign.co.uk

Printed in Great Britain by CPI Group (UK) Ltd

Cover photo courtesy of Trevor Smith Photography Limited

The right of Steve Cowens to be identified as the author of this work has been asserted
by him in accordance with the Copyright, Designs and Patents Act 1988.

Papers used by John Blake Publishing are natural, recyclable products made
from wood grown in sustainable forests. The manufacturing processes conform
to the environmental regulations of the country of origin.

Every attempt has been made to contact the relevant copyright-holders, but some were
unobtainable. We would be grateful if the appropriate people could contact us.

Written in remembrance of all Blades fans
no longer with us

'We are Bladesmen, we are Bladesmen
Super Bladesmen, from the Lane'

AUTHOR PROFILE: STEVE COWENS

 Steve Cowens was born in Sheffield in 1964, and he works and lives there today with his wife Debbie and their two children. He recalls going to his first game at Bramall Lane in 1970 and had his first season-ticket in 1974. Throughout the 80s and 90s, he was a recognised top face amongst the notorious and violent hooligan firm the Blades Business Crew. Today, with his life firmly away from his violent past, he has become a successful author, having penned the bestselling *Blades Business Crew*, a shocking diary of a hooligan top boy. He has followed this up with his recently self-published *Blades Business Crew 2*. In between, he has contributed to titles such as *30 Years of Hurt*, *Terrace Legends* and *Hooligans*. He is currently writing his first fiction book.

He selects Tony Currie as his all-time favourite Sheffield United player and lists his hobbies as keeping koi carp and managing a successful adults football team in the Sheffield leagues.

CONTENTS

THE BACKGROUND

In Sheffield, it's simple: you are either red or blue; a middle ground does not exist in our great city. Sheffield's football divide, and the fierce rivalry that goes with it, has led to numerous arrests and jail sentences, countless injuries, near-fatalities and tragically even the death of an innocent United fan. The hatred between the two clubs has seen the use of weapons in battle including acid, petrol bombs, knives, bats and distress flares alongside the more common football weaponry taken from pubs, such as glasses, bottles and pool cues. Other cities sharing two football teams don't seem to have the intense problem that Sheffield has; in Liverpool, for instance, the Scousers can share the same pubs and ends on match days, but, in Sheffield, that is simply not possible. The Steel City divide has even been known to split families and ruin friendships.

But why do the Sheffield clubs hate each other with such a passion? Although both clubs' fans share a mutual dislike for their rivals, in the 50s and 60s, some fans from both teams used to go to Hillsborough one week then Bramall Lane the following week. My granddad was one of those fans and, although he definitely went to watch Wednesday lose – well, he *hoped* they would lose – he really went to watch a game of football. Something changed during the late 60s and early 70s – perhaps it was the explosion of gang culture, when teddy boys, skinheads, rockers and mods made it seem cool to be part of a gang, or maybe it was simply part of the social unrest amongst young men that was so evident at the time.

1

Sheffield became famous throughout the world in the 19th century for its production of steel; more notably it became the flagship of worldwide stainless steel production. This fuelled a tenfold increase in the local population during the Industrial Revolution. Sheffield gained its City Charter in 1893 and was officially titled the City of Sheffield. International competition inevitably saw a decline in local industry during the 1970s and 80s. This, coupled with the fact that Maggie Thatcher's policies triggered the collapse of the national coal industry, lead to a reduced population in Sheffield.

Commonly known as the city of seven hills, Sheffield is surrounded by stunning countryside and the city itself has more trees per person than any other city in Europe. Sheffield is England's fifth-largest metropolitan area with a population of 1,811,700, most of whom are from a working-class background, which helps make the city's people some of the friendliest, most welcoming people on our shores.

It has also bred football fans that will fight for their clubs' territory and pride. This pride is often channelled into violence and derby day is not a place for the fainthearted. Even both clubs' non-hooligan fans (some of the shirters) will forget their usual peaceful demeanour and fight for their clubs' pride. The games themselves are not enjoyable occasions for either side's fans, as the fear and apprehension of losing make the games tense and fraught affairs. The workplace on Monday morning after a derby is always dreaded by the losing side as awaiting them are smug grins and smart comments, ingredients that make the actual game itself less than enjoyable. The depth of this feeling carries through to the players and staff of the teams. They know just how much winning or losing this fixture means to their supporters.

Both sets of fans refer to each other as 'pigs', a derogatory term which originated in the late 70s. Both sides can explain their reasoning for this: Wednesday say they call us pigs because United's red and white shirts actually remind them of streaky bacon, while United fans argue that Hillsborough (Swillsborough) was actually built on a piggery, a fact backed up by local history books.

Local history society books which can be viewed at Sheffield Central Library state:

The Wednesday football club first played its games at the Olive Grove sports ground in Heeley before moving to a new stadium in the Owlerton district of Sheffield. The first ordnance survey maps mark the nearest building to the stadium as Swine Cottage. They also show another farm on Penistone Road, just south of where the north stand is situated which is thought to have been a large piggery [still is!]. Pork farming is thought to have been practised in the area since the early 1800s and did not cease until around 1900 when the city's rapid expansion put an end to pork farming in the area. At its height the Owlerton piggery, as it was known, provided work for more then 50 employees. Initial discussions about a new nickname soon began after Wednesday's arrival at Owlerton. In reference to their new home most of the clubs officials were in favour of 'the Owls', taken from Owlerton stadium. However, another suggestion was also very popular. In view of the area's strong tradition of pork farming, a popular grass roots alternative was 'the Pigs'. Although the name Owls prevailed, many working-class supporters continued to refer to their team as the Pigs. A popular song of the time went, 'They may be Owls to some, but they'll always be Pigs to me'. This song was performed in music halls across South Yorkshire. As late as the 1920s and 30s, fans used to welcome their team on to the field with characteristic grunting sounds [they still do that!]. This peculiarity was once referred to by BBC commentator Edward Milburn, who famously described Hillsborough as a sea of grunts, moments after the Wednesday won the First Division title in 1932.

These facts show why and who the pigs are in Sheffield but, of course, Wednesday fans will never let the facts get in the way of their piss-poor argument about the colours of our shirts.

Sheffield itself has areas where each club has strongholds, some of which are actually on each other's doorsteps and invasions into hostile territory have often ended in conflict. Be it a one-on-one fight outside a local pub, a 10-on-10 youth brawl on the back streets

of town or hundreds of hooligans seeking conflict on derby day, the rivalry will often manifest into violence. One thing's for sure, after 40 years of trouble between the two sides, the city is as divided as ever when it comes to football.

	Total arrests since 2000	Arrests for racist chanting	Arrests for offensive weapon	Alcohol-related arrests
UNITED	584	3	2	133
WEDNESDAY	544	12	10	178

So, what can be taken from these Home Office figures and what picture do they paint? United have had 40 more arrests at their matches than Wednesday but Wednesday have had 45 more alcohol-related arrests. Does this mean that Wednesday fans drink more or can't handle what they are drinking? The latter I think.

Also Wednesday have had ten arrests compared with United's two for carrying offensive weapons. Does this mean that Wednesday need to fight with weapons more than United? Finally, Wednesday have had 12 arrests for racist chanting. Does this mean Wednesday fans are more racist than Blades supporters? Through experience, I think that Wednesday are definitely the more racist group, certainly amongst the hooligan element anyhow. United's firm has been pretty much multicultural since I first put on a pair of Diadora Borg Elites in 1981.

Wednesday had quite a few blacks with their firm in the 80s but, by the mid-90s, they were almost totally a white firm. Quite a few people have tried to tie a few Wednesday lads' link with the far right as the main reason why Wednesday seem quite a racist firm in this day and age. I don't really subscribe to that general consensus of opinion. Wednesday's link with Chelsea and the far right is indeed evident but I know the lads who are linked and they had black mates within their firm during the 80s.

Likewise, during the early 80s, United had a group numbering around 10 lads who would be seen at National Front marches and

they played a big part in an attack on an IRA rally that marched through the streets of Sheffield. Yet these same people would sit and drink with black lads within our firm and fight side by side with them if need be. The reason that I think that Wednesday have been tarred with having a racist element within the firm is it's easier to be racist when you don't have a black or Asian geezer within your group or as a friend and this is exactly why the race issue has emerged within their mob.

Going back to the statistics, when the Home Office released significant funds for an intelligence-led unit designed to use new legislation with a view to obtain banning orders through the use of civil courts, South Yorkshire Police decided that the breaking up of the BBC was priority number one. The intelligence-led funds led to lads being banned in big numbers with most of the main faces copping three-year bans, even though some of the evidence against them was poor to say the least. The police knew that, to challenge these orders, any charged lad would have to cough up four to five grand. They wanted to rip the heart out of the BBC and, to a certain extent, they succeeded.

South Yorkshire Police Chief Inspector Eddison told newspapers that the BBC had gained notoriety in the 80s and 90s and were widely regarded as one of the leading football firms in the country at that time. He added that, because the BBC's hardcore had grown up with each other, the police had found it hard to infiltrate the gang and that the top 12 members of the BBC had been eliminated from match-day activities. Eddison told how the police had gained the most banning orders in the country and that they are recognised nationally as a role model of good practice, cough! By the middle of 2006, United had received 63 banning orders by way of conviction and 22 by way of complaint through the civil courts. Wednesday, in the meantime, were left to their own devices for a time, as the OB concentrated on their main cause for concern, the BBC.

After the banning of 85 United lads, the police then turned their attention to Wednesday's firm the OCS. They also copped a load of bans, one major result the police had was when around 50 Wednesday

were caught on CCTV in Doncaster attacking a pub which contained around 10 Doncaster lads. This led to just under 20 lads being banned through video evidence. In total, United have had 242 banning orders and Wednesday 158. New funding has been ploughed into football banning orders again this season (2009-10), an outrageous use of public money by the police. United have had another 26 lads served with these bans since January 2010.

THE STEEL CITY – 'IF YOU KNOW YOUR HISTORY'

As most people are aware, Sheffield boasts the oldest football club in the world in Sheffield FC and the second oldest in Hallam FC. Founded in 1857, Sheffield FC became the flag bearer of football clubs and, by 1862, 15 more clubs had been formed. The Football Association was founded in 1863, and the London-based association adopted Sheffield FC's rules and regulations. By 1867, Sheffield FC added the corner kick to its rules and also introduced a fixed crossbar rather than just a line of tape which had been used previously. Wednesday and United actually started life as cricket clubs which later added football club status to their name.

The Wednesday Football Club was formed in 1867 in the Adelphi Hotel on Arundel Street (that hotel has got a lot to answer for). The cricket club always had Wednesdays as a day off, hence the name Sheffield Wednesday – fuckin' stupid, if you ask me. Years later (1889), Sheffield United cricket club formed a football team to give its members something to do during the winter months. In truth, the cricket committee did not like football and at first they treated the idea of starting a football club with complete disdain. But the cricket club was losing money hand over fist and it needed to start to generate much-needed income. On 22 March 1889, my life and love Sheffield United FC was born. Wednesday FC were not at all happy with these events for two reasons: first, they didn't think the town was big enough to support two teams, but more, importantly, they saw United as a threat to their existence. What also didn't help

7

matters was the fact that United recruited some of Wednesday's players. Because of a poor response to an advertising campaign aimed at hiring new local players, the first United side was made up predominantly of Scots.

United's first competitive game was in September 1889 against Notts Rangers at Meadow Lane, Nottingham. William Robertson placed his name in the history archives of Sheffield United by scoring our first ever goal in the 4–1 defeat. We also lost 13–0 to Bolton, although, as an excuse, our keeper, Charlie Howlett, lost his spectacles in the six-inch-deep mud with the game evenly poised at 6–0! Bramall Lane hosted its first home game for United that same year. With United struggling in their first term, the Wednesday side had reached the FA Cup Final and won the Championship. United were looked on as the paupers but the red side of Sheffield were determined to make a name for themselves, even if it was just to shut up the more established Wednesday outfit.

The following year saw the first ever Sheffield derby and, just before Christmas, United travelled to Wednesday's ground, the Olive Grove, for this eagerly awaited showdown. A crowd of 10,000 was swelled by a huge firm of 300 United boys dressed in the latest flat caps – only kiddin'! Despite taking the lead, United lost the encounter 2–1. The return game at Bramall Lane in January 1891 saw United gain revenge in a 3–2 win witnessed by a crowd of over 14,000. The two rivals hadn't got off to the best of starts off the pitch. Wednesday were bitter that United were undercutting them with what they charged fans to see home games. United were likewise incensed when their bid to join Wednesday in the Alliance League was rejected, and they thought that Wednesday had influenced the decision. United went on to join the Northern League instead. In 1892, both Sheffield sides reached the final of the Wharncliffe Cup.

Wednesday refused to play the game at Bramall Lane, so the tie was cancelled. United argued that Wednesday's refusal was due to the fact that in the previous season United had walloped Wednesday 5–0 at the Lane. After that game, United fans had made a piss-take funeral card which read:

BLADE VERSUS OWL

In Loving Remembrance of
THE SHEFFIELD WEDNESDAY FOOTBALL TEAM
Who were safely put to rest on Monday, October 26th.

Wednesday returned the compliment after beating United 4–1 in the return and made their own cards up to the same effect – see they've always copied us: funeral cards, balloons at matches, giant flags, flares, songs; you name it, they've copied it.

On Friday, 13 May, both United's and Wednesday's bid to join the Football League had been successful. Wednesday went straight into the First Division with United only deemed fit enough to join the Second Division and so the history of Sheffield's two famous clubs had begun.

Interestingly, at this time, both clubs were nicknamed the Blades. The name Blades actually came from a gang of young thugs who had been hired by publicans during the 1882 Sheffield riots to disrupt a planned march by the Salvation Army. The thugs were nicknamed the Sheffield Blades and the name was transferred to the football teams. United later changed their nickname to the Cutlers but, when Wednesday switched grounds from Olive Grove to a new ground at Owlerton, they also took up the nickname 'The Owls'. United then became known as the Blades.

Looking back through the history books, it seems the first recorded incidents of trouble at a Sheffield derby went back as far as 1892. During the game, it seems both sets of players left the field of play and jumped into the crowd to join in fighting between rival spectators. Police had to break up the disturbance but the deadly rivalry seeds had already been sown. For the next few years, the derby games were prone to disorder.

The next recorded incident of trouble brought up the name of a certain Blades legend, goalkeeper William 'Fatty' Foulke. At 6'2" and weighing in at over 20 stone, Foulke was an intimidating figure for any opposing centre-forward and, although, in those days, it was fair play to shoulder-barge the keeper either into the net for a goal or to the floor, I can't see Foulke suffering from too many barging centre-forwards.

Foulke's name will live on in sporting folklore, especially in the red and white side of Sheffield.

Foulke was the heaviest recorded keeper; he went on to play for England and at the latter end of his career he signed for Chelsea but by that time his weight had ballooned to over 25 stone.

One of Fatty's main dislikes was Wednesday, and crowd trouble happened during the derby game at Olive Grove in 1897 during a United v Wednesday game. Foulke had been subjected to a torrent of abuse from Wednesday fans that had gathered behind the goal – you can just see it, the first rendition of 'Who ate all the pies'! During the course of the second half, Foulke had had enough and jumped into the Wednesday end to persuade the snorters to shut up. The game was still going on as Fatty waded through the crowds, bless him.

THE STEEL CITY DERBY – RESULTS, FACTS AND FIGURES

- United have won 45 games, drawn 38 and lost 41

- United: goals for 171, goals against 164

- Biggest United score was 7–3 in the 1951–52 season

- Biggest Wednesday score was 5–2 in the 1928–29 season

- United have won the FA Cup four times to Wednesday's three

- United have only won the old First Division Championship once throughout their history, while Wednesday have won it four times

- Wednesday finally won a game at Bramall Lane in 2008, after 41 years and 12 bites of the cherry.

- United did the double over Wednesday in 1991 and 2006. Wednesday have recently ended their double drought in the 2008-9 season; the last one before that came in 1913.

- Wednesday won the old League Cup in 1991

- United have been above Wednesday in terms of final league placing since 2001.

WEDNESDAY RULE OK

Not many people will argue that Wednesday had the lion's share of battle victories during the 70s. Their mob, the EBRA (East Bank Republican Army), had big numbers, and in those ranks stood some big hitters. The SRA (Shoreham Republican Army, later to become the Shoreham Barmy Army) themselves had some good lads but nowhere near the quality and numbers that Wednesday could produce. Many a time, especially in the then named County Cup games (a Cup competition between Rotherham, Doncaster, Chesterfield, United and Wednesday), both teams would infiltrate each other's Kop, with Wednesday amassing big numbers on United's Shoreham End.

The United lads gallantly tried to defend our turf from the invading snorters but they would often finish off second best. I was far too young in those days to get involved in the combat but I do remember looking up at our Kop from the John Street terrace during games with Wednesday; they had more on our Kop than we did and they seemed to hold the central ground as well.

Sheffield in the 70s was a hotbed for trouble at football. In 1973, United fans topped a football league of shame. The United hooligan element had seen 276 arrests, with Wednesday finishing third in the table with 258 arrests. So, over a season, the two clubs had seen arrests totalling 534. Sheffield was fast becoming the home of football-related violence. The year before the table was published, there was large-scale disorder at United's games throughout the season. In April

1972, Newcastle's visit to Bramall Lane led to 54 fans being arrested, the return game saw a further 83 locked up, then a month later another 30 arrests were made during the game with Manchester United which saw running battles on the Shoreham Kop as Manchester's Red Army battled it out with the SRA. When Chelsea's visit produced another 41 arrests, Sheffield United games had now become a policeman's nightmare. The stark reality of it all was in just four United home games there had been a total of 192 arrests.

Over at Hillsborough, Manchester United's visit in the same season produced 113 arrests, although, of that amount, over 30 were juveniles. What is interesting is that the numbers of police allocated to the games at this time were around 120, although by 1976 the number of police keeping order at football had doubled.

At the Sheffield derbies nowadays or a high-profile game, over 280 police are now on duty, when the violence is nowhere near as bad or as out of control as it used to be.

So, although Wednesday may have held sway in our city through this period, it was very much in evidence that United had a large hooligan element. One of United's older lads takes up the story about those days and perhaps the SRA's best effort against the stronger EBRA.

EGG DAY

One thing I learned very quickly was everyone's hatred of Sheffield Wednesday. My school had been predominantly Blades and the few pigs caused little or no animosity between the two but the feeling on the Kop was different.

'Fuckin' Wednesday bastards' could be heard as the old man in the white coat took the large tin numbers around to the alphabet scoreboard at the Lane and the score was in Wednesday's favour.

'I hate them blue and white cunts' was also regularly voiced, and the more we heard the sayings and got more into the scene, the more we grew to hate them as well.

At the following game, which was at home to Notts Forest, a plan was literally hatched. Hats off to the bright spark that

came up with the idea but word spread around the Kop like wild fire. That word being to take as many eggs as you could carry to the derby game at Hillsborough in a few weeks' time; an invasion of their Kop was planned and a new song rang around the Kop:

'Don't forget your eggs

Don't forget your eggs

Ee-hi-adio, don't forget your eggs!'

Egg Day soon arrived, one Saturday in September 1966, four 15-year-old Dronfield lads sneaked into Hopkinsons small holdings egg coup, their mission 'the great egg snatch'. Scores of chickens roamed freely around the sheds and outbuildings, laying eggs willy nilly in makeshift nests. After collecting a carrier bag full, they caught the bus to Sheffield to meet up with around 250 fellow Blades who were meeting in the Pond Street bus station at midday. I had been in town since 11am, armed with a carton of eggs, obtained by leaving a note out for my mother's milkman. Many of the Blades arriving also carried boxes of eggs. We set off on the three-mile trek with our banners, flags and eggs, picking up small groups of lads on the way as we walked through town. There wasn't a copper in sight. We showed off our eggs to each other like they were some kind of invention that no one had seen before. 'Look at them fuckers for eggs then!'

Reaching the bottom of Penistone Road, about a dozen or so Pitsmoor lads carrying a large banner joined us. The odd egg was chucked at any passing Wednesdayite we saw. On reaching the ground at half past one, we queued outside the Penistone Road End, which was Wednesday's East Bank Kop, and paid the one-shilling entrance fee. I emerged at the other side of the turnstiles to see a group of Blades telling the lads that the coppers were at the back of the open Kop, searching everyone for eggs. The word must have got out about the plan we had hatched. I hid my eggs in some bushes and walked past two coppers searching dozens of youths as they entered the Kop.

'Got any eggs?' the copper asked me, patting my bush jacket. A couple of cartons lay at his feet.

'No,' I answered.

'Go on then, in you go.'

At least 10 lads had sneaked by as he did this. I waited a few minutes, walked back out and collected my eggs, then, when I passed the same copper again, said, 'You've searched me once.'

The ground was all but deserted except for us; we stood at the back of the Kop directly behind the goal waiting for the pigs to arrive. The plan was, at ten to three, the shout would go up, 'Sheff United – hallelujah!' and we would release our eggs en masse at the Wednesday fans below us. By two o'clock, 50 or so Wednesday had gathered in front of us, which proved too tempting for some of the trigger-happy Blades and a few rounds of ammo were released into their ranks. By 2.30, the ground was filling up, more Wednesday, more Blades and more eggs entered the stadium. At ten to three, 40,000 fans were in the ground and as the mass of Blades began singing and swaying the cry went up: 'Sheff United – hallelujah!' It was a sight to behold, nowhere to run, nowhere to hide, it was 'raining eggs, hallelujah'. A great roar greeted the teams as they took to the pitch. Wednesday banners had yellow slime running down them.

'Scrambled eggs, scrambled eggs!' we chanted at the egg-covered Owls. Our ammunition was now exhausted, so we turned to coins and other missiles, such as stones from the banking behind the Kop. One of the young Dronfield lads (who later went on to have a distinguished career in the police force) was removed and thrown out of the ground by his later-to-be colleagues. The game ended in a 2–2 draw but the Blades had scored what we all thought was a late winning goal, only for it to be disallowed for offside. We left the ground en masse at the end of the game and marched down Penistone Road towards town, chanting, 'We were robbed,' but still laughing at the few egg-stained Wednesday fans we saw.

SHEFFIELD WEDNESDAY, 1967

The infiltrating or 'taking' of Kops was now becoming commonplace. So Sheffield Wednesday's visit to the Lane in September was expected to see them infiltrate the Shoreham End in big numbers and that intrusion had to be met with some serious resistance. A Blades meet was arranged for midday at the Howard Hotel across from Sheffield's train station. Fifty or so Blades stood outside the pub with a lot more inside. Half a dozen Dronfield Blades joined the throng.

The Blades lads were buzzing; their hatred for Wednesday knew no bounds. Word was out that Wednesday were meeting up at the same time in Fitzalan Square, around 800 yards from our meet. A few lads who turned up confirmed that there was indeed loads of Wednesday in the square. In those days, it never entered our minds to go up and confront them; the fighting was to take place in or around the ground.

After half an hour, we set off to the ground; it was considered important that we got in before the Owls mob. On the journey an assortment of weapons were picked up: bricks, iron bars and lumps of wood all collected from building sites along Shoreham Street. On arriving at the ground, 30 or more Blades sat on a wall outside the turnstiles on John Street. Yet more Blades arrived in ones and twos, swelling our ranks to 150 or more. The turnstiles weren't open yet, so all we could do was wait.

Word soon came through that a big Wednesday mob had been

seen walking down the Moor end of the city centre. This meant that they would arrive at the ground via Bramall Lane at the opposite end of John Street. Sure enough, a mass of blue and white appeared at the other end of John Street and slowly walked towards us. Judging by their numbers, it was equal.

Blades leaped to their feet as one and sprinted towards them. Both mobs reached the players' entrance which was halfway along John Street. At this point, as the two mobs squared up, Wednesday turned and ran! Nobody chased them far, nobody said, 'Let's do this,' 'Let's go back to the Kop'; there were no leaders, no one was in charge. United's mob looked to have an average age of 18 as none of the older suities or rockers was with us. Maybe it was the fact that Wednesday were invading our territory or just the sheer hatred we had for them, but it was the first time our young lads had 'done' Wednesday; we were coming of age. We calmly walked back to the Kop and sat back down. We were defending our Kop, kids playing war games. It never entered my head I might get hurt.

The Wednesday mob didn't go far. They appeared again soon after; this time they didn't get as far as the first time as we chased them again. The turnstiles opened at 1.30, we piled on our Kop and, instead of heading for our usual place at the front behind the goal, lined up at the top of the steps at the back of the Shoreham. I didn't have a clue what would be going through Wednesday lads' heads. Did they have leaders? And, if they did, would they still come on, having already been run twice? Sure enough, they emerged and started queuing outside the Kop.

From our vantage point, we could see out on to the street. Everyone stood waiting for them to come walking up the 100 or so steps that lead on to the top of our Kop (or 'angina hill' as it was commonly called). The first 20 or so that emerged were greeted with a hail of rocks and bricks. They hid behind a wall at the bottom. They could actually enter the Kop in the bottom corner via the kids' enclosure but no matter which way they tried they were fucked in our opinion, as we held the higher ground and pelted them with anything to hand. Where were the coppers? you ask. Nowhere is the answer; they didn't fancy the prospect of trying to

get in the middle of hundreds of armed-to-the-teeth rampant teenagers. Four, five, six times, the pig fans tried to get to the back of our Kop but each time they were beaten back.

Finally, after an hour of chaos, the police arrived and surrounded the Wednesday mob and actually walked them up our Kop! We charged down and threw everything we had at the two sets of pigs. The coppers were just as bad as their newfound mates but they also turned and fled under the barrage. Ten minutes later, more plod arrived. This time they mingled in with us and watched for any missile throwers who were immediately arrested. This allowed the police to bring up the Wednesday mob without it coming under attack. They were then placed at the right-hand side of us. The ground was about full now with both groups being swelled by more lads joining their ranks. Wednesday had obviously gathered a lot of the missiles we had thrown and returned fire. The Kop became a missile battlefield.

'Mcduff', the eldest of the six Cordell brothers (three were Blades and three were Owls), wore a hunter's white pith helmet with the words 'Blades' written on the front. He'd borrowed it from me after my mother had purchased it at a jumble sale. It was lucky he had it on, as a large rock crashed into it causing a big dent on the side. Lads from both sides were led away with head injuries to be treated by the St John Ambulance volunteers stationed pitch-side.

There weren't many black lads around at the time but one black lad called Mick Grudge hung around with the Heeley mob. Mick was a Wednesdayite and was at the forefront of the Wednesday mob dishing it out to any Blades that came near him. His fellow Heeley mates, Herman and the rest of them, had seen enough and, even though he was a mate, laid into him, forcing him back into the crowd. I can only remember one black lad with the Blades at that time; his name was Arthur, he wasn't really black, just dark looking.

I'm ashamed to say it now but in our ignorance we were terrible racists at the time and used all sorts of names we wouldn't use now. Parents even told you if you didn't behave the black man would get you. We even sang awful racist songs. But, in our defence, we really didn't know any better. It wasn't until the very early 70s that we

began to meet and get to know black lads in pubs and clubs in town. I began to realise that we were all the same and in all walks of life some were good, some were bad, no matter what colour the skin.

The game kicked off before 36,000 crammed into the ground. The fighting continued and both managers made loudspeaker appeals for calm. No one gave a fuck, we were having fun! With the game well under way, things calmed slightly but still the odd missile hit the target and some lad who couldn't be treated on the spot was whisked off to hospital. Most Wednesday fans had left the ground before 'iron lungs, legs of plastic' John Ritchie scored the late winner for Wednesday (their last victory at beautiful downtown Bramall Lane by the way). We left the ground, pissed off at the result but proud that we had successfully defended the Shoreham. We did our usual walk up The Moor into the town centre but no mobs of Wednesday were around.

Front-page headlines read: 'SIX HOSPITAL CASES MAR RITCHIE'S DERBY WINNER' and all the information in the detailed report had been gathered from lads who took part! Their names and addresses were added on to their accounts – imagine that now! Everything was detailed from the meeting place of both mobs to the chase along John Street. United's chairman played it down as high spirits! The national newspapers picked up on the story on Monday morning and, according to the tabloids, Sheffield United topped the league table for arrests and disorder, fuckin' great stuff, top of the League at last.

SHANDY PANTS

During the 70s, Wednesday had a leader, not in terms of fighting ability, but a sort of cult figure who went by his nickname of Shandy, or Shandy the pig, as Blades called him.

When I first started going to the matches, it wasn't long before you got to know the top, or most well-known, pig lads, and Shandy was certainly one of the most well known. In the 70s, a song would ring around the East Bank: 'Shandy, Shandy, I walk a million miles for one of your smiles, oh, Shandy', and if you had seen his smile then you'd realise that even Wednesday fans have a sense of humour. He was known well right across the city, both by the legions of football fans, no matter what colour their allegiance was, and also by a large percentage of the population at large. The main reason for this was that Shandy had unusual features, and I think that's enough said on the subject, and wherever he went his rasping voice would chant, 'Wenshdee! Wenshdee!', his hair lip giving the enemy name a new sound. One thing about Shandy, though, was he was a laugh to have a drink with and I spent many an hour being amused by his tales of prowess among the hooligan world that we lived in.

He was often in the company of Blades lads and entertained us with his heroic stories of the Wednesday supermen led by himself, Super-Shandy. He lived in Hackenthorpe – still does, I think – and he knew most of the United lads from around that way; he also knew that we would ridicule him all night, not for his looks, but for

his team, which tells you a lot about the problems with being a pig in our city in those days.

One thing United lads never did and that was hit or bully Shandy; no, we were better than that, we respected his faith to the blue and white. The last I heard of Shandy was that he had been hit by a bus while crossing the road in one of his many drunken binges; a shame really that a lad who had a lifetime of ridicule and verbal abuse for being a pig could suffer further misery. He recovered somehow. I don't know about the bus though.

Shandy loved a drink and one time we took him around town after bumping into him in the Penny Black in town. We plied him with drinks, mainly shorts, until he spewed all over, pissed his pants, then passed out.

One of many stories from Shandy folklore: Shandy was once in the Birley Hotel, pissed as usual, and blurted out to the watching public, 'I think that there is summat up with my water system.' He then ordered a pint of whisky and supped the lot straight down. Suddenly his face turned from the usual arrangements of odd colours to bright green, he then pissed, shit and spewed up all at the same time, then collapsed. The ambulance arrived, and, as they were attempting to take him into the ambulance and off to hospital, he started coming round and started to shout, 'Are we going to Gillingham, is this the bus?' It so happened that the pigs were playing Gillingham the next day, and Shandy was having none of it, he escaped from the no-doubt relieved grasp of the medics and ran off down the street. We never did find out if he got to Gillingham.

We all remembered Shandy from the Testimonial games at the Lane in the 70s. At one particular game the pigs had taken our Kop, to add insult and humiliation to our lads Wednesday had Shandy hoisted up on to a crush barrier, singing, 'Shandy, Shandy, I'll walk a million miles for one of your smiles'. The 50 or so Blades who had bothered to turn up came in at the back and laid straight into the pigs, Scattering hundreds of the bastards until they realised how few of us there were, they charged back up the Kop surrounding us and we would have been battered if the coppers had not rounded us up and thrown us out of our own ground. It was not a good time to be a Blade.

WEDNESDAY, MY PART IN
THEIR DOWNFALL

Through the title of this chapter, I am not trying to say *I* was the main reason that we overtook a few years of Wednesday rule, far from it. I played my part to the full but I was just one of a new breed of game youngsters that got together in the early 80s who took it to Wednesday and eventually overpowered them. Through the years, I have been arrested five times for Wednesday/United-related trouble.

I was born into a family of big Blades supporters, and my granddad was the foundation of my love of United. He was as biased a Blade as you'll ever see. United could lose 5–0 but it was never the team's fault; no, the opposition were dirty players or the referee never gave us a thing, any excuse to defend his beloved club.

My cousins were all Blades and, when the new South Stand was built in 1974, we bought season tickets together for this stand that seemed a million miles away from sticking our faces through the white railings and hanging our scarves from our wrists on the John Street terrace. (In 2006, when United had plastic seating fitted to the South Stand, they sold off the old wooden seats. I went down and bought the very same seat that I'd christened in 1974, when United drew 1–1 with Derby County. The seat has been fixed to a wall overlooking my koi carp pond in the garden.)

At 15 or 16, I got into the piss-poorly named new romantic scene and started going to clubs like the Crazy Daizy on High Street and the Limit on West Street. I stopped well fuckin' short of putting

21

makeup on like a lot of lads did who were into the scene. I'd dance the night away flicking my stupidly overgrown fringe to the latest tunes like Visage's 'Fade to Grey', Spandau Ballet's 'To Cut a Long Story Short' and Kraftwerk's classic 'The Model'. The clubs not only played the new romantic stuff, they also played great music from the Jam, Clash, Madness, the Cure and the Specials.

The Crazy Daizy had a bad reputation for trouble and my dad had warned me about going in the club, after all I was only 16, and 16 then ain't the 16 it is now. The club had seen a lot of trouble between rival groups of blacks and whites but, as a 16-year-old, I thought I knew better. It was in the Crazy Daizy nightclub that I had my first taste of violence Sheffield Wednesday style. One of Wednesday's older lads who I didn't know from Adam at the time came up to me and demanded, 'Take that fuckin' badge off or I'll smash you all over,' referring to my Blades badge.

I refused and the Wednesday lad sloped off. Later I was punched from the side while having a piss in the toilet, then volleyed into the piss-troff by the Wednesday lad and his mates. The bully was a well-known knobhead called Granville who ran coaches for Wednesday's firm and was one of their main actors. I think the incident left an over-riding impression on me and a hatred of Wednesday that hadn't been as strong as it was before the incident took place.

A year after the Crazy Daizy attack, I was in Steely's (Roxy's) nightclub when I got talking to a lad called Kav who worked with me. My new romantic clothes had now been replaced by Slazenger and Pringle jumpers and Adidas trainers. Kav hung around with a lot of Wednesday and probably their main lad at the time was a big black fella called Harry. He saw my United badge and spat lager on it. The young Blade went for him and I was bundled away by Kav. No doubt I would have been mullered but it was my shirt and club that had been spat on. Kav later fucked Wednesday off and not only became a great friend of mine, he became a great United lad too.

I also remember Wednesday coming in the Red Lion at the bottom of West Street and basically the 50 or so of them battered the 10 blades in there. I was 17 and the little posse of Blades were mostly pups and Wednesday's main actors thought it funny to knock

the fuck out of us. More recently, Wednesday thought it funny to smash one of our game lads all over with bottles when 100 of them went in a pub while we were at West Ham. No, that's not bullying, it's fuckin' shite.

What I'm getting at is I was subjected to the bullying side but didn't go on and on about it in *BBC*, in fact, I never even mentioned it. It happened on both sides, as shit as it is. In a Wednesday book, it seems to focus on United being nothing but bullies – it's bollocks and the author knows it. OK, United had a couple of lads that overstepped the mark but so did Wednesday.

During the same period that United were supposed to be big-time bullies, 50 of us walked into the Golden Ball in town and in doing so 15 Wednesday were trapped in the corner, did they get battered? Did they get a slap? Did they fuck, in fact a few arguments took place and I and a few of the townies stood firm against the out-of-town Blades who wanted to smash Wednesday there and then. One thing's for sure, if the boot was on the other foot, the boot would have been used.

THE CASUALS ARE COMING

Wednesday knew they had the upper hand but their arrogance during the late 70s and early 80s was to prove their downfall. It was quite weird at times in our city; both sets of lads would often drink together in the Blue Bell in town. People like Smids from United were good mates with Bender from Wednesday and in certain situations the two groups would drink in the same pub without a hint of trouble.

Leeds United's visit to Hillsborough in September 1982 confirmed this when an 80-strong United firm went in the Blue Bell on High Street. Inside were over 100 Wednesday. Both groups didn't really mingle together: our mob was at one end of the pub, the other firm were at the opposite end and the middle ground was for the few people that knew each other, keeping a sort of peaceful barrier between the two mobs, as there was no doubt a few who wanted to knock seven shades out of each other but in the name of Sheffield they bottled their hatred up for once. Even though Sheffield turned out over 200 mixed lads, they would not fight side by side as this day proved.

Leeds actually got into town and Wednesday left the Bell to engage them in combat. United stayed put, which, looking back, was weird really. News came back that Wednesday had been done by Leeds and that Leeds were heading our way via the hole in the road. We left the Bell via the back doors and in the little alley between the Dove and Rainbow and the Bell it kicked off with

Leeds. Ribina shoe shop was raided and stiletto heels were used by United's lads against Sheffield's most hated city. The stilettos were the last thing Leeds had to worry about as Trimmer had a ratchet screwdriver and he twice plunged it into the back of the neck of some poor Leeds lad.

Leeds backed off and we argued that we had done Wednesday's work for them as they weren't up to it. Later that night, the unlikely peace between Wednesday and United turned into violence as both sides clashed in town. It was probably the last time the two groups tolerated each other. It had been a situation that seems unbelievable nowadays and one that most lads didn't want in the first place but, because a few respected lads knew each other and got on, the others tried to keep the cart on the rails.

The shoots of a new breed of fan at Bramall Lane were beginning to stir around this time. United's plight on the pitch was at an all-time low, and defeat to Walsall in the final game of the 1979–80 season saw the Blades ply their trade for the first time in English football's basement, the Fourth Division. Wednesday fans mockingly call the day United were relegated 'Thank Givens Day', after Don Givens missed a last-minute penalty that would have kept United up.

Perversely, the relegation actually made the club's fans stronger; everywhere we went we took big numbers and, to 16-year-old lads like me, it was an ideal time for serving an apprenticeship in terms of football violence. The youngsters, of which we had many, surfaced into this new world, a world of tennis, golf and designer wear and fighting at football, the Casual movement had erupted on to the scene and, with it, a new breed of football hooligan.

Wednesday, for their part, failed to see this new breed emerging in big numbers across the city. They treated our firm with contempt and that was Wednesday's downfall. Three years later and with numerous battles under our belts, we were ready to take it to Wednesday and take it to Wednesday we did, with bells on.

The older United lads began to realise that these young lads in Fila and Tacchini were well up for the challenge and a new optimism swept the hooligan corridors around Bramall Lane. It was time for a shift in power in the Steel City.

THE TURNING POINT

The general consensus of opinion is that the shift of power from Wednesday to United occurred in 1985. My view is that, one winter's night in 1982, the fear myself and the rest of our main youngsters had for Wednesday was lifted after we had stood our ground against Wednesday's main firm that night and created a massive shift in attitude within our pups.

The peace that had existed for the Leeds visit three months earlier had dissolved that same night as the two groups had clashed later in town. With Wednesday wounded that the Blades firm had had the audacity to even think of taking them on, they took it upon themselves over the nest few months to start smashing in everything that was red and white. Our firm of youngsters had discussed on numerous occasions about how and when we were going to take over who runs the show in Sheffield. For most of us it was bravado because we were still only 16- to 18-year-olds, I for one really talked the talk but deep down I knew I wasn't really ready to walk the walk, yet.

Anyhow, around 25 of our young trendies were heading from the Penny Black pub in Pond Street that night to go and meet up with the rest of the older lads who had settled down in the Blue Bell on Sheffield's High Street. As we walked up, around 40 Wednesday came around the corner and we bumped straight into them. We were edgy as Wednesday belittled us by spitting at us and telling us to 'get home as it was past our bedtime'. I was looked up to by a few

of our youngsters because I'd got myself a bit of a reputation for being game. So, in an act of bravado, I waded into Wednesday.

Our pups all followed me into battle and Wednesday were shocked at our attack. They back-pedalled a couple of yards but those couple of yards may have been a couple of miles as we had surprised ourselves in moving these snorters back. I admit at the time I was bricking it, after all I was only 17 and some of the geezers we had run into were double our age. The police thankfully came to our rescue, as Wednesday came back at us but we had done enough and I can still see the handshakes and high fives that our lot shared as we walked up to meet the rest of our firm. I was shouting, 'I fuckin' told you we could do them cunts.' Although we hadn't actually run Wednesday, we'd done enough and the fear and respect we once had for their firm was lifted.

On entering the Blue Bell, we couldn't tell the older lads quickly enough of our semi-result. Sensing that Wednesday would probably be thinking twice about our up-and-coming firm, the older lads left immediately and headed down to the Penny Black. The 60 of us ran Wednesday back inside the pub after they had initially spilled out into the street to engage in combat.

The gamest Wednesday lad and the last to retreat was a black guy called Delroy, who has since passed away having suffered asthma attack. The pub was totalled and a couple of United's main actors got lifted, one of which was Eyes.

That in my view was a major victory for the morale of our youngsters and we never had the same respect for Wednesday's firm again.

With friendships between United and Wednesday firmly put to bed. Trouble between the two groups became more frequent than at any other period in time. Over the next couple of years, a power struggle evolved; one week Wednesday would come looking for the Blades mob, the following week United would go on the hunt. By 1984, it was a level playing field, and the battle for supremacy had at last begun, but, by 1986, United's firm had all but taken over. Wednesday still had the odd result and turned out big numbers to try and counterattack this new breed of Blades thug but the damage

had been done; the contempt they'd had for United's firm had come back and bitten them on the bollocks. There was no turning back for our firm and, like a fox after a rabbit, we wouldn't let up until we were totally sure the job was complete.

WEDNESDAY HOSPITALISED, THE HUNT IS ON

In 1985, a fight on London Road with a few of Wednesday's big hitters led to a year of trouble and a year in which me and a lad called Howie were number one on Wednesday's hit list. It all started late one night in the Lansdowne pub. Around 10 young United lads, myself included, entered the pub.

Inside, standing near the door, were six Wednesday lads, three white and three black geezers, whose reputation went before them. It was evident from the start that they were out to cause some bollocks ... and bollocks is what they got. As we were all relatively young, Yifter, the senior Blade among us, took it on himself to try to pour oil on troubled waters.

This didn't happen, and, when one of the black blokes wanted to fight Yifter outside, he took up the offer, even though you could see in his eyes he didn't fancy it one bit; fair play to him, though, as none of us wanted trouble with this group but his pride carried him through. Everyone headed outside and I deliberately held back and was the last one out.

As the two groups squared up, the Wednesday lads were calling all the shots about how we were wankers and hadn't got the bollocks to fight them. They had their backs to me so I walked through them, turned and faced up a yard away and without warning I chinned the nearest one to me. He went straight down and wasn't getting back up by the look of him. It kicked off and, despite the odds now being two to one in our favour, they had a right go. One was shot in the

chest at point-blank range with a distress flare and one by one they were overpowered. Four of their group were left unconscious in the middle of the road with two taken away by ambulance.

I knew straight away that there would be serious repercussions; these game lads had lost some face and anyone there that night would be on their shopping list. Sure enough, my name came out along with Howie's, when 10 Wednesday informed two Blades that we were both dead meat, then the two Blades were twatted. Another United lad was assaulted in Sinatra's nightclub by one of the black lads; he was out with his girlfriend and lost a tooth in the attack. This was seen by many as totally out of order, but it also sent out the message that they meant business. The week after the assault in Sinatra's, United attacked a few Wednesday in the Hallamshire Hotel on West Street in revenge for the aforementioned wrongdoing. Both incidents were out of order but now the gloves were off and the rules between the two firms were that there were no rules.

To make matters worse, around two months later, a group of 15 blokes were out celebrating a stag night one Friday on London Road. They began singing Wednesday songs and, although a few of them were known to the young United firm that were drinking in the same pub, the 20-strong Blades firm steamed into their rivals with chairs and glasses. One was left unconscious with a broken jaw and a couple were arrested.

Again Wednesday vowed revenge and rumours of Wednesday coming down to London Road in big numbers to sort out this young Blades firm gathered pace by the minute.

MOLOTOV MADNESS,
SIX MONTHS OF MADNESS

One Friday evening in late autumn 1985, 30 United lads were drinking in the Pheasant Inn on London Road. Nothing was different really, same lads out, same pub crawl, but this night was to be the start of two months of hostility between United and Wednesday that got seriously out of hand. The rumour mill had been in overdrive, Wednesday were turning up here, there and every-fuckin'-where.

That night, we got a tip-off, via the pub phone from a Blade in town, who told us Wednesday had up to 50 lads in town and they looked like they were heading our way. Sure enough, Wednesday walked a firm straight up to the Pheasant, it was like they wanted to try to stop this young Blades firm in their tracks and show them who was boss – wrong! When we realised our foe was on our doorstep, the pub emptied, with the snooker cues exiting as well. Hand-to-hand combat broke out in the middle of London Road and Wednesday were backed off before they turned and ran. One of their main men got captured and ragged a bit, as did a lad who had his dreadlocks ripped from his scalp Red Indian style. They were pinned on the wall of a pub on London Road as some sort of trophy with a little written sign underneath that read, 'Wednesday dreads, ripped from head'! Another Wednesday lad was laid out unconscious and we were concerned about the state of him. Some of ours laid him out in the recovery position and tended to him until the OB showed. Wednesday had regrouped in the Roebuck in town but

United had tasted victory and wanted to finish this Owls firm off, for one night anyhow. We went up and, as Wednesday poured out of the pub, we put them to flight again.

The following weekend, 50 of us went up West Street to search for the snorters. Wednesday were in the Saddle just up from the Limit and the pub was attacked with Wednesday getting out in the doorway only to be overpowered. A few Wednesday were assaulted later on as they stood in the queue to get in the Limit. It all got a bit silly really; it wasn't safe to be either a Blade or Owl around this time.

The code of conduct, if ever it has existed between the two groups, was shot to pieces as it became a no-rules affair with reports of both Wednesday and United lads attacked in town while out with either non-hooligan mates or girlfriends. The tit-for-tat attacks carried on weekly, with Wednesday being run off London Road twice more. The third and final time Wednesday were run, they didn't even stand long enough for a punch to be thrown, and I knew at this point that we had got to them mentally.

Then the following Friday we heard through the hoolie-vine that Wednesday were turning a big team out to launch an attack on our London Road territory; they were going to put us in our place once and for all, or so they said. Because there had been plenty of trouble in the previous month or so, the OB had a large presence in the area so we would have to be at our cunning best to get any action from the night. Around 100 of our firm were plotted up on London Road when I arrived.

I had made elaborate plans and I'd bandaged my leg up and carried a crutch even though I had no injury. We had been told that Wednesday would be well and truly tooled up so it was a case of meeting fire with fire. A few United lads had also taken the threat seriously as three baseball bats were hidden behind the fruit machine in the Pheasant. As always, we had people on patrol in cars. The scouts had clocked Wednesday and they had similar numbers to us. Wednesday's plan was to come on to London Road via the back-walks and avoid coming in through town.

The OB were all over London Road like a rash and we knew that we might have to take a few arrests tonight, but business needed to be

taken care of. To be honest, Wednesday had been lost off our radar. We had no idea where they had gone from the last sighting and things started to get tetchy. Then news of Wednesday's whereabouts came from an unexpected source, a copper's radio. Bingo, we now knew that the Wednesday firm were heading up St Mary's Gate.

Four of us jumped into Frankie's car to suss out their mob. Two distress flares were loaded as we drove off. Wednesday were clocked on Denby Street entering the Sportsman Inn. A distress flare was shot in their direction. The Wednesday firm cheered as the flare rose above their heads and crashed into the pub wall. Our lot were literally 300–400 yards away tucked up and waiting for news. We headed back and relayed the news. We had to get the OB away from the Pheasant, so, in a cunning plan, we sent 20 lads down London Road towards the Lansdowne.

Sure enough, the OB followed. The rest of us headed off in dribs and drabs to meet up in the Sheldon car park and then walk down towards Wednesday en masse. As we got closer, the snorts sussed us and started screaming at the top of their voices to their colleagues inside the pub. It was at this point that a few of us started to jog towards them. One of our main actors shouted for everyone to walk and keep quiet. It was a bit weird and didn't get the old adrenaline pumping like normal as we casually walked towards Wednesday who were by now going crackers in the road.

Once within throwing distance, Wednesday threw the lot at us, it was a case of covering your face as you couldn't see the missiles in the dark. The roar went up and our casual walk was no more as we all hurtled down at them. Later, Wednesday maintained that the OB ran them back into the pub and left us alone; in truth, Wednesday had started to do one before the OB arrived and the plod actually came from behind us and ran through, clubbing anything in their way. The police came from everywhere and I limped off as the plod steamed everyone. As I hobbled around the corner, I bumped into Sam. Then, as we made our way back to London Road via another street, 10 of Wednesday's main boys came around the corner; they had missed the battle.

'Run again, you mugs.'

They came at us but I just tucked the crutch under my arm and my limp became a sprint, it's a miracle! Miracle over, as I ran around the building and straight into four Old Bill. Shit, crutch back to the floor and limp back in fashion. Sam copped a clip but I was left and told to clear off.

Later that evening, a Blade was blinded in one eye as he was hit with a glass as we attacked a pub with Wednesday inside. Ten lads had been arrested that night, eight were Blades and two were young OCS lads. The two Wednesday lads had been arrested while carrying four petrol bombs in a rucksack; I knew them both and they were obviously doing other people's dirty work, as they didn't even have it in them to fight at the time, never mind throw a petrol bomb. While the two of them were on remand in Hull Prison, they were attacked by a couple of Blades.

Later, they both received two years in a young offenders' unit. The petrol bomb was a frightening and sinister new development in the war for supremacy between the rival groups. Two days after the tear-up with Wednesday, I popped in the Sportsman during my dinner break. The Shaw family had just taken over the pub and Graham the landlord showed me a bag of sharpened triangles of lead that Wednesday had left under the seats. They would have no doubt blinded someone if they had hit their target.

The trouble and arrests, and even the fact that one Blade lad had permanently lost the sight in one eye, didn't stop the trouble continuing. Two weeks later, a group of 20 Blades attacked around 10 Wednesday in a pub on West Street and chased them into the women's toilets. Things had got seriously out of hand.

The assault on the black lads on London Road had not gone away. I'd got fed up with the whole affair and figured if I was going to get it then so be it.

After United had visited Huddersfield Town, once back in town the 50 of us went in the Penny Black. We had a quick pint and started to drift up town to our usual haunt, Silks. I was about to go when Eyes came over and told me to fuck off as Harrison, one of the black lads who had been laid out on London Road, had just walked in the other side and was asking if I was out. I thanked

Eyes and waited until everyone had gone, then got another pint and went and sat with Eyes and Harrison. I'd got to face this head on.

Eyes was looking at me, puzzled why I hadn't gone. To cut it short, after around 10 minutes Harrison asked me my name and I told him. All 6'3" of his boxer frame stood up.

'Fuckin' get outside,' he demanded.

'Look, I know you're here for me so I've stayed and come over when I could have fucked off and I'm not going outside.'

He sat back down, looking a bit perplexed by the whole affair. He asked me if I was on London Road that night and told me his mate was going to kill me. The mate he was referring to was another lad who'd been knocked unconscious that night. Unbeknown to them, my football team had drawn their team in the Cup in two weeks' time, so I told Harrison that if they wanted me I'd be playing in that game. We ended up having a couple of pints and I think he admired my front and honesty.

On the Sunday morning of the game, I felt like a man who'd just had his last rites read to him. To make matters worse for me, I had broken my right hand during a fight in town in the previous week. I was determined to play and taped loads of cotton wool around my cast, I didn't want to be seen as if I was bottling out and I had to be strong for the rest of my team who were nervous to say the least.

The ref passed my cast but, as we warmed up on the pitch, no opponents had arrived. Then, with five minutes to kick-off, eight cars screeched into the Concord sports centre car park. Twenty-five blokes, mainly blacks, marched up to the pitch accompanied by a few dogs straining at the leash.

I copped for a few verbals but was determined not to be intimidated and played my usual physical game. We won the game 4–0 and I was pleasantly surprised at how many of their team came and shook my hand at the end of the game. Even the lad who had been laid out on London Road came and shook my hand. The ice had been broken and, fair play to them, I was in an uncertain position but they chose to give me respect. I'd already got respect for them as

I'd seen how game they were in the incident on London Road but they gained my respect as men as well that day.

Just as we thought we'd got away relatively scot-free. A huge explosion rocked the small wooden changing room. Only me and Shotgun were left getting changed as most of ours had either left in their kit or had changed in record time. Mitch had thrown an army stun grenade (not an air-bomb firework as written in the book *Blades Business Crew*) at the entrance door of their changing room. They all came steaming around to confront me and Shotgun who was still sat in his pants – now nearly filled with brown runny stuff – as a load of heads appeared at our door demanding to know what the fuck that was.

I got up and pointed up Concord Park towards Mitch who was by now 100 yards away and still gathering pace as he ran. A few of them laughed and the ice had finally been broken. I know them all now and we share a beer whenever we bump into each other nowadays. A few years after this event, all of them stopped running around with the Wednesday firm.

ATTACKED WITH PETROL BOMBS

The aforementioned petrol-bomb incident had me thinking about where all this rivalry was leading to, death? Not long after the incident that saw two young Wednesday lads jailed for carrying the petrol bombs, another Testimonial had been arranged, which would be played at Hillsborough. We had no intentions of going to the game but every intension of giving it to Wednesday that night. Our numbers that night were around 60 lads. After having a couple of drinks in the Penny Black, we set off in dribs and drabs towards Hillsborough. We knew where Wednesday were drinking and our plan was to go straight to that pub after mobbing back up. We snaked our way through the quiet back streets towards the Kelvin flats where Wednesday were. On nearing the pub, we tooled up with bricks and so on. Then one of the lads went in the pub to get Wednesday out in the street. There was no OB around at all. We prepared for battle only to be disappointed in the fact that Wednesday had left the pub.

We were now in a dilemma; a lot of the lads had planned to go home after the tear-up and, as we would have to wait another two hours before the match finished, a few lads drifted off. But around 40 of us sat tight.

Then unexpectedly the OB came in the pub and had a nosy around. It was at this point I heard one of ours say, 'If they find them, my prints will be all over the bottles.'

Another Blade said, 'You should have worn gloves like I did.'

It transpired that two of our lot had been across to the petrol station and bought some petrol. They got four milk bottles and stuck some rags in the top. It was thankfully the last time petrol bombs were used between the two firms.

The OB made us go back into town under escort, two bombs were left and two carried under coats even though we had a 20-man police escort. Everyone mumbled that, when we reached the bottom of the flats, we would make a break for it and run into the flats. It was every man for himself until we met back up later in the Dove and Rainbow. The plan worked with most of us getting away, leaving a few still captured by the plod.

Everyone met up as planned at the rendezvous. We'd lost the plod. We knew which way Wednesday would walk back into town and roughly what time they would arrive, so we set off and holed up on a little slip road. The streetlight was smashed as we threw bricks up at it and then waited in the darkness. One of our lads waited across the street on his own then he gave us the nod: Wednesday were here.

I peeked around the corner and Wednesday were walking directly towards us with two police vans following behind them. Perfect. The trouble was one of Wednesday's main men was walking well ahead of the rest and he spotted us and shouted. We came out of the darkness but our surprise had been rumbled and police screeched up and chased us. It was only natural to go back to the original meeting place. I was pleased when I got there that our lot used their brains and almost everyone was still together. Wednesday were by now walking up past the courts and, just as we were going to attack them, the OB sussed us and ran us again. This actually helped our cause as we ran up behind the church and came out on High Street just as Wednesday got to the bottom of it. Both mobs ran at each other. I'd forgotten about the two bombs until I saw one lit and thrown at Wednesday. Luckily, it didn't go off but it had the desired effect as Wednesday backed off, then we ran them down the road with only Dinga standing his ground.

ALL'S FAIR IN LOVE AND WAR

The following weekend, Wednesday tried to get around the back of the Lansdowne pub on London Road. They got sussed and were run back into town, with only two lads standing their ground but probably wishing they hadn't. One of the youths who had stood was a lad called Bacon, quite appropriate for a Wednesday fan! He was getting a bad beating and then two United lads sprayed him with lighter fluid and tried to set him on fire. I jumped in and grabbed Bacon and escorted him towards town. He was understandably very shaken by the events and kept repeating that the Berties (Blades) had tried to flame him. He asked me to walk him into town as he didn't want to be left. I ended up walking him right up to the Limit club. Incidentally, one of the twisted fire-starters who had tried to set fire to Bacon was a lad called Peachy and, in an amazing coincidence, Bacon moved next door to Peachy six months later. The first time the two met as new neighbours, they struck up an understanding that they should not bring trouble to each other's doorstep.

As I bid Bacon farewell outside the Limit, he insisted that I came in so he could buy me a drink. This was going to go one way or the other: I'd either earn respect for what I had done or I was going to get splattered all over the gaff by the pissed-off Wednesday lads who I knew would be inside the club. Bacon told me that, if Wednesday started on me, then he would fight at my side. Touching as this was, I still headed down those stairs thinking that I was mincemeat. To be fair, a lot of Wednesday came over and chatted, and they were all

right lads really. That night, I think I earned a lot of respect off Wednesday; of course, there were still a few of them lurking in the background with that 'let's kill him' look on their faces but, fair play to them, I wasn't touched.

Bacon came over with a can of Red Stripe; he had taken his top off as it stank of lighter fluid. Underneath he was wearing a T-shirt with the slogan 'Gas the Blades' and a cartoon-type drawing of a queue of Blades going into the Nazi gas chambers to be gassed by the guards who were in the Wednesday blue and white.

'If I'd known you had that on, I would have let you burn, you cunt,' I joked with Bacon.

The T-shirts were made by a Wednesday lad called Lebby, who was good mates with a Blades lad called Webby and the two of them made T-shirts that totally took the piss out of each other's club. Some were the same with just the teams turned around, while others could only be adopted by one side; the 'Gas the Blades' was one such shirt.

Unfortunately, Webby was paralysed after diving into a shallow pool abroad. We had a benefit night for him with a few bands playing, one of which was a group of United lads who called their band Like Ice, Like Fire. My pal Paul Heaton also did a terrific impromptu solo set, even though I'd promised him he wouldn't have to sing, but to be fair he made the night special for Webby.

Hundreds turned out at Bramall Lane's executive suite, where United's boys and the few Wednesday that had turned out put aside their differences for the night, and rightly so. A couple of grand was raised to buy Webby a computer that he could work using his head. Sadly, Webby died two years later.

Going to the Limit was always a precarious move for most Blades. I could usually go in without much of a problem as I could have a chat and a beer with most Wednesday, although obviously there were some Wednesday lads that I had no time for and no doubt they had no time for me. I only had grief in the Limit when I went in with United lads who couldn't accept the fact that their fiercest rivals were in the same club.

One night in the late 80s, we had been up West Street on the lookout for Wednesday. The Stocksbridge Owls had given it to one of our lads the week before so we went on the hunt. After no success, we all went in the Limit. The 25 of us included a Forest lad called Boatsy; he knew GJ, who was a game United lad. They had met at an England game and have been friends ever since.

The club started to fill up and 10 of our 25 had melted away, leaving our numbers seriously depleted. Wednesday started to come in the club and gathered in their usual place near the toilets. This made pissing a hazardous move. Our lot were convinced that Wednesday were going to launch an attack so we stood with our backs to the bar with many of our number concealing bottles in their coats. A little pep talk between ourselves confirmed that everyone was up for it if it came on top. I went for an uncomfortable piss, the type of piss where you slash all over your trainers as your head is turned as you look over your shoulder.

A mixed-race Wednesday lad I knew came in and said, 'Steve, I think you had better get out here, quick.'

I dashed through the crowd to see that Wednesday had surrounded our lot at the bar. When I was alongside my colleagues, I turned to face Wednesday. One of their old school told me to get these cunts out. I shrugged my shoulders and told him that 10 of our lot had disappeared and that the ones left were staying. There was an ugly atmosphere but I glanced around at our little crew and their faces painted a picture that I wanted to see: we were up for it.

Arguments were breaking out all over and it was only a matter of time before the balloon went up. Then a young Wednesday lad leaned through and tried to grab a United pup called Tiler, shouting, 'He was there last week when I got battered.'

I grabbed both of them and told them to go and sort it out. The Wednesday lad's arse went so I told him, 'Shut it then, all mouth and no bollocks.'

I had a quick chat with three of Wednesday's main actors and agreed we'd leave after finishing our drinks if they moved away. Fair play to them, we were outnumbered and surrounded but ready to face anything that they had in store. We left half an hour

later, so a potential flashpoint was averted and this was no mean feat, as, at the time, United and Wednesday were at each other's throats, big time.

But another time I went in the Limit, it didn't really work out that well ... and that's an understatement. Badger and I were in Sinatra's one night. We were well pissed and, mainly because of this, we decided to walk the 200 yards up Calver Street and have a couple in the Limit. I think we both knew it would end in tears but there you go. Badger is a great lad; he's game as fuck and we know we won't leave each other's side if it kicks off. The only trouble with Badger is he can be an obstreperous cunt when he's had a few gargles. We'd only been in the Limit 10 minutes, and, as I chatted to a couple of lads from the Woodthorpe Estate, Badger started fighting with a Wendy lad. He was getting hammered at first but somehow got back on top. I'd got my back to the fight as I was trying to keep it one on one as there was a lot of Wednesday hovering over the fight. But, when a Wendy lad booted Badger in the face, I immediately chinned him.

The lot went up. Bouncers lobbed Badger and the other geezer out and left me to battle my way out. I was throwing punches at an alarming rate as I back-pedalled through the masses. I got dropped a couple of times but jumped back up and steamed in. The Limit had steep stairs leading down to it, so I thought, if I could get to the top, me and Badger could have a pop as Wednesday came up the stairs after me. The trouble was, as I got up there, I saw Badger curled up in the middle of West Street with three Wednesday playing football with his body. I had to think quickly and get into them. I managed to sidewind one to the floor and Badger got to his feet; then we waded into them and had them on the move until reinforcements had us on the back foot.

We were battered already so we stood and traded, until the plod pulled up and everyone scattered. Me and Badger ran down a dark alley at the back of the Dickens pub. We stood under a streetlight to survey the damage. Both of us had black eyes and our shirts were hanging from our backs, Badger was worse off than me, but he'd copped for a pair of size nines in the clock.

In the taxi home, I asked what had started it. He told me it was because of his wife's best mate. She'd gone out with the Wednesday lad and he had hit her. Fuck me, I thought, I've been brawling because of a lass I hardly know. Saying that, I don't like women beaters. I've never laid a finger on our Gert in all the 24 years I've known her, even if I might have felt like it sometimes.

Incidentally, the lass whose honour Badger was defending by the way had been on *Blind Date* and they showed her on the beach abroad with the bloke she'd chosen as her date. As they splashed around in the sea, she came out with this beaut: 'Why does the water taste salty?'

Jesus, every time someone from Sheffield goes on the television, we get shown up.

Around this time I was getting a bit of grief off a couple of United lads for being quite pally with a few Wednesday. I couldn't understand it and it got to me at times. Yes, I could have a chat with a few snorters, but, when it came to it, they and I knew that in battle there were no friendships and I'd be in the frontline for my team and mates. I think what peeved a few United lads was the fact that, if we went in a pub and there was only a few pigs in it, I'd walk straight over and talk to them to sort of show our lot that bullying a few lads was out of order. Mind you, not that Wednesday did me any favours back. I've had two unfriendly visits from them at football on Sunday mornings, they've come to my workplace and they've phoned my work and mobile with threats, so maybe I should have just done the same in return, but it's simply not my nature. But being a fair lad towards Wednesday got me into a few scrapes with both sides, so I couldn't win really.

In most firms, there's good and bad lads, and United and Wednesday are no different.

Most Friday evenings, me and Badger would go down town with a few pals, non-hooligan lads. On this particular evening in 1989, I ended up in the cells after trying to help out a Wednesday lad. As a suited and booted Badger and me walked between bars, we bumped

into an out-of-breath Wednesday lad called Tesh. He told us that he had been out on Chirpy's (one of Wednesday's main actors at the time) stag night and they had clashed with United's lads. Wednesday had been chased, so we offered to walk Tesh back up to the Limit on West Street.

As we got on to West Street, we bumped straight into the Wednesday firm who were hanging around on a street corner opposite the Limit. As they all came menacingly around us, I saw a lad who had done a naughty one a few months earlier and went at him. We steamed into each other and I was then bombarded with punches as the rest of them decided it was party season. It was on top, as me and Badger fended off blows while trying to get some in ourselves. I lost my Armani jacket in the struggle, but Badger managed to get it back. We had to retreat and, to be fair, if it wasn't for a Wednesday lad called Jester I would have had a few more injuries than the fat bloody lip I'd gained.

I thanked Jest but was on one. We headed off in a taxi for the Leadmill where we hoped we would find some of our lads.

Five of our lads were outside and told us that the rest of our lot were either inside or had gone to the Music Factory on London Road. I was in no mood to wait around and the seven of us headed up into town. Although the lads with us were good lads, I could tell they were ill at ease but all I had in my head was that I was going to run into Wednesday no matter what.

Sure enough, we walked straight into the Wednesday mob outside the Wopentake club. I stood with my arms outstretched, as Wednesday saw us and came running our way. Although we were severely outnumbered, I wasn't shifting and I screamed at our lot to stand. To be honest, I don't think they did but I was out in front as the first wave hit me. I windmilled in but was engulfed in a sea of knuckles and boots. My shit demi-wave perm was pulled from my skull and I blame Wednesday for my going bald later!

Then the punches stopped and I was dragged to the floor. The OB had arrived. I was thrown into a police van along with five Wednesday lads. The lad who had punched me in the first fracas sat opposite me and we looked each other up and down.

Down at Bridge Street Police Station, I was slung in a cell. On the

floor curled up was none other than Mr Stag Night himself, Chirpy. He was fast asleep so I walked over to him and gave him a nudge with my foot. 'Wake up, Chirpy, the Berties are here.'

Chirpy jumped awake and his face was a picture when he tried to focus, then refocus on me, as he realised through his drunken slumber who was standing over him.

'Cowensy, what are you doing here?'

'I'm your solicitor, what do you think? Your mates have just mullered me in town.'

It seemed that the whole of my body was aching, even my eyelashes hurt, or so it felt. I sat down beside Chirpy and we chatted. He was all right and this was the first time I'd had the chance to have a proper chat with him. He told me that Wednesday and their firm had cost him his first marriage. I reassured him that, if she couldn't understand a man's need to stick up for his mates and club, he was better off without her. Chirps was old school, code of conduct and all that. I shook his hand as he was released. I think we both went up in each other's estimation that night.

The first time in court I was put in the dock with them. I shouted the usher over and said that I was not a part of this group and had actually been fighting against these cunts. A few of them laughed at the comment but I was dealt with separately. However, I did take note of the address of the lad who had been the main instigator that night. In the end I was fined 160 quid but that wasn't the end of it.

Around a month or so later, I was driving home from training at Bramall Lane. As I drove up Frecheville, I spotted a face I recognised – the very same Wednesday lad, who was walking with another one of their boys. On instinct, I slowed but realised that Colly was in the car with me and it was nothing to do with him. He knew something was up and, after I'd explained, he told me to turn around and we would sort it. I drove past them and pulled up a side street, got out of the car and waited. They walked past oblivious. Colly walked swiftly past them and turned, as I tapped the Wednesday lad on the shoulder.

'Not got 30 of your pals with you now, have you?'

He pushed his arms out in front of him and, to be honest, I had won the fight without throwing a punch. We actually get on pretty well now.

It wasn't the first time I ended up in trouble trying to help Wednesday lads. On Christmas Eve 1987, I ended up in the cells again, this time because I stopped two Wednesday youngsters from getting battered.

It wasn't unusual for United and Wednesday to get together in town on Christmas Eve for a festive tear-up. These get-togethers started in 1979 and died out some 10 years later. I never bothered turning out for a few reasons, the main one being that no one wants to be locked up on Christmas Eve. It was a time for my family and, no matter who United played on Boxing Day, I never turned out, preferring to go to the match with my family.

Anyway, on this particular Christmas Eve, I had to go to town to get my wife a present; usually I'd got it sorted early doors, but for some reason I'd left it late this year. I met up with my mate Nigel who was in Gossips, along with around 15 other United lads. After a couple of drinks, the two of us walked to Fargate, and my plan was to go to Next and buy her indoors a new suit.

As we walked down Fargate, we saw around 20 lads who we immediately recognised as a group of United lads who called themselves the Suicide Squad. The squad used to go to United games totally independent to the rest of the firm; they were no strangers to trouble and had a lot of game and handy lads. I knew most of them and, as I glanced over, I saw them rush over and it kicked off in a shop doorway with two young Wednesday lads. We jogged over and I recognised one of the lads getting roughed up. He was a game little sod called Winky, and his elder brother was a main face with Wednesday.

I jumped in to protect him, shouting, 'Leave it out, there's only two of them.'

The squad were all drunk as skunks and one grabbed a white cricket hat from my head; it had the United badge on one side and BBC embroidered on the other, and I was quite attached to it. To cut it short, the big lad who had snatched my hat wouldn't give it

back so I nutted him with a beauty; it was my only option because I couldn't hit him as I had a pot on my right hand. It kicked off a bit as a couple of his mates tried steaming me. The OB came running over and apprehended me. I pleaded my innocence and explained that my hat had been nicked. The plod let me go with a warning to behave or I would be locked up.

I then saw the lad who had snatched my hat – he was stemming the flow of blood from his nose with it! I ran over, jumped up and kicked him. I was promptly arrested and thrown in the police van.

One of the officers in the van was Peter Springett. He'd played in goal for Wednesday and was now the community bobby around Bramall Lane. This was just at the start of the football intelligence officers and Peter knew most of the United lads, me included.

'Your luck run out, Steve?'

'Looks that way.'

(He sadly died later from cancer and I had full respect for this man.)

At the station, I was charged with being drunk and disorderly, which was a laugh as I'd only had two cokes. But I ended up going Guilty and was fined.

That wasn't the end of it, though, as there was still the matter of the stolen hat to be sorted. At the end of that season, I was part of a big BBC mob that were walking back up to the station after a game at Huddersfield, when someone shouted, 'Cowens.' It was one of the squad, who informed me that his mate wanted a word. It was the lad who I had butted on Fargate four months earlier. It turned out he wanted to fight me so we arranged to meet up back in Sheffield. At the meet, we had a fight that seemed to go on for ages until the OB clocked us and we ended up shaking hands. All this because I had stuck up for a Wednesday fan!

One of Wednesday's lads at the time was a lad called Slimey; he was the type who didn't know how to conduct himself and the code of conduct never entered his head. He was a main actor with Wednesday and most of the lads in our firm hated him with a passion. Personally, I didn't really have a view on the lad, until the day he turned up with his pals one Sunday morning in 1987. What got me about it was that, months earlier, me and Kav had

bumped into him and another Wednesday lad on Chapel Walk in town.

'He's just walked down there, that Steve Cowens,' the Wednesday lad informed Slimey just as we had walked back up.

'Yes, I have,' I said and Kav walked straight up to Slimey and asked him his name. Slimey denied who he was, even though we knew full well it was him. So, in a two-on-two situation, Slimey didn't want to know but thought it was OK to turn up at one of my Sunday football games tooled up with four of his mates.

I was warming up on the pitch with four of my team-mates when I noticed five lads walking briskly towards me. One was Slimey, and the others had scarves around their faces. I knew straight away what the score was and shouted to my team-mates to watch the rest as I went to greet Slimey. Straight away, he pulled a steel cleaver out of his crombie coat. I screamed, 'You fuckin' divvy.'

As I squared up, Slimey and the rest of them closed in on me. I quickly noted that two had bats and one was holding a large pop bottle. I tried to boot Slimey and a Wednesday lad tried to twat me with his bat. He slipped on the wet grass and I booted him. It was on top but I was putting on a good show, despite none of my team mates coming to my aid, which shocked me, especially as two of them, Holder and Batesy, were United lads. Then they all came at me at once and I had to turn and run. At the side of the pitch, there was a cricket square that had been fenced off for the winter. I ran over and pulled a four-foot-long rustic post out of the ground. I turned and jogged towards the five lads, who stopped in their tracks. I could see they weren't too sure now.

'Come on, we're all tooled up now,' I shouted.

As I went at them, one threw the Tizer bottle at me. It smashed on my knee, but I didn't really feel anything at the time, as the adrenaline was pumping like mad. I ran at them with the post held above my head, and they turned and ran. My team-mates who had previously frozen, then joined the chase. I just missed Slimey with the post as I tried to bring it crashing down on him; good job I missed really. The rest of our team were now walking up to the pitch and they attacked the fleeing Wednesday lads. My leg went numb

and I looked down to see my leg covered in blood caused by a two-inch cut just above my knee.

The muscle had frayed and was protruding from my leg, but a few stitches in hospital had me good as new.

I was fuming, though; there was no fairer Blade than me when it came to inter-city rivalries and this was how they repaid me, I thought. I vowed to find out the names hiding behind the scarves and to get revenge.

Later that year, I was one of 40 United lads heading down to the Music Factory from town. Kav and myself were 100 yards in front of the rest when who did we bump into but Slimey. He was all suited and booted and out with his workmates. I challenged him and he pleaded that he was out with his workmates and didn't want any trouble. *I* didn't want any trouble when I was playing football, but I'd got it anyway, thanks to him and his cronies.

The rest of United's lads came around the corner as me and Slimey were arguing.

'I'm gonna get it here, aren't I?' Slimey said as he saw our lot approaching.

'No, we're not like you cunts, it's me and you,' I said.

The United lads saw Slimey and a few went for him; I mean, he really wasn't liked at all. For some reason, I found myself holding my mates back and sticking up for Slimey. I must be mad! The thing was, I didn't want us to lower ourselves to his level. I could just see it in the pub the following week: 'Forty Berties did me in town while I was out with workmates, fuckin' wankers.'

Anyhow, Tricky wanted Slimey bad and, as I tried to hold Tricky off, I knew deep down that I had to let him go or fall out with him and I wasn't falling out with a mate over Slimey, he wasn't worth it. Tricky bashed Slimey in a one-on-one, a situation that would never have happened if things had been the other way around.

Around two months after the attack at the Sunday-morning football, I was invited out on a Wednesday lad's birthday. Tinny was friends with a lot of United's lads. They had grown up together as friends on the tough Woodthorpe Estate. Tinny would often travel

to United's away games, and I'd stuck up for him at Man City once when a few United lads wanted to do him in. The lads who were a few years older than me were petty criminals and were always on the lookout for an earner; while the rest of us just wanted a fight, they would often rob sports shops and pubs. Tinny also liked an earner and came along with our sticky-fingered brigade. In 1983, in Doncaster, two United lads robbed 10 grand from the upstairs of a pub, and both got lifted a week later. One of the lads arrested was actually a professional with Rotherham United and a good mate of mine. The then manager of the Millers (George Kerr) had to go to court to put in a good word for our lad.

Tinny's birthday left me with a problem. I was bang at it with Wednesday at the time and I'd still got the attack at the Sunday football bouncing about in my head. What didn't help was the fact that the names of my attackers had been given to me by another Wednesday lad who I put a bit of pressure on. I knew that the same lads would be out on Tinny's birthday. Anyhow, I turned up but was convinced I was going to get it sooner or later that night or I'd bring trouble on to myself through not being able to get the football attack out of my head. I'd put a small United pin badge on to show my colours and walked in the Blue Bell on High Street as large as life. Around 30 Wednesday were inside, and it was like one of those westerns when a stranger walks into the town saloon. I uneasily made my way to the bar. Tinny was leaning against it and shook my hand.

'Listen, Tinny, what do you want to drink, as I've just popped in to show my face, mate,' I said, checking out the mumblings of the Wednesday lads over Tinny's shoulder.

'Look, Steve, it's my birthday, and if any of these start with you they can have some of this,' he told me, pulling a lock knife from his pocket.

Titch and Migs, two of Tinny's Blades hooligan mates, came over to me. I felt a bit more at ease with two United lads who I knew would stand by me. The night went all right but I still had the nagging doubt that, as the beer flowed, a few Wednesday would get some Dutch courage. Fair play, though, I had no trouble and actually

got on well with a lot of them, and one even grassed one of the others up as one of my attackers at football.

I pulled him and he was papping it; he bought me a drink and explained that Slimey had said that it would be a one-on-one with me that day and that he only wanted a bit of back-up in case the rest of my team started.

Later that evening, I took two Wednesday lads called Shen and Dinga into the Music Factory. The Factory had a lot of United lads in who weren't happy to see the two Wednesday lads and they wanted to do them in. I argued that it would look really bad on us that I had been out all night with them and they'd looked after me, so I had to look after them and I didn't want to fall out with mates but that's how it had to be. The two Wednesday went after about an hour, which, to be honest, was a relief for me, as I felt like I was babysitting and couldn't even go for a piss without worrying what would happen.

The following week on London Road, the usual 30 or 40 of us were out. Luey told me that Pud had been slagging me by calling me a pig lover. In truth, he had a bit of a point, because most of our lot wanted nothing to do with anything blue and white. I pulled Pud and ended up chinning him, as he called me it to my face. This really upset me, as falling out with my own firm and mates was the last thing I wanted. I couldn't get my head around the fact that I had had more grief with Wednesday than most, yet I was being slagged. I lost it for a while and vowed that I was done with all the bollocks.

A few weeks on, Pud and me made up. Pud later got arrested in Bournemouth, and who was the first one trying to get him off? Me. I managed to talk the plod out of nicking him and our friendship was thankfully back on track.

BAD DAY AT BLACK ROCK

Just as we thought we had put Wednesday in their rightful place, we got a nasty shock when Wednesday ran us after the Tony Kenworthy Testimonial in 1987. Maybe we had adopted the same disregard for Wednesday that they had had for us a few years earlier. One thing is for sure, that night we got caught out by a Wednesday firm that were desperate for a result against us.

That night was by far the worst I have felt after being run at football. Such is the hatred and rivalry in our city, even Testimonials were an excuse for both firms to have a dig. In the previous couple of years, we'd had Wednesday off quite a few times, so, on the night of Kenworthy's Testimonial, we didn't expect to be going home with our tails firmly between our legs. It's no good trying to gloss over the events with excuses: we got done, simple as.

Everyone gets turned over from time to time but it's a bitter pill to swallow when it's your fiercest rivals that have had you on your toes.

Neither firm had gone to the game, although I went and was well pleased with myself, as I acquired Kenworthy's shirt on the pitch at the final whistle. Kenworthy had been a United centre-half for 12 years after coming through the youth system. I liked how he played; he took no shit, was physical and played with his heart on his sleeve. He and another tough character, Scotsman John McPhail, forged a successful no-nonsense centre-half pairing.

The few years leading up to this game had seen us leg Wednesday's

firm on numerous occasions, so we were pretty confident that we had now got the upper hand. It never entered our heads that we would end up on the back foot that night.

After the match, we'd arranged to meet up at the Lansdowne at the bottom of London Road. It was quite a mixed United mob that stood outside when I arrived. There were a lot of passengers and lads who didn't really want to fight but felt it was their duty to show their face as, after all, this was Wednesday. In all, around 70 lads set off into town via the back-walks to avoid the police's attention.

Of that number, around 35 of the crew were our regular lads, enough to take care of business, I thought. Once in town, we emerged at the side of Henry's wine bar. We caught sight of Wednesday who were further down the road at the side of the not-so-aptly named Peace Gardens. The pre-brawl roar went up and we ran towards the Wednesday firm. Wednesday had around the same numbers as us and we traded punches in the road. They backed off a little as a distress flare dissected them; a leading Wednesday lad was bouncing about in the road holding a knife out in front of him. United's firm surged and Wednesday started to wobble; at this point, I thought we had them on the go but, fair play, they held it together.

I had ended up at the side of the brawl and it was at this point that I realised that the 30 or so passengers we had with us were stood 20 yards behind the actual fighting and were just prancing around shouting. This meant that Wednesday had more lads up for it and, in their first actual charge, Wednesday had United's frontline on the move. I ran in from the side and punched one but they had us on the hop. I watched with dismay as Wednesday ran United despite cries of 'STAND'. Spenny, Hilly and myself looked on helplessly as our firm legged it. Herman who was an older Barmy Army lad stood on his own and Wednesday dragged him to the floor.

We went to his rescue as Wednesday's vultures ragged him, while the rest of their firm continued the chase. Herman was furious and mumbled that he had finished with United as he dusted himself down; he was as good as his word and never turned out for United again. He'd been on the scene for two decades and was as game as they come but this day saw him retire from his hooligan days.

Hilly, Spenny and I ran up behind the Wednesday firm who were in hot pursuit of our lot. We were half hoping that United would turn it around but deep down we knew that, once you turn and run, you never get yourself back together. We could hear the sound of more brawling and, as we ran up at the back of Occasions nightclub, six Wednesday lads known to us came into view. The three of us were on one and I rushed forward to square up to them. One went to pull a knife out but Hilly knew him well and screamed at him to put it away. As we squared up, I ran and punched Lewis, a tall Wednesday Casual. He stumbled back and we ran at them making them do one.

Despite our little victory at the end, we knew we had been done and I went home totally dejected by the night's events. Six arrests were made that night and a United youngster was stabbed during the brawl. I couldn't sleep that night which shows the depth of feeling and how much being top dogs meant to us. I vowed that it would be a one-off and that we had to bounce back and prove that we were still number one.

WEDNESDAY'S COP OUT

Wednesday's result after the Kenworthy game no doubt added a new enthusiasm into their firm. They thought they had stemmed the tide but it just proved to be a false dawn. Desperate to follow up the running of a Blades mob, they started doing a few naughty ones like turning up tooled up to attack a group of Blades who used to have a kickabout together. But revenge came the following Friday in the shape of an attack on a well-known Wednesday pub which resulted in two Wednesday lads being hospitalised. Things got very tetchy in Sheffield around this time.

Every now and again, South Yorkshire Police would let both Sheffield teams play on the same day, which, on one occasion, cost me a day in the cells.

Across the city, towards Barnsley, out in the sticks, is the home of Wednesday, whose home is Hillsborough or Swillsborough as we Blades prefer. Their visitors in February 1987 were West Ham and following their team were one of the most respected firms in the country, the ICF. Visiting Bramall Lane on the same day were Plymouth Argyle, a non-event on the football hooligan calendar. That must have been the police's reasoning for letting both games go ahead on the same day. Our firm were a bit in limbo during the weeks leading up to the game but in the end no arrangements were made, as we saw West Ham as Wednesday's problem. A big Wednesday turnout was expected so we decided to meet up in the Penny Black straight after our game, reasoning that we could

get into town first and plot up and wait. Also, any West Ham firm would have to walk past the Penny, so it was ideal on both fronts. Wednesday must have had a firm's meeting and I reckon it went like this:

'We'll meet in the Blue Bell and jump West Ham as they come into town.'

'No, let's go down London Road at 12 o'clock; there'll be no Blades about so we can take the piss a bit and it'll save us getting mashed in by West Ham. All those in favour of London Road, raise their hands. Carried unanimously, London Road it is!'

That morning, I knew a handful of our lot were meeting in the Dodgers pub near the train station. I drove down in my car, reasoning that I could have a look-see if the West Ham firm were around or Wednesday for that matter. When I entered the Dodgers, around a dozen United lads were playing pool.

I got restless and went for a drive around town to see if any firms were around. As I drove along Arundel Gate, I saw a good mob of 100-plus boys heading away from town towards Bramall Lane. On closer inspection, I realised that it was a Wednesday firm and the alarm bells told me that they were out on a Blade hunt. It was only midday and Wednesday knew full well that no Blades firm would be around in any numbers; it was a total cop out by Wednesday. They had a good mob out but chose to avoid any confrontation with a West Ham mob.

I tracked the OCS until they got near London Road, then sped around the back of the Lansdowne (our pub at the time) and ran inside. No one was in except my mate Badger. I grabbed him and told him to get out quick. Just as we got out the back door. Wednesday came in the front. Badger was 40 seconds from hospitalisation. We jumped in the car and headed back to the Dodgers.

Only a handful more of our lot were gathered inside. I hurriedly explained that Wednesday had a big team out and were on London Road. The odds against us were heavily stacked but we had to go and defend our patch. We parked up at the Sheaf on Bramall Lane and walked the short distance to London Road.

A quick body count showed 23, but a good 23. We started encouraging each other to stick together and not to leave anyone.

'Start running and someone's going to get battered by them,' I reasoned.

As we approached from a side street, the landlord of the Pheasant gave us all the nod. His body language told us that Wednesday were just around the corner. We couldn't see them and they couldn't see us. This actually suited us and we ran on to the petrol-station forecourt and armed ourselves with whatever we could. For my part, I emptied the sand out of a steel bin, zipped up my hood and prepared for battle. Some of the lads got fire extinguishers. It was pretty obvious it was going to come on top but, if we could just take them by surprise, we might just get ourselves a result from the top drawer. And take them by surprise we did! I ran around the corner swinging the steel bin like a demented hammer thrower. Wednesday were shocked and, as everyone steamed in, they backed away. Our numbers didn't really matter at this point, as Wednesday had no idea how many we had coming around that corner and you could see this in their faces.

A couple of our lot were bluffing by shouting more imaginary boys to join our plight from around the corner. Wednesday regrouped outside the Tramway and came pouring back at us, with bricks and bottles raining down. Reefer copped a brick straight in the face and staggered away from the frontline. I tried to stand my ground by swinging the bin in front of me. I remember thinking the cardinal sin for a hooligan: 'Where's the fuckin' coppers when you want them?' It was on top big time.

By now, I'd got them all around me and some had even gone past me in the brawl. I was in that bad situation where, if you run, you have a good chance of getting tripped and a certain beating but standing any longer was not an option. I threw the bucket to try to give myself a yard to do one. As I turned and ran, someone clipped the back of my legs causing me to stumble. One tried to grab me and I punched him in my panic to get away, my arse twitching like a rabbit's nose.

Our little firm were being chased down London Road with the

sound of 'OCS, OCS' ringing in our ears. We ran towards the Lansdowne and Pete the landlord was standing in the doorway issuing our lads with bats and pool cues as they hurtled inside. Howie and myself didn't have the chance to get in the pub, as our lot crushed through the doors, so we ran around the back. The pub was totalled.

The two of us at the back of the pub loaded up with rocks and launched our attack as we ran back around and threw our ammo at the Wednesday masses that were attacking our pub. The OB screeched up and Wednesday started to walk away as the coppers got their shit together. Most of our lot came out of the pub and insults were exchanged.

I shouted over to a Wednesday lad I knew, 'What was that about? West Ham too big for you?'

As Wednesday were escorted back into town, we put the word out that everyone should meet up at the Lanny straight after the game. Revenge time. After the game, around 70 Blades had met. To be honest, it wasn't the best mob we've had and it reminded me much of the firm we had out for the Kenworthy debacle. We headed to the Penny Black in town. News soon came through that Wednesday were drinking in the Yorkshireman pub at the top end of town. Without further ado, we set off to war.

I walked to the pub with 15 others as the rest hid in the Peace Gardens. We wanted to get Wednesday out on the street; there was no result in just attacking the pub. The plan was to get them outside by backing away as far as the end of the road and the rest would then run up and join us. We went to the doors and Titch shouted inside, 'Come on, Wednesday, we're here.'

Wednesday threw glasses at the door and we backed away into the street. Our hidden crew had got restless and came charging around the corner – a good plan ruined. 'BBC, BBC,' echoed in the dark street and the pub was smashed to bits, even the big heavy double doors were ripped from their hinges. Wednesday defended the doors by launching whatever came to hand. It went on for ages and, by the time the plod turned up, a lot of our lot had walked away. Four Blades and one Wednesday were arrested at the scene.

No result could be claimed by us as we hadn't done anything other than attack a pub.

One week later, a coach full of United lads were pulled over by the police on the Sheffield Parkway. Four lads were arrested including myself. I was locked up for six hours, questioned twice and release without charge. I'd been grassed up by one of my own.

WEDNESDAY CENTENARY, 1989

The 1989–90 season was United's centenary year. To celebrate, a pre-season friendly had been arranged with the old foe, Sheffield Wednesday. The game was to be played in August at Bramall Lane and would be a nice warm-up for our now very strong firm.

On the day of the game, we met as usual in the Pheasant on London Road. When I turned up at midday, there were only around 40 of our firm gathered in the pub. Wednesday were meeting at the Arbourthorne Hotel, a pub situated on a tough council estate around three miles from beautiful downtown Bramall Lane. Wednesday had been making big noises that they were turning everyone out and this new Blades firm were going to be put back in their place after taking over proceedings in Sheffield. A few telephone calls were made and I spoke to a top Wednesday lad. He told me that Wednesday had about 150 lads out and that the firm they had was the best they had turned out for many a year. I could tell by the tone in his voice that he fancied their chances but then again so did I. It was agreed that Wednesday would make their way down to the Earl of Arundel and we would head for the Sheaf; hooligan kick-off time was arranged for 2.30.

With more of our lot turning up by the minute, by one o'clock we had well over 100 lads out and, to be fair, they were all our main firm of mid-20-year-olds who were by now seasoned thugs. Our average age at this time was probably around 24, while our rival firm's

average age would have been 30 to 35. To us, it didn't matter about the numbers or quality Wednesday had out, as we knew that we would steam into them and, when you have over 100 lads who are all of the same mind, then Wednesday were going to struggle to cope. In truth, man for man, Wednesday probably had a harder firm than us but this was football violence and it didn't matter how handy individuals were, the firm who wanted it most were the ones who were going to come out on top.

One of our scouts pulled up in the car outside the Pheasant and told us Wednesday were on the move and also confirmed they had a massive team out. Good, no excuses then, I thought. They were keeping their end of the deal by heading to the Arundel, so we supped up and headed for our appointed destination, the Sheaf. We'd split up into twos and threes as the plod were all over London Road like a rash and we didn't want to attract their attention by walking en masse to our destination and ruining our chances of an off.

Everyone was buzzing and well up for it outside the Sheaf, as lads went around encouraging each other and shaking hands as if to confirm the tightness of our firm. Bang on 2.30, we set off. I walked in front with Tiler. We both knew that neither of us would back off an inch, so we bounced in front of our firm whose strides were getting quicker and longer with every step.

The Sheaf was only 500 yards from the Earl but not visible until we walked around the corner. We were by now 300 yards from the Earl and Wednesday spilled out of the pub and began running up towards us. We fanned and our quick walk soon became a jog. I looked at Tiler who was running down parallel with me. 'Don't stop, straight in,' I yelled but Tiler didn't need telling. I was just getting the old adrenaline pumping through my body. Wednesday did indeed have a great mob and, to be honest, I thought we were going to have a big job on our hands to shift them along; the least I expected was a toe-to-toe battle as Wednesday had turned every face out.

'BBC, BBC' was shouted with an aggression I had never heard before.

Wednesday completely filled the road and pavements. Around 10

black lads were fronting for Wednesday. I knew most of them and they were respected geezers in our city, but this was football and it wasn't about individuals, it was about who wanted it most, who was the gamest, who had the bottle.

As the two firms got within launching distance of each other, glasses, bricks and bottles filled the air. We didn't slow in our charge. The two front rows tore into each other but Wednesday had committed the cardinal sin of stopping their charge and standing flat. Big mistake — it's the first sign of loss of nerve.

Anyhow, Wednesday had managed to get 100 yards from the pub so perhaps the bog hiders missed the action but Wednesday started to lose nerve and backed off. I ran and hit one just as he was turning to run; he went down but was back on his feet and running in a split second. They were screaming at each other to 'STAND' but we'd got them on the hop and continued our assault on the disappearing Wednesday line. That sight of Wednesday's best firm in total retreat was a buzz and a half. A game lad called Zack had stood on his own and was copping a beating from around 10 of our lot who had captured him. I ran over and pulled a few of our lot off him; fair play to him, he was the *only* one with the bollocks to stand his ground, and kicking him into the middle of next week was the last thing he deserved.

I escorted him to the sanctuary of the surrounding roadside trees. He shook my hand, muttering that Wednesday were shit. I ran to join up with the rest of our firm who had totally written off Wednesday's firm. In that one 45-second brawl, we had proved we were still the top firm in Sheffield. They had turned out every face and every big gun they had but our young Casual firm were too strong and too game. A lot of their older heads seemed to disappear from their ranks after that day.

The OB got the bedraggled OCS firm together and marched them slowly to the ground. Quite a few of us waited near the top of Bramall Lane, as we wanted to mock their firm and rub the result in as much as possible. The OCS made a token effort to break from the escort as a few of us were shouting 'runners' and 'shit Wednesday'. The half-hearted attempt at breaking free was greeted with a cheer

from our lot; they had had the chance to dance but failed. We went in the ground but a lot of United's lads didn't bother. Wednesday for their part sloped off into town under the OB escort.

The game itself was a boring 0–0 draw only highlighted by that tosser Carlton Palmer getting sent off and effectively ruining his chances of playing for his country. Just how he ever pulled an England shirt on only Graham Taylor will ever know.

Around two weeks after the game, Housey, Vinny and myself were in Josie's nightclub when in walked the whole Wednesday squad. We couldn't resist and started giving some pig players the verbals. Palmer was my target but he successfully rebuffed my attack with the line: 'It's always been my ambition to play for England and I've probably blown my only chance to play for my country, so please leave it out, mate, I'm gutted.'

He'd shut me up with that as he looked genuinely hurt by the fact that, by being sent off, he'd been left out of the English team. He's still a tosser, though; the one thing I really hate about some footballers is the fact that they become big-time Charlies and, in my opinion, Palmer fits that bracket with bells on.

Anyhow, after the game, we scanned the streets and went looking in town for Wednesday, but no luck, the Wednesday firm had melted but deep down we knew they would have to try and get some face back. The small groups of our firm all eventually met up in a city-centre pub called Silks, which was our usual haunt at the time. Every Saturday night between six and eight o'clock, you'd find anything up to 300 lads in there depending on our opponents for the day. As I went in, it was packed with around 250 United; don't get me wrong, not all of these were our firm but a lot of the others were Barmys who would get stuck in if need be.

I was surprised to see Zack and around six of the black lads who had been run along with the Wednesday firm earlier standing at the bar. Zack again shook my hand but, just by having a look around, I could see that a lot of our firm were unhappy to say the least at their presence. I mentioned this to Zack; the one thing that I didn't want to happen was our lot to smash the fuck out of seven lads. It's a no-win situation really: you don't give it to them and you're mugs;

you do give it to them and you're bullies. The Wednesday lads left and it was obvious they would return with the rest of the OCS.

In situations like these, we needed a couple of lads that were leaders who could think on their feet and who had enough respect that the rest would listen, but we were all more or less equal as we had that many game lads who all tried to have a say but what we needed was a Chelsea Hickmott-type figure to sort us out. The reason I'm mentioning this is the fact that I was trying to get us to split into two groups with one group heading just down the road to the Three Cranes, which was only 100 yards away from Silks. I was trying to think on my feet as I knew the OCS would turn up soon and there was only one exit point from Silks, so, if Wednesday did appear, we would struggle to get everyone outside.

Sure enough, the 10 or so United who were stood outside came in screaming that our foe had arrived. Objects crashed against the pub windows and 'Wednesday, Wednesday' echoed in the street. Everyone headed for the one exit door. United lads were rammed together like sardines and the unfortunate ones nearest the door were pushed towards the Wednesday firm as they attacked the doors. What also went against us was the fact that Wednesday had tooled themselves up from roadworks just around the corner, which gave them a ready-made arsenal, but, to be fair, we would have done the same thing; never look a gift horse in the mouth.

Inside, it was bedlam as we tried to get out but the front lads were taking the brunt of Wednesday's attack and quite a few of our lads got hospitalised. It also didn't help our cause that Tony's rottweiler dog was biting everyone around it, as it went into a slavering frenzy.

I managed to battle towards the front and, in a surge, around 15 of us got out; we were instantly attacked in the doorway and backed down the road. It was suicidal really, as bricks and bottles crashed into us and the steel spikes that are used for roadworks' red and white tape were used against our little surge. To make matters worse, the Wednesday lads who had been in Silks 10 minutes earlier came up behind us with around another 10 lads in tow.

We now had to run through another attack and I managed to get through with a punch landing on my shoulder as I ducked. We turned

at the bottom of the road to see another surge as Tony and his dog ran into Wednesday. I think at this point Wednesday had exhausted their ammo and were looking to get away, as the OB were closing in but my memory of Tony and his dog running into Wednesday is still vivid.

To be honest, Wednesday had backed away from the pub doors, whether it was because they had had enough of the onslaught or the fact that the OB would be here in minutes I don't know. It wasn't the end though, as the police screeched up. The Wednesday lads headed towards us as we jogged back up the street.

A very young Lester Divers (RIP) then dropped one with a roundhouse kick, as the 15 of us squared up to Wednesday. Lester wanted his name left in my first book and actually told me prior to a Wednesday game that he didn't give a fuck and didn't want his name putting in as Forest or the other disguised name I used. That moment when Lester dropped a very respected and handy lad confirmed that this man was special and he would become probably the most respected lad United's firm has ever seen or ever will see for that matter. He's gone now but his memory lives on.

The dog was set on a couple more Wednesday and one was badly bitten as he tried to crawl into the Mucky Duck pub. The hospital was full of wounded football thugs. It even kicked off in casualty to end a very violent day in Sheffield's hooligan history. Wednesday argued that they had made the day a draw but in reality we had sent their firm packing and attacking a pub doorway was nowhere near enough to gloss over the fact that we had battered them in the head-to-head on the street.

SUNDAY, BLOODY SUNDAY

The trouble with running and playing for a football team was the fact it made me an open target for Wednesday. It fucked me off no end that Wednesday could stoop as low as to come to the Sunday football for trouble; they knew I had standards and I certainly wouldn't lower myself to visit houses or workplaces or phone people's houses or mobiles. To me, the game we were in should have been left to the streets. I had four Wednesday lads visit me at my work saying that someone claiming to be me had been phoning their houses threatening them. They knew that was not my style and, to be fair, they said the same but wanted to know if I had any idea who might be responsible. On the flip side, one of their lads called Belly was followed home in a taxi once by three of United's lads and was jumped outside his home, so I suppose the argument can swing both ways.

Anyhow, in 1985, my Sunday team had some great characters – Shotgun, Mitch, Nobby, Kav, Norm, Housey, Sainey and Nudge – who were all involved with United's firm at the time and this often led to trouble.

Wednesday's main actors had a team called the Shakespeare, who used to meet on the steps just outside the Penny Black, while we used to meet inside the pub via the back entrance. It was a recipe for disaster really. Then, one Sunday morning, outside the Penny Black, they attacked a car being driven by one of our team which was the last one to set off for our game. Bats were used and the car

was badly damaged. It was unfortunate for the lad behind the bar, as he'd lent us the car because we didn't have enough transport to get us to the ground and he wasn't impressed when he saw the state of his car when we returned.

The following week, I told everyone to bring a bat as we were going to do Wednesday in. It was quite funny as all our lot turned up with straight arms, as everyone had a bat up their sleeve, although not half as funny as when Nobby walked in the pub carrying a six-foot boating oar.

'It's the only thing I could find,' he said smiling through the gap in his teeth.

Wednesday didn't turn up, which was lucky really, as our team would have been looking at a few reprisal attacks from their firm and, being based at the Penny Black, we were sitting ducks. They never met there again.

Three years later, our team was again targeted, although I think they had come to teach me a lesson as I was bang at it on Saturdays and had got myself a reputation, which was either good or bad depending on how you look at it. Most of the same lads mentioned earlier were still playing for us, so, when a Wednesday lad let me know that their firm were planning to attack me and the team on Sunday morning, I had to let the team know. It was a no-brainer really, as we were playing the Arbourthorne Hotel, a pub that a lot of their lads drank in.

I got asked by quite a few of our lads if I wanted them to turn out. I thanked them but said that I didn't, first, because I didn't want a pitched battle on my behalf and my team kicked out of the league, and, second, if it did kick off, then we would be targeted even more. I believed it was totally out of order.

The Sunday morning came along and our team were not their usual jovial selves as we walked into the changing rooms at Arbourthorne playing fields, which was not surprising really. Because I'd punched an opponent a few weeks earlier, I was suspended for the game and had to stand on the sidelines.

My team talk went along the lines of winning the game and letting

me worry about the off-the-pitch activities. I wasn't exactly carefree but I've always had a 'what will be will be' attitude. If I was going to get it, then someone was going with me, as I had placed an insurance policy in our medical bag.

We quickly took a three-goal lead as Arbourthorne concentrated on legs rather than the ball, and it was obvious that some of their players were in on what was about to go off. One of the Wednesday lads called Gossip had been down earlier on a recon exercise accompanied by his Doberman. I'd walked straight up to him and made small talk.

As half-time approached, I glanced up at the Vulcan pub which overlooked the pitch, and saw around 30 Wednesday come down the hill towards the pitch with a Rottweiler and the aforementioned Doberman in tow. My dad was standing next me and he was my first thought. I knew he wasn't going to stand there while I got mullered but he is just a normal bloke and trouble is not his forte; my mum's harder than him! He pleaded with me to fuck off as we were a good 100 yards away across the pitch.

Wednesday sauntered down to pitch-side. Just as they got to the touchline, Holder, a Blade lad who played for us, chinned one of their players because he was giving it the 'you're dead now' shit. A lot of players got involved and Wednesday ran on the pitch making strange caveman-type noises.

Without thinking, I ran across the pitch to help my team-mates. The referee restored order by repeatedly blowing his whistle like he was about to self-combust. He sent Holder and one of their players off. Holder is one game lad and I've never seen him take a backward step. He actually went and fought a Wednesday main face in a one-on-one in Norfolk Park one evening. No one knew about it but he was truthful enough to tell us after that Errol (the Wednesday lad) had won the fight, albeit by shoving his thumbs into Holder's eyes.

Anyhow, Wednesday started pointing across the pitch at me and a few started to walk around. My dad was getting very distressed so I walked away from him towards the oncoming foe. I wanted to get some distance from my dad because of the beating I thought I was about to get. There was no way I was going to run. Fuck that!

The old adrenaline was pumping as I approached the first few Wednesday. One of Wednesday's main geezers greeted me with 'wanker' – nice.

Another lad booted me on the back of my legs from behind and, as I glanced back, he shouted, 'You're shit.'

I shrugged my shoulders and replied, 'I'm shit? Thirty of you lot for me?'

As I continued to walk to the main bulk of Wednesday, and to a Wednesday lad called Chirpy in particular, they must have been stunned by my front. Chirpy was a leading Wednesday lad, with whom I would later share a police cell for the night, although at this stage I'd never spoken to the man before. I thought, if I was going to get it, which was a very good possibility, then I wanted to know who we would be dealing with at a later date.

'What's happening, Chirpy? Thirty of you for me?'

'We'd heard Shane and Luey played football for you,' he said.

'They don't play football, for fuck's sake, man.'

They looked a bit perplexed about what to do next. I couldn't help but think that they had dropped two of United's main lads out of their arses to excuse turning up.

'Come on, let's go,' Chirpy said.

Fair play to Wednesday, they could have smashed me into the middle of next week but chose to go and for that I was grateful. I walked back around the pitch to my relieved dad.

'Jesus, son, what did you say?'

'Just forget it, Pop, it's sorted.'

Just another day in life on the edge of a city totally divided by football.

Some 10 years later, my Sunday team had become a very good side and we progressed to the best standard around. The faces in our team had changed completely but we still had a few United lads who liked a bit of terrace dancing.

Our first game in the Meadowhall League, as luck would have it, was away at the Sportsman against a team from Stannington. I knew a Wendy lad called Mack had something to do with running them

and that they were mostly of the blue and white persuasion. In the build-up to the game, we'd heard rumours that Wednesday were turning a firm out for us, even though we had a few Wednesday lads in our side.

It left us with a predicament; do we go up to Stannington firmed up or do we just take the team? It was our first game in a new league and I could see the lot kicking off and us being kicked out of the league before we'd even begun. So much hard work had been done in the pre-season to get us into a position where we could compete, not only on the pitch but also financially.

A lot of United's lads had got wind of Wendy turning out for us and my mobile received quite a few offers of help including one from our main man Lester Divers who offered to bring his team up, as he called them.

In the end, we decided to go up with just the team and to just treat it as another game. Well, almost … On the day of the game, every one of our players had a rounders bat in his bag; I'd told them that they were for protection only and not to pull them out unless they had to.

It was a Thursday-evening game and we had to make our way across Sheffield in the rush hour. Their ground was 12 miles from the city centre, and, although we tried to keep together, I lost the rest of the lads and then got lost on the way to the ground. I pulled on to a side road just after Stannington to try to get my bearings as we headed out of Sheffield towards Dungworth. The side road had around six riot vans and two dog vans parked in a line, but I didn't think anything of it, as the area wasn't familiar to me and I thought there must be a cop shop on the road. I later found out those bizzies were for us.

I read my street map and got my shit together, then started to drive the two miles to the ground. On the way my mobile went. 'Steve, you better get here quick, there's loads of them and a few are tooled up.'

Good job we'd got the bats, I thought. I pulled up into the car park of the ground and quickly got out of the car, my bat up my telltale straight arm.

Our opposition stood 30-handed on a bank and some numpty was stood there swinging nunchuks around like a pissed-up dickhead Bruce Lee. I stood in front of them posing like Eubank used to do. A few motioned my way, so I prepared for kick-off.

Suddenly, Bolly shouted, 'Steve, watch it.'

I thought some more were coming up behind but, no, it was the plod who were hiding in the trees filming us with a camcorder. Then police came from everywhere, it was well over the top.

Raggy and a few others walked up to my car and threw their bats on to my back seat, which was good of them. The referee had heard about the impending trouble and had decided not to come. The police were keen to get the game out of the way so one bobby offered to ref it for us.

I didn't fancy playing with more police than spectators around the pitch, and, to be honest, I wanted out of there as my car was full of bats.

'We've had to set up a special operation for this,' one copper moaned to me.

'I can't help the fact that these divs have forgotten we're supposed to be playing a game of football,' I replied.

We set off back to Sheffield with an escort Kenneth Noye would have been proud of. Every time I went around a bend, I threw another bat out of the window, much to the amusement of our two Wednesday-fan team members who were in the car behind me. So, that was that, our first game called off and an eight-vehicle police escort back to Sheffield. Sound!

Back at the pub, I phoned the Sportsman at Stannington and asked for Macky. Someone came on the phone and started having a chirp.

'Look, just because I run the side doesn't mean all the lads are BBC, far from it. Don't forget you've got to play at our ground; we've come in this league to play football, nothing else. Let's make sure that, next time we play, there's none of that shit, OK?'

He agreed.

When we played them at home later in the season, the police came but kept a low profile. There was no trouble and they came and had a beer after the game. The ice had been broken and we could get on with the football again.

UNITED'S DOUBLE, PART 1

The build-up to this game in November 1991 was electric; it had been almost 12 years since the last competitive game between the clubs. On the advice of the police, the game was moved to a Sunday with the kick-off at midday. Police had also demanded that every pub within three miles of the ground be closed after the game. The authorities hoped that trouble would be minimised and, to be fair, it worked. Both sets of fans and boys had nowhere to go before or after the match.

I took my usual seat in the South Stand just behind the dugouts. The atmosphere was unreal, our boys were scattered all around the ground, with the largest group of around 250 situated in the John Street terrace. A young United lad came down the steps of the stand with blood running from his nose. I shouted over to him and he told me he'd been twatted outside by Wednesday. Then, seconds later, a Wednesday lad called Lebby who I knew pretty well walked down the steps with his mate. Sometimes, in the game I was in, you get carried away and I did on this day. I threatened Lebby and went across the seats towards him. He looked at me as if to say, 'What are you doing?' Lebby was old school and always frontlined for Wednesday on the streets and I should have given him a bit more respect than I did.

A few weeks later, I bumped into him in town and was man enough to go over and apologise and buy him a shandy!

Anyhow, at the match, another United youngster came down the

stand and shouted to me that Wednesday were in the concourse at the back of the South Stand. I immediately jumped up and ran up the steps, only pausing briefly to shout to Tap, Lewis, Pud, Tiler and a few others. Without really thinking or waiting for that matter, I ran down the gangway on to the concourse. To my left and towards United's Kop stood around 40 Wednesday. I started jogging over towards them. They were all stood around eating pies and drinking Bovril. It was most of Wednesday's main firm with no bits of kids with them. A quick glimpse back and I realised I was on my own, for the time being at least. A few Wednesday spotted me and fanned out with their arms outstretched. I continued my jog, then thought, fuck it, in for a penny in for a pound. I just steamed in. My arms and legs were going like the clappers as I fought with Wednesday. I was just thinking how well I'd done to stay on my feet for so long when, under a barrage of punches, kicks, pies and Bovril, I went down. Immediately, I tried to get back up but the boots were flying in and the old hands over the head and face was my only option until the much needed help came. A shout of 'Come on' confirmed reinforcements had arrived. Tiler, Luey, Tap and around six or seven more came steaming in.

I jumped back to my feet and it was game on. We were well outnumbered but the lads we had fighting were all game as fuck, plus, as the concourse wasn't that wide, we could go toe-to-toe with Wednesday's frontline. Fists and boots lashed out as we battled it out with each other, neither side giving an inch. Wednesday were getting in each other's way but we had more room to manoeuvre. I ran in a couple of times landing punches as I did. Then I caught sight of someone coming from the side of me; just in time I threw a right-hander, which connected sweetly. As he reeled back, I realised it was Mifter, a lad I knew reasonably well. He's a handy lad and, fair play, he knew the score, no love lost in battle.

Stewards and police came flying in and it was time to ring the bell on this tear-up. The match had kicked off, so we took up our seats.

By half-time, word had spread around the South Stand. I didn't need a pie as I had enough during the first half as I picked lumps of steak and pastry off my coat. Around 30–40 had wormed our way

through the crowd towards where Wednesday were. The OB were all over the shop but let us mingle together; a few insults were exchanged but there was no violence, as one punch would mean one arrest. I saw Mifter, and his eye was completely closed. I said to him there was no offence; he just nodded but naturally looked a bit pissed off. If I had copped for one, then I wouldn't have held any grudge and nor did Mifter.

Lads were giving each other grief: 'You're shit, Wednesday.' 'Fuck off, Bertie, we'll see you up West Street later.' 'Me and you, let's take a walk,' and so on.

A lot of plain-clothes plod mingled in and both firms' footie coppers kept a close eye on who was doing and saying what. The game finished with a very up-for-it United team beating the much more fancied Wednesday outfit 2–0 (Whitehouse and Deane). The Blades had four Sheffield lads in the squad, Bradshaw, Ward, Hoyland and Dane Whitehouse. Not only were they Sheffield lads but they were all avid Blades fans and can be seen at the Lane from time to time with Dane not missing many games.

To me, that was the difference in the two teams: passion. In an extraordinary moment during the second half, Wednesday's Nigel Jemson was punched on the touchline by a Blade who took a dislike to him. I knew the lad who did it and he was carted off to the cells. He never got banned or even had to go to court. When I asked him later why he'd punched Jemson, he said that he hated Wednesday. Fair enough.

A lot of United's lads headed up Ecclesall Road afterwards, for two reasons: Wednesday might be knocking around up there but the main reason was we wanted to celebrate and there was plenty of licensed burger bars where we could have a beer or ten. The beer flowed and the singing began, with everyone in great spirits.

Walk tall, walk straight and look the world right in the eye,
That's what my momma told me, when I was about knee high,
She said, sonny, you're a Blades fan, so hold your head up high.
And as you're walking down the street, poke a pig fan in the eye.

BLADE VERSUS OWL

As usual, a few did one without paying. Later that night, we went around town and headed up West Street in search of our foe. Wednesday must have gone home with their little pink curly tails placed firmly between their legs.

UNITED'S DOUBLE, PART 2

I knew that the BBC would turn out big numbers for this game in March 1992; there was a much better chance of a dance for the evening game at Hillsborough than there had been at Bramall Lane. The fact that United had sold their 7,200 allocation in hours meant that a lot of Blades bought tickets for Wednesday's Kop and seats, so trouble was guaranteed. At teatime, 300 BBC and other Blades had gathered in two pubs in town.

The plan was to drink our way to Hillsborough and hit the back of their Kop around kick-off time. The OB were all over us like a rash. Ten riot vans backed up by plod on horseback and foot monitored our movements. Then the march to Hillsborough was on. United's mob looked impressive as it stretched out along Penistone Road for over 200 yards. I knew that, when we hit the crowds at the ground, the plod would have to be on top form to stop us breaking from the escort. Sure enough, around 40 of us broke out and, in trying to get us rounded back up, the escort fell to pieces. We were now all over the place, on enemy territory and up for a ruck.

Bang outside the Wednesday Kop, it went off. Hundreds of Wednesday fans were in massive queues at the turnstiles.

'BBC, BBC,' rang out and to be fair a lot of Wednesday were prepared to fight against this intrusion. The BBC went about their work and battles raged right along the back of their Kop as the United firm had split into smaller groups. I ended up with 20 others towards the top end of Penistone Road.

A lot of Wednesday who were walking down from various pubs like the Gate and the Travellers ran up to join in the battling. We ran into them football style and they had a good go. Another surge in from us and we ran them. One stood his ground and was beaten to the floor.

At this point, I thought we were going to get done as Wednesday had regrouped and, as more and more numbers swelled their ranks, they came charging back at us. There seemed to be hundreds of them but we stood firm and traded. I copped someone's size nines in the bollocks, and I nearly spewed up as the pain of my nads being rattled had me bent double. The OB managed to get control by forcing United's firm across the road. I sat on a wall cupping my bollocks.

Seven United lads were nicked; one was Shammy whose dial was all over the front page of the *Sheffield Star* when he went to court. They were all banned from attending for a period of one year.

I was in a bit of a dilemma at Hillsborough, as the OB tried to force us to the away end, as I'd got a ticket for Wednesday's stand. Around 25 good lads had obtained seats towards the Kop end of Wednesday's North Stand. When I got inside, I met up with the rest who had sensibly ignored their seat numbers and sat right at the back so, when/if it came on top, we had the high ground.

We had a great view of the fighting as it broke out on Wednesday's Kop. Hundreds of United fans had infiltrated it and it was kicking off all along the front as fans battled it out. The police took ages to sort out the situation and, just as they had removed one lot of Blades, it would kick off again.

It just shows the depth of feeling in our city when two really young lads, who were dressed in United tracksuits, gave Wednesday fans the wanker signs along with their dad as they were escorted around the perimeter track after being ejected from the Kop.

United came out and I stood in proud admiration of our fans. It was like a scene from the San Siro as a dozen red distress flares lit up the Leppings Lane End. Thousands of balloons bounced around and two massive flags were passed along the end. I was proud of my fellow supporters and the atmosphere they created was second to none. The team rewarded such great support with a fine 3–1 victory,

with Sheffield lad and staunch Blade Dane Whitehouse notching again along with two from on-loan Bobby Davison. Each United goal had been greeted with sporadic fighting all around the ground.

At the final whistle, we stood on the seats clapping the team off and generally going shitpot-crazy.

As the crowds vacated the ground, we could see trouble at mill in the shape of a load of Wednesday lads coming up towards us. We just waited patiently for them to get within reach of us. Wayne then roundhouse-kicked one in the side of his face and he was sent crashing over the seats. That was it; we all surged over the seats at them and they in turn surged over the seats in panic to get away. They were falling all over each other and pulling each other back in their haste. Outside, we mobbed back up at the petrol station as planned and the 200 or so of us walked the three miles back into town. In town, clubs were packed with Blades celebrating a famous Sheffield double.

Forty-two fans were arrested during the night: 37 Blades and five Wednesday.

Fighting between the two rival mobs was at its height around this time, and the early to mid-90s saw trouble involving the BBC and the OCS escalate into weekly encounters. Both groups started to concentrate more on each other than on the teams they were playing. We could have a game with great potential with, say, Barnsley away but the Beeb were more interested in staying in Sheffield because Wednesday had Grimsby at home and they would be turning a firm out. It got ridiculous.

Even Friday nights had started to see regular trouble. The police started to get sick of it, so arrests became more commonplace as the OB sought to stop these marauding mobs of football thugs. Charges got more serious, and the police adopted a new tactic of getting lads on a higher charge with the view that they might accept a lesser charge later in court. An offence which would usually carry a charge of threatening behaviour was upped to a charge of affray, which would be today's equivalent of violent disorder. When they hit the courts, the lads were offered the choice of having the charge dropped

to threatening behaviour. A lot of lads accepted this and the police started to see a few results in court rather than the 'Not Guilty all the way' attitude that football lads had previously adopted.

Two nights in late 1992 proved how things had changed in Sheffield as the power had swung well and truly in the BBC's direction. One Friday evening, 20 of us were drinking in the Ironmongers pub at the back of Trippet Lane. It was a pub we had never been in, so the layout was new to us, which led to three of us being on the top level and the rest of our lads settling down at the bottom end. We'd only been in 10 minutes when Wednesday came steaming through the doors, and two of them were brandishing some kind of cosh. Pud was nearest the door as the three of us tried to battle the Wednesday firm back outside. Our lot were slow on the uptake but then came running to our aid, which was just in time really as Wednesday were in the pub and it was on top for us. The United mob tabled and chaired the rival mob back outside and, as Wednesday regrouped outside the entrance, we got ourselves together and ran en masse straight into the Wednesday mob outside. It was dark on the streets so difficult to assess the numbers we were facing but at an estimate they looked around 30-strong.

Punches were exchanged in the doorway of the pub but Wednesday were backed out into the darkened street. We flew into them and had them backing away. Then they turned and ran with two of their number captured and pulled to the floor. They copped a bit of a beating as we screamed at Wednesday to come back for their mates. Wednesday regrouped outside the Blue Bell pub and we charged up at them. They held the higher ground but we went into them in a frenzy; we'd tasted victory and weren't letting go now. Wednesday ran again and this time we chased them right on to High Street where they again tried to stand their ground. I hit and dropped one who was known to me; Chirpy and Quinny came running to his aid but the damage – and Wednesday – were well and truly done.

A month later, Wednesday were at home. They had been making a few noises that they were going to go to Silks later that night to do the Berties. United had heard that Wednesday were meeting on

the Wicker that day and, although the turnout was low in numbers, the BBC firm numbering just under 20 headed down to the Brewer on the Bridge pub on the Wicker. Wednesday were further up the Wicker and got wind of this cheeky Blade mob and decided to go and teach them a lesson. United spilled out to greet them and fanned out across the road. Sensing the Blades mob was not at its strongest in terms of numbers, Wednesday charged forward. The BBC stood firm and a full-scale toe-to-toe battle went off. Wednesday's numbers were 40 to 60, depending on who you talked to, so we'll say the 40 of them got run the length of the Wicker. It was a great result for the BBC and even they had surprised themselves with the result as the numbers were not good. The battle had shown the gulf that now existed between the two fierce rivals.

TEAMING UP

Although United lads have had the odd guests come along with the firm, they have never mobbed up with anyone else. I couldn't turn out with another mob. I'm United and that's it really, although through the years I have forged lots of friendships with lads from lots of different clubs.

In 1985, Chelsea visited Hillsborough in the League Cup, and a Wednesday lad had been slashed before the game even started. I went along with two United lads and Tinny, who was Wednesday. Chelsea came in the seats behind us; they shot a flare in the air and attacked. Wednesday spilled on to the pitch, but four lads stood their ground – me, the two Blades and Tinny. I used my United golf umbrella to repel the Chelsea firm that swarmed over the seats.

A few years down the line, Wednesday forged an unlikely allegiance with the London club. Through England games and political beliefs, a few of Wednesday's main men had become pals with a few of Chelsea's.

In May 1993, Chelsea visited Bramall Lane; it was a game we were all looking forward to, especially with Chelsea's links with Wednesday. In the season prior to this game, United had played Chelsea at Stamford Bridge in the FA Cup quarter-final. United had taken a good firm not only for Chelsea but also because Wednesday were also in the capital that day with a game at Arsenal. As usual, the rumour mill had it that Wednesday and Chelsea were teaming up to do the Blades. We were hoping they would, as a Wednesday firm mixed in

with Chelsea would only weaken the London firm but, in truth, most of us knew that, even if Wednesday did turn out with Chelsea, it would only be a few of them.

Suffice to say that only three Wednesday were with the Chelsea firm that day. I know a few Wednesday lads that have told me that they would never turn out with the Cockney cunts, as they called them. Likewise, I'm pretty sure that Chelsea's main actors would not want to team up in any kind of numbers with another club; it's just not the done thing. United have never teamed up with anyone and never will.

That day in London has been well documented, so I will move on to the day at Bramall Lane, when neither Wednesday nor Chelsea can deny that they held each other's hand.

On the final day of the 1992–93 season, United turned out a big firm for their Chelsea counterparts and any Wednesday they had in tow. In truth, we were left frustrated before the game, as mobs of United split up and tried to find some opposition. After the match, we had news that Wednesday and Chelsea were in the Nursery Tavern on Ecclesall Road. Because of the massive police presence, we met up away from town in Sharrow straight after the match. It was argued that we would be able to slip through the flats towards Ecclesall Road without getting sussed by the OB.

The 200 BBC had a quick pint then set off to our target. The plan was working as we had not been seen by the police. We had made it on to the bottom of Ecclesall Road when the police came from everywhere, we were 300 yards from our target and it kicked off with the OB. Quite a few United lads were nicked and a few sustained injuries as police on horseback backed up by dog handlers quelled a mini-riot. A few of us retreated to a pub at the bottom of Ecclesall Road.

After 10 minutes, when I knew the coast had cleared a bit, I set off to walk to the Nursery. Badger came running up behind me and came along. Inside were around 30 to 40 Chelsea along with perhaps seven or eight Wednesday. We had a few amicable words and told the Chelsea lot that, unless they moved on, there would be no terrace dancing going off today, as our lot had just been at it with

the OB while they had been sitting tight supping their stronger-than-usual lager tops.

Badger and I then went down to London Road to join up with the rest of our mob who were sat in the sunshine outside the Pheasant Inn. News soon came through that the police were escorting the southerners and friends towards town. We ran around the back and headed towards them through the supermarket car park. As soon as we saw the escort, we charged but were met by mounted police who charged at us followed by the bollock biters. If I had been in charge of the police that day, I'd have left Chelsea to their own devices and left them to get the mother of all shoeings but, of course, the police are there to stop trouble, although I've often thought that, if they let a few firms get a kicking rather than protect them, then it would make them think twice about showing again. Maybe this is the way forward?

Anyhow, frustrated at our fruitless attempts to get at Chelsea, we headed into town. Our numbers were still high, although the day's events had probably reduced our firm's numbers by half. Then, at around nine o'clock, news came through that Chels-nesday were in Berlins. This actually meant we could kill three birds with one stone as there had been trouble between our lads and the Berlins bouncers in recent weeks. The plan was to attack the front and back doors of the club simultaneously after sorting the club's CCTV cameras out. The plan worked fine and the CCTV was ragged down. One United lad was actually nicked later as the camera showed a perfect image of his contorted face pulling the camera downwards and away from the club's doors.

The trouble was those at the back of the club didn't know when the attack would start and, as the front doors were steamed, the 25 at the back stood around like lemons until the OB chased them from the back of the club while it kicked off at the front. The bouncers used bats and CS gas to repel the attack, while Wednesday and Chelsea bounced around as well. The OB came from both directions and, as a result, eight United lads were nicked and charged with affray. No bouncers, Chelsea or Wednesday were arrested and

Above: Myself sat outside Bramall Lane, reflecting on a past of violence and a future away from it.

Below: A sea of red and white cheer the team on to the pitch before our FA Cup semi-final with Wednesday in 1993.

Above: Are you Wednesday in disguise? A Blade takes the piss during the derby at Bramall Lane in 2005.

Below: A civic reception was held for the triumphant United team to celebrate our return to the Championship after a 12-year absence.

Above: Myself, centre (cap), stood on top of the dugouts after our 2–0 win over Wednesday in 1992.

Below: The infamous game vs Leeds United in 1989. There was wide-scale disorder throughout the day. Here Blades fans spill from the John Street terrace in an attempt to get at Leeds fans on the away end.

Top: Alan Quinn becomes the first player to score for both clubs in a Sheffield derby.

Above right: Michael Tonge shows Wednesday fans where the ball went in their net after scoring in our 2–1 win at Hillsborough in 2006.

Left: Typical Warnock, celebrating our 1–0 victory over Wednesday in 2005.

one well-known Wednesday herbert drove around in a police van picking out Blades, tosser.

Not long after this, the same club's bouncers somehow got hold of a dossier of 14 United lads' details, containing mug shots, names, ages and addresses. The bouncers photocopied them and handed them out to Wednesday. A Wednesday lad I knew well phoned me and told me about what was going off and passed me a copy. Six of the lads on the dossiers received threatening phone calls from either the bouncers or Wednesday lads. One of our lads even had a crude petrol bomb thrown at his house wall. Whoever gave the bouncers these files wants his bumps feeling!

Matters were building to a head. The bouncers had formed an allegiance with Wednesday and the club barred Blades, while it was rumoured Wednesday had been served free drinks to help protect the club from Blades hooligans. Then two Blades were assaulted in the club, one was out with his workmates and the other his girlfriend. It was the last straw.

The following Saturday, up to 30 United walked up to the club. On seeing the bouncers at the back of the club, they charged in and the bouncers had to dive over the bar for protection. Two of them were badly beaten and the bar area sustained substantial damage as optics were smashed up with bar stools. The bouncers were informed by the last Blade to leave that they would be back if there were any more beatings of United fans.

The week after, I went in the club, along with six others. There'd been a definite mood swing and things eventually calmed down.

But, just as it calmed down at Berlins, things changed for the worst at the Music Factory. We always went in the Factory on a Saturday night but one weekend United lads were barred. It was unclear why this happened, but I think it had something to do with bouncers wanting to control who sold drugs and who didn't. Of course, the bouncers had no control over the United lads but the two groups had got on fine really. There had been very little, if any, trouble at the club but it was well known that two United lads were doing a roaring trade with the disco biscuits (Ecstasy). It started to get messy and the club was attacked weekly. In one attack the club

was emptied as CS gas was used by United's lads. A firearm was also discharged inside. It culminated in the Sheffield bouncers refusing to work the door as some heavy people got involved. A new security team were hired from Nottingham and, according to reports, they were not to be fucked around with. But this was like a red rag to a bull. The bouncers were attacked two weekends on the trot, and chased inside. The minibus in which they travelled up was set on fire one night. During it all, I'd kept out of it really. I was up for fighting for the Blades but not risking arrest so people could sell drugs.

Arrests were made as hidden cameras were set up outside the club the week after bouncers had used baseball bats to protect themselves as they were attacked again. The following week, the cameras captured the BBC's attack on the bouncers in which a distress flare was fired at them and again CS gas was released. Four United lads were later arrested and charged, one under the Firearms Act.

SHEFFIELD'S BIG DAY MARRED BY DEATH OF AN INNOCENT FAN

This was probably the biggest game Sheffield football had ever seen. In 1993, United pulled Wednesday out of the hat in the FA Cup semi-final. The FA, in their wisdom, had chosen Elland Road as the venue for this massive match. The other semi-final, which was between two other fierce rivals, Arsenal and Tottenham, was deemed by the powers that be to be a big enough game to be held at Wembley Stadium instead of Villa Park, while we had to be content with fighting over the then Leeds capacity of 28,000. There was uproar in our city as both Wednesday and United fans argued for the game to be played at the home of English football as well. Radio phone-ins were jammed and a massive petition was delivered to Soho Square.

The pressure put on the FA was immense and, eventually, they relented, so the game would be played at Wembley.

Such was the demand to see the game that both clubs quickly sold out their 35,000 allocation and, in truth, both could have sold a lot more. This was going to be Sheffield's day, and rivalries and passions were running high. Pleas by both clubs and police for a trouble-free game were well intentioned but, to be honest, there was more chance of Rangers and Celtic having a love-in than a load of Sheffielders forgetting the hatred they have for each other.

Our firm was buzzing. Everyone had planned to travel down in various modes of transport with a meet in Leicester Square organised for the evening before the match. I went down in a van of lads from around our way.

After we'd dropped our bags off at the hotel, we went to meet the rest of the lads. The meet was surrounded by OB when we arrived. Packed inside were around 400 of our firm. Rumours were doing the rounds that Wednesday were meeting up with a few of Chelsea's lads, but our hopes of getting it on with them diminished as soon as I saw the numbers and quality we had out. The frustration that no Wednesday were around and the fact that the best firm we had turned out in years were going to have to be content with a drunken singsong was too much for some. United lads clashed with the police and a bit of a battle took place which saw the arrest of several United lads. We headed back to the hotel in Canary Wharf.

Bert, being Bert, decided to do the daft Northerners in London sketch; he jumped on the steel sheets in the middle of the escalators that lead down to the tube. Straight into Eddie the Eagle Edwards pose, he quickly picked up speed as his Kickers burned rubber: 15mph over the first no-smoking sign; 20mph over the next, then the last one at the bottom proved too much, and, 25mph, bump, fly, crash!

Bert hit the power-off box at the bottom neck-first and at such a speed that his legs buckled over his back and he sent pedestrians flying all over. I ran down, knowing he was badly hurt. He got to his feet but hadn't a clue where he was, and the amphetamines he'd consumed didn't help as he tried to focus on me as I held his head. He had a hole in his neck that was so big you could see the veins dangling down and his windpipe. He started to moan and I was just reassuring him that he'd be all right when Patch sidled up and casually said, 'Fuckin' hell, Bert, tha's got a big hole in thee neck!'

With this, Bert collapsed and fainted. He was rushed to hospital and later came back to the hotel looking like Tutankhamen.

Next morning, the feeling was immense. I'd never felt like this before a big game and, what's more, I was convinced that the Blades would turn the snort beasts over. United's firm that day was unreal, 600-strong and some top-notch geezers. I saw Wednesday's firm before the game and there was a bit of a clash at the top of Wembley Way but nothing to get excited about, just a couple of punches and the OB had it wrapped up before it had begun.

STEEL CITY RIVALS

In a heart-rending moment before kick-off, a United goalkeeper called Mel Reece took a slow and painful walk around Wembley perimeter track. Reece had developed cancer and a few weeks later he had gone. Sheffield, for once, was united during his walk, with Wednesday fans standing and clapping him around the pitch. It brought home that, after all, football was just a game and life was much more important.

In the 2005–06 season, two Wednesday fans were sadly killed as their car crashed on its way home from Coventry. Despite fears that United fans would disrupt the planned minute's silence before the derby game at Hillsborough, the fears were unfounded as both sets of fans observed the minute's silence impeccably, with United fans showing their class by standing and clapping straight after it.

A couple of hundred Wednesday divs in the South Stand at the side of the away end immediately started singing, 'Die, piggy, die die,' which showed them up as clueless cunts, who have no idea how to conduct themselves; maybe the three pints of shandy before the game had affected their judgement.

Wednesday won the semi-final at Wembley 2–1 after extra-time but, in truth, they mullered us and, but for an outstanding goalkeeping display by Alan Kelly, the score could have been embarrassing. The gulf between the two sides on the pitch was there for all to see; off the pitch the same gulf between the two hooligan firms was also evident as United had 10 times the numbers of our rivals. After the game we mobbed up on the embankment and walked a massive firm down Wembley Way. I hung back to take a photo and saw Wednesday's little firm surrounded by police who also outnumbered them. The BBC disappeared into the tube station and headed off towards Victoria Station with the hope of bumping into Chelsea.

The semi-final had been a magnificent spectacle: 78,000 Sheffielders lifting the roof in a brilliant display of colours. However, tragically, the day was overshadowed by the death of an innocent United fan in the car park after the game. A group of Wednesday hooligans started some trouble with a group of innocent United fans, and, in the altercation,

a Blades supporter was assaulted by Sonny, an older Wednesday lad who should have known better. The United fan, who had no hooligan connections, later died. In court, Sonny received a two-year custodial sentence for his part in it. What should have been a celebration of Sheffield football ended up being overshadowed by the tragic death of a Blades fan.

NEAR-FATALITY AT STEEL CITY CUP

The now defunct Steel City Cup was the brainchild of one Reginald Brearley. Brearley was United's chairman between 1981 and 1995. In theory, the idea of having a trophy made and an annual game between the two clubs was a good one. Little did Reginald know that both sets of rival hooligans would be rubbing their hands at the thought of the set-to, and the competition would almost cost a Wednesday lad his life.

This particular game was to be played at Bramall Lane. Nothing happened prior to the match, in fact, we were a bit gutted that we hadn't seen or heard anything from the OCS. After the game, we headed into town and met up in Silks, 70-handed. Wednesday were on the blower saying they were on Ecclesall Road and for us to go down for a pop. By 6.30pm, we'd had enough of the grunters' calls and decided it was time for action; once again, we had to go to them.

As we congregated outside Silks, a taxi pulled up and Badger, Holder, Paul and Matt jumped in, shouting to meet up in Champs which is just up the road from the Nursery Tavern where we thought Wednesday were holed up. The trouble was that the rest of us had to walk to the taxi rank in Fitzalan Square, I say walk, but it quickly became a run in our eagerness to get it on. Unbeknown to us, Badger and the three other Blades had been chased as soon as they got out of the taxi. Wednesday chased the four of them right down a side street and Badger had to jump in the stream to avoid capture.

Seven taxis were filled and the taxi I was in set off first. When we got down there, it was obvious something had gone off. We got out of the taxis without paying and ran at five Wednesday lads standing on the corner of Champs. They were shouting down the road and, as I ran around the corner, the Wednesday firm were returning after chasing Badger and co. I went straight into them as they ran at us. The first lad who came my way got dropped; I knew him pretty well and had dropped him twice before in rucks, but, fair play to him, he never held a grudge when I bumped into him a few months later, and he knew it wasn't personal, just business.

As more Blades joined in the melee, Wednesday ran; some went back down the road they had just come up, while others were chased towards the Nursery Tavern. I joined around 10 others and chased around the same number of pigs towards the Nursery. Tiler had run past a few Wednesday in his haste to punch one and was dropped by a sidewinder from Granville. Tiler being one of the gamest lads around, he jumped back up and, although he'd got his Trevor Berbick legs on, he tried to fight, as Wednesday tried to launch a counterattack. Me and Housey were straight into them and they turned and fled again, only turning briefly outside the Nursery to throw some bottles that were left on the outside tables. Two bottles crashed into me, then a third crashed into my chest as I covered my face, this fucker hurt me big time.

Wednesday backed into the pub doors and rammed it shut. I dropkicked the door and it flew open. Wednesday defended the door with stools and glasses. The sirens were getting louder; then we realised they were so loud that they were actually at the scene. As hooligans, we've all done the innocent walk away with a 'it wasn't me, guv' expression on our faces, and that's exactly what I did as I mooched off.

It wasn't until later in town that a few of the lads said that a Wednesday lad called Teeney had been sparked out and looked in a bad way. Indeed, he was in a bad way, the intensive-care type of bad way. Teeney is a huge mountain of a man, but, unbeknown to us, further up the road from where we were fighting, he was knocked

to the floor and a United lad had been out of order in smashing him in the face with a big lump of concrete.

Next day, it was headline news. TV and radio reported how a Wednesday lad was fighting for his life in intensive care.

Thankfully, he came around and made a full recovery.

Later that week, eight United lads were dawn-raided by the OB. One of the arrested lads was Badger. On the actual night it had all happened, after he was chased through the stream by Wednesday, he'd gone straight home and missed all the battling. His wife wanted to know why his clothes were all soaking wet, so, like a cunt, he told her that he had been on Ecclesall Road and, because he was going home early to his wife, me and a few others had thrown him in a stream.

That fib bit him on the bollocks as, when the OB raided his gaff, he'd gone to work, so his missus told them there was no way he could have been in any trouble as he was on Ecclesall Road that evening and had come home wet because his so-called mates had thrown him in a stream. In short, she'd grassed him up. The OB naturally suspected that Badger had washed his clothes in the stream to get any blood off them. Badger's missus even told the OB what clothes he had on so they took them for forensics. So the moral of the story is, don't go bullshitting your Gert when something serious happens.

No one was charged with Teeney's assault which also put paid to some of our lot being convinced that the Beeb had a coppers' nark in their ranks.

ATTACKED AT HILLSBOROUGH

On 12 December 1999, I had gone with three Everton mates to watch their game against Sheffy Wendy. My pal Mitch Ward had signed for Everton and had got us tickets, I'd never give Wednesday a penny of my money unless my beloved Blades were playing there. I'd arranged to meet a Wednesday mate called Macky in the Masons Arms on Hillsborough Corner. In all, there were seven of us – three Blades, three Everton and a Wednesday fan.

Earlier, Everton had around 40 lads in the Howard Hotel but I'd told Macky that I would only come up with a few lads as otherwise it could get a bit hairy. Little did I know …

We met Mack and had a couple of beers but we ignored his advice to walk to the ground with him and his mates. We set off through the Hillsborough shopping precinct, but, just as we were walking up the street towards the ground, Raggy got punched from behind. We spun around to see around 25 Wednesday lads launching an attack on us. After a brief scuffle, we had to do one to a skip that I had spotted further up the road.

The Wednesday fan with us simply did one, but I've no problem with that as he could hardly fight with us against his own team, could he? I was first to the skip and leaned inside to find the most poorly equipped skip in battle terms and I salvaged the only three decent-sized bricks I could find, although I suppose I could have pulled the cut-down conifers out and hid behind them!

Wednesday were approaching so I ran at them while the rest of

our little group frantically groped around to find something that might even this fight up a bit. Rob shouted for us to stand with our backs against the footpath wall. I thought it was a bit of a stupid idea but, actually, when you think about it, that's exactly what we should have done.

One Wednesday lad screamed, 'Cowens, you're taking the piss.'

If I'd been taking the piss, I'd have taken a few more of Everton's firm up to Hillsborough than the three of them, but, to be fair, looking back, I can see his point of view. I wouldn't have liked a few Wednesday taking three Chelsea up London Road.

The golden rule when you have something in your hand is to keep it, especially when it came on top like this situation. But, like all the best-laid plans, it went out of the window and I threw one at a Wednesday lad called Qauz. It smashed into him and I found out later that it had broken his arm. The trouble was one of them picked it up and lobbed it back at me. The plod screeched up and, to be fair, it was on top for us. My Everton pal, Rob, was arrested as he stood in the road with a brick in each hand.

I went over to remonstrate with a few Wednesday lads I knew. 'You're out of order, it's typical of you lot is this.'

I got into an argument with a lad who was showing off in front of his mates and the OB. I vowed the next time I saw him he was getting one, and that vow ended up getting me locked up some six months later.

A Wednesday lad came over and said, 'Steve, I'll try and get your mate off.'

Fair play to the lad, as he went straight over to the cop car that was holding Rob and put his ten-penneth in to try to get him a royal Sheffield pardon. Now this fella wasn't liked at all by the red and white side of Sheffield as not only did he like carrying a knife but he also liked using it, and at least two United lads had been plugged by this man.

Rob was set free, as, in reality, he had done nothing except try to stand his ground while under attack, fair's fair.

Everton went on to win the game 2–0 which cheered me up a tad. Afterwards, we caught the tram back to town and went in the

Hallamshire Hotel on West Street for a drink. I was still on one as I told Pete that, if I saw them later, I was going straight into the lot of them arguing that Wednesday were out of order for attacking us. Pete reasoned that we shouldn't have gone up Hillsborough in the first place. I said that we had been in the Masons over an hour and that Wednesday knew we were there but still waited until they could jump us from behind on the streets. In reality, I knew Pete was right but it really pissed me off because I knew a lot of the Wednesday main actors who were there and actually got on reasonably well with a few of them. That fact had now gone out of the window as I wanted revenge. A few Wednesday put it about that I had been dropped in the earlier altercation. I never got touched, never mind dropped. If I had, I would've said, as an unexpected free punch from behind should drop anyone.

Later, we met up with 30 BBC in town. At around 10pm, news came that Wednesday had actually come into town for once and were drinking just up the road from us. As everyone vacated the premises, I argued that it was no good just attacking the pub as that would achieve shitesville.

Our lot held back at the end of the road as four of us, including two Everton, walked into the pub doorway. Wednesday had seen us and started bouncing around all agitated. I informed Tesh and a few others that the misters were here and to get outside. I knew, in reality, that Wednesday would sit tight as they pushed and pulled each other, screaming at the tops of their voices. Our lot came running up and, as they arrived, so did the OB. Wednesday threw glasses at the windows from inside, just why only they will know. The OB pushed us back down the road and I got my third and final public warning as a firm shove from Dibble told me it was time to go. Time was on my side and I would get my chance one day. Unfortunately, when the time did come, it ended with me sat in a police cell for the eighth time in my football career.

ON ENGLAND'S GREEN
AND PASTURED LAND

Both Sheffield clubs have quite a big England following nowadays, but that hasn't always been the case. In the early 80s, it was United who had the bigger turnout in terms of lads. It has been known for both sets of lads to clash abroad and one such incident carried over on to a train journey home when two small groups of rivals clashed at Euro 2000.

Back home in Blighty, the Blades and Owls hooligans have clashed on countless occasions after England games. One such fight came after England had beaten Scotland 2–0 during the Euro 2000 Championship playoff game up in chilly Jock-land. On the day of the match, I went down to the players café in Attercliffe along with a mix of 20 non-hooligan and fully fledged hooligan mates. Ten minutes prior to kick-off, around 40 BBC lads walked in to watch the game. Afterwards, we decided to go to the Wellington pub in Darnall and have a few drinks with the Beeb and the Darnall massive.

As we walked across the car park, a well-known black United lad was on the blower, arguing loudly. He was on his mobile to a pub on the outskirts of Sheffield. Wednesday were in there and on the other end of the line was a leading Wednesday lad. After threatening to go up and teach the Wednesday lad a lesson, the United lad jumped in a taxi with three others and said he was going to the Wellington. When we got in there, he wasn't around so I asked Luey if he'd gone up to sort the Wednesday lad out. I knew that it would

end badly as four United lads wouldn't be enough to sort this out and I knew that Wednesday would see this as a golden opportunity to do them in. Sure enough, news came through that the United lads had been attacked and one was seriously injured and on his way to hospital in an ambulance but not before the United boy had broken the Wednesday lad's jaw.

The BBC were fuming and taxis were ordered. I was in two minds: all my close mates were going into town, but it was not long after Wednesday had attacked me and a few mates up Hillsborough prior to the Everton game, plus the fact that I thought about Wednesday attacking the four United lads who had been game enough to go up there without being mob-handed. I made my decision and followed my heart.

We arranged to meet up in a pub about a mile away from where Wednesday were. We knew full well that the plod would be around and getting to Wednesday would not be easy.

At the pub, the OB clocked us and drove off so we knew we had to move quickly. The bus stop was just outside and, as a bus came into view, we decided to jump on it.

The bus pulled up 30 yards from the pub and I got up to get off first. I could see around five police vans across the road in another pub's car park. This threw the BBC who, unbeknown to me, had started crossing the road to the other pub. I headed for the pub where the first incident happened and 20 lads stood outside. Three dog handlers stood in the car park along with a few other plod. On seeing the activity, the Wednesday lads were in an excitable state. As I headed straight to the pub doorway, one shouted, 'Who are these? Are these 'em?'

'Come on, boys.' I ran at the doorway.

They threw a few glasses at me and, as our lot had realised their initial mistake, they came charging into the car park as Wednesday backed into the pub. It was then I was smashed over the head with a riot baton and I had a police dog hanging from my arm. The riot squad kicked the shit out of us; no grumbles like, but I saw several of our lads with their heads split open. I managed to get out of the car park at the top end.

It was quite funny really, looking back, as a Wednesday fan from around our way had been out to watch the match with us and, because he didn't know anyone, he just followed me up to the pub doors. He was on all fours in the car park getting mullered. He actually got away by crawling through a prickled hedge and looked like Steve McQueen did when he got tangled in the barbed wire in *The Great Escape*. To top it off, he was off work for three months after badly damaging his knee. We joke now when I see him and ask if he fancies coming for a beer. His reply is always 'Fuck that!'

I'd got a massive bump on my head, a gashed hand caused by a dog's teeth and I wondered how I'd ended up in trouble again, but then again I quite enjoyed myself!

IN THE CELLS AGAIN

Wednesday have a thing about Derby. I'm not sure why or how it started but, if there's one match Wednesday are guaranteed to turn a firm out for, then it's Derby away. In February 2000, Wednesday took big numbers down to Pride Park. The estimates were 200-plus and all their old school would stick on their Hi-tec trainers and come out for this one. Wednesday had been putting it around that on their return they were going to 'do' the BBC. Of course, talk is cheap but we knew that, with the numbers Wednesday had out, we had to take the threat seriously and make sure we didn't get caught with our pants down.

After United's home game with Tranmere, we headed down to the Royal Standard. A few of our lot had been in constant contact with the snorters firm. There's hardly any lads from each firm who actually have mates in the rival mob; I can only think of two United lads that are mates with any of Wednesday's active mob. Personally, I have never had any mates who run with Wednesday, although I'll be the first to admit that I was one of only a few Blades that could go in places like the Limit and not get the shit other United lads have. I could have a chat with the Wednesday lads and they showed me respect, so they got it back.

Quite a few United lads didn't like the fact that sometimes I'd talk to a Wednesday lad or the fact that I could go up places like West Street and drink in the same pub as them without any bollocks. I actually ended up fighting on two separate occasions with United

lads who had slagged me off for being a bit too close to a few of Wednesday's mob, and had been arrested that Christmas Eve when I tried to stick up for the two Wednesday youngsters on Fargate. Wednesday lads seemed to forget at times that I was a fair lad who didn't like to see anything that was out of order on either side. It didn't stop Wednesday doing some shite things to me but I saw it as their problem. I'll always carry a code around with me; it's just the way I am. I'd actually got a bit of time for a few Wednesday lads, but, as for some of the others in their firm at the time, well, I wouldn't piss on them if they were on fire.

One thing both sets of lads knew was that, when it came to a United v Wednesday set-to, I'd be on the frontline for the Blades firm.

Anyhow, around 90 United had assembled in the Standard, it was a high-quality mob and as I scanned around the pub I realised that this mob of United were all tried and trusted, and I knew that it didn't matter if Wednesday had 500 lads out, this firm of BBC were going nowhere.

The two groups were in contact and Wednesday agreed to come to the Standard as soon as they landed in Sheffield. There was no CCTV and the pub was close enough to the station to get it on before the OB had the chance to get their shit together.

We also knew that deep down a big firm of Wednesday would have an awful lot of passengers tagging along. They wouldn't know what had hit them in a major 'off'.

Wednesday were watched out of the station but, instead of heading our way, they unsurprisingly headed into town. We were revved up and gutted at their movements.

Tap got on the blower to them: 'Where the fuck are you going'?

They said they were meeting some more lads in town. Like the 200-plus of them weren't enough.

After half-an-hour, everyone was getting restless. It was evident that, if we were going to get it on, then we would have to do the hunting as usual. As soon as we set off, the OB were on our case. Wednesday had plotted up on Division Street which is precisely where we headed for. As we headed up Trafalgar Street, which leads

directly on to Division Street, around 50 OB had blocked the road off. Our mob still approached. I hung back with around 10 others, who were going to go around to the next road. But, before we moved off, the OB and United's mob kicked off.

Fair play to the Blades mob for having it with the OB. What we didn't realise was that United's lads had clocked Wednesday at the top of the road. United lads were getting dropped by the OB's batons but getting back up and running in again. A few bizzies were pulled to the ground and attacked with their own batons. A United lad was knocked clean out and lay prostrate in the middle of the riot. I had never seen anything like it or a United mob so frenzied. If Wednesday had been of a like mind and run down the road behind the OB, then the plod would have had no chance of stopping the two groups, but, to be honest, I couldn't see if the OB were stopping Wednesday at the top of the road. The 10 of us started to jog to the next road that led up to Division Street. As we ran up, a couple of taxis containing Wednesday lads drove past and stopped at the traffic lights. Zuey was first to suss them and the taxis were attacked before they drove off at speed with the Wednesday lads giving us the fingers out of the back window.

Then someone shouted, 'Wednesday are here!'

I screamed at everyone not to shift. I rounded the corner to see the first few Wednesday coming down the road. The OB screeched up and proceeded to block this road off as well. It was at this point I saw one of the Wednesday lads who had attacked me and my Everton pals at Hillsborough. I thought of my last words to him on that day and, true to my word, I ran forward. It was stupid really, as he was stood behind three plod, but, because I was on one and the old red mist had descended, I ran through them and punched him. I didn't connect as well as I'd have liked, so I went forward to kick him but the OB pulled me back and I fell to the floor with the plod diving on top of me. As they pushed me face down and tried to handcuff me, I heard somebody shout, 'They've got Steve!'

The next thing I knew was that United's lads attacked the OB in an attempt to get me free. I got caught in the crossfire as officers held on to me while hitting out with their batons. At one point, a

copper had his baton ripped from him and I managed to break free, only to be grabbed again. I ended up being dragged down the road; my knees were bleeding and I'd lost my mobile in the melee. Despite the lads' bold efforts, I was arrested and cuffed while bent over a parked car. Fair play to the arresting officer, he was game as fuck and, despite him and his colleagues coming under serious attack, he'd got his arrest. I actually apologised to a WPC as we drove to the cop shop; she was shaking like a leaf and looked terrified. She half smiled but it was clear she was severely shaken by the experience.

So I ended up back in the familiar surroundings of Bridge Street nick. It's at this moment it hits you. I'd been around long enough to use a bit more savvy, and you think of the stupidity of the arrest, you think of your family at home, you think of all sorts of shit.

After six hours in custody, I was released into the dark. I had a violent disorder hanging over me if any CCTV had captured any of my actions. Over the next few days, local press and TV made the events into major headline news. Five police officers had been injured and one detained in hospital over night. Fifteen people had been arrested in the city's worst outbreak of football-related trouble in years. I was eventually charged with threatening behaviour – result. I went Guilty in court and was fined 100 sovs. Was it worth it? Not really, the punched lad and I are back on speaking terms and in reality we shouldn't have been up Hillsborough that day.

Sometimes you are in the wrong place at the wrong time and you can't avoid what comes your way. That certainly was the case when I got arrested again in 2008.

One of United's old school lads had developed a form of cancer behind his eye. As a way of helping him out, we decided to run a charity evening. I arranged for two bands to play and, with the help of a few others we sold the place out with 250 guests – including my mate Cass Pennant, who came up from the smoke, boxing Blade Curtis Woodhouse and Blades legend Dane Whitehouse. It was a special evening that made me proud to be a Blade, as we were all as one. Sometimes internal bollocks creep into United's firm, it's just a couple of lads really but it develops like a cancer and can get out of

hand, but to me, United are at their strongest when we are as our name: UNITED.

Anyhow, on the day I got locked up I'd picked up all the tickets, posters and flyers and planned to meet some lads to hand out the tickets and put a few flyers around the pubs. United had got Cardiff at home so a lot of us would be out due to our love of the Welsh. I met SG, the lad who had cancer, and he was very sincere in his thanks, so much so that tears welled up in our eyes as we hugged.

Now I don't usually go into town much anymore; I always seem to find trouble and I'm not that keen on drinking down there anyway. But after meeting SG I decided to have a few beers with him and a few other United old-school lads. Later that evening we ended up in the Swim Inn on West Street; in total seven of us sat drinking near the doorway. It was 11 o'clock and I nipped outside to make a quick phone call. As I stood in the doorway I glanced to my right and noticed around 20-plus lads bouncing towards the pub. I immediately recognised a couple who I knew were Wednesday; one, who is a good geezer, came and shook my hand. The rest weren't so friendly and, as I stood with my back to the door, they started bouncing around. The lads came running to the door and the two groups squared up. Wednesday had just returned from Swansea. The lads who were with me were as game as fuck, and it wouldn't matter if we faced an army. We weren't going anywhere. Asaba, a good Blades lad, smashed the first Wednesday lad who ran towards us and I followed suit, knocking another to the floor. The lad who Asaba hit was out for the count, we followed it through and ran into them as they backed away, shouting, 'Stand!'

We were now in the middle of West Street. Wednesday tried to get their shit together and came running back at us, but we stood firm, traded and had them on the back foot again. This time we followed it through; I copped a couple of punches as I traded blows with them. Despite their superior numbers, they couldn't cope. We continued to go forward and move them back. I ended up with around four Wednesday in front of me and went at them; all of a sudden I'm on the floor, with the OB on top of me. Now if I'd been in Wednesday's position I'd have given a warning about the OB

coming up behind, but I suppose we're a different breed with regard
to rights and wrongs. It was still kicking off around me as I was
being cuffed up, a very brave Wednesday lad shouted, 'Cowens, I'll
kick you in the fuckin' head!' as I laid face down with a copper's
knee in my back.

I was frogmarched to the van and slung inside. The arresting
copper asked me my name and as I told him he said, 'I thought you'd
given all this up, I'm mates with XXXX and XXXX who play
football for you.'

'Wrong time, wrong place,' I replied, adding, 'I'll never leave
my mates.'

After 10 minutes I was made to stand in front of the van as CCTV
was trained on me.

'Can you let us know what you've got this lad doing?' the police
said over the radio.

The arresting officer said he was going to see if he could give me
an on-the-spot fine, but it was out of his hands. He added that
they'd just followed Wednesday up for the train station and that he
couldn't believe five of us had just ran them. (I explained that there
were actually seven of us!) Another 10 minutes passed and I was still
sat in the back of the van on West Street, some 40 minutes after
being nabbed. Then a copper jumped in and started writing
something out. 'Fuckin' result!' I thought as I signed for my £80
on-the-spot fine.

'I might start getting back into this caper if it only costs me 80
sovs,' I joked. So that was that, I'd been arrested again. The usual
bollocks came out: I'd been dropped by a Happy Mondays
Wednesday lad, when in fact I never went to the canvas except
when the OB got me down. Instead of giving praise out for us being
game as fuck, they have to tell bollocks to their little Burberry-
wearing mates. (At least the good geezer amongst 'em told it how
it was.)

Like I say, wrong place, wrong time. I enjoyed it though!

It must be a dream to play for the team you support. Imagine running out wearing the famous red and white stripes, with the crowd singing your name, enough to make you burst with pride. No other player/fan fits the bill more than United's former employee Dane Whitehouse. Dane's career was cut short by a terrible challenge by Gareth Ainsworth who was then at Port Vale. The following season, Dane's father Sid steamed on the Port Vale players' coach and tried to apprehend Ainsworth for what he felt he had done to his son.

To me, Whitehouse epitomised what being a Blade is all about – loyalty, passion and pride. All Dane wanted to do was pull on the United red and white and go and give his all on the pitch. Big-money moves were offered to Dane but he never wanted to leave the club as United were and still are in his blood. So imagine the feeling he had when he scored in both our League wins over the Owls in the 1991–92 season.

Dane was one of four Sheffield lads who played in the derbies that season, with Carl Bradshaw, Mitch Ward and Jamie Hoyland making up the quartet. If ever pride and passion won a football game, then it was that season, as the heavily fancied Wednesday side who had a team full of superstars were missing one ingredient: some Sheffield Steel, as the Blades ran out deserved winners 2–0 and 3–1. One of the Wednesday players from that era was a left-back called Phil King.

A month after the 2–0 win at Bramall Lane, I was drinking in

Henry's wine bar in town on a Christmas works do when the whole Wednesday team walked in, and they were also having their Christmas do. I couldn't resist the chance to give out a bit of light-hearted banter. So, when Chris Woods stood behind me at the bar, I offered to buy him a beer; he politely refused but I insisted.

'OK, cheers, I'll have a bottle of Sol,' he said, not wanting to hurt my feelings.

I got the Sol, and turned and went to give it him, but, as he went to take it, I quickly pulled it away, saying, 'No, you'll only drop the cunt!'

He was rightly pissed off and, as he noticed my United enamel badge on my jumper, he sarcastically replied, 'Very fuckin' funny.'

'Not as funny as your performance at the Lane last month,' I retorted.

Now I'm not proud of giving him some stick as I was pissed at the time and wasn't letting the chance slip. I told him I was only having a laugh and gave him the drink. I eventually got talking to quite a few of their players, including John Sheridan, Woods and the aforementioned King.

They were top blokes really and, although you hate them when they are playing against your team, I actually found myself enjoying their company. King had me laughing when he got on about how intimidating Bramall Lane was during the derby. He then quizzed me about why all the fans in the John Street terrace were calling him a piggy cunt whenever he took a throw-in. When I told him that's what we call Wednesday in general, he was relieved that it wasn't just him and said, 'I thought it was me who they thought looked like a pig!'

We had a good laugh and the Wednesday players asked me to join them in Josephine's nightclub. I declined but they had made a good impression on me, even though they played for the other side.

Not all meetings between players and fans have a happy ending. In the same bar, a few years later, United were out again on a Christmas do. Wednesday's game against Coventry had been called off and 50 Wednesday lads decided to have a drink around town. They eventually ended up in Henry's where the United team were

enjoying their night out. This was a Dave Bassett side so it had to have its fair share of loons in it.

One bloke that fits that bill perfectly is Billy Whitehurst, a fine gentleman and a scholar. Billy had been famously described by Alan Hansen in his autobiography as the hardest player he's ever faced and admits to being terrified of him on the pitch. So, when the Wednesday boys started abusing the United team, Billy took it upon himself to sort the situation out. Vinnie Jones's car was damaged outside the bar and Billy politely asked who top boy was.

A lad I know called Lewis dropped the bollock of his life by going outside with Billy and, less than a minute later, big bad Billy was back in the pub with the matter sorted.

Although it's rare for United and Wednesday hooligans to become involved with the opposition players, it does and has sometimes happened. Wednesday fans were none too happy when Alan Quinn was attacked by two United lads outside Sheffield train station. They reasoned he was an innocent player and the assault was bang out of order. So, when Quinn swapped his trotters and grew himself some hands so he could play for the Blades, the boot was then on the other foot. Quinn then ended up in trouble during a late-night fracas in a local pub in the Wednesday hotbed of Oughtibridge.

The rival players themselves have been known to swap punches when bumping into each other in nightclubs. Although these incidents are few and far between, I know of at least six times when rival Sheffield footballers have exchanged blows.

One player who has had more than his fair share of woes in our city is a lad called Carl Bradshaw. Bradshaw was born into a proud Blades family and ended up getting a professional contract with Wednesday. At first, Wednesday fans hated him; after all, his leg was emblazoned with a Blades tattoo.

They eventually warmed to him after a series of wholehearted displays. Bradshaw then went back to being a villain, as Dave Bassett signed him and to Brads it was a dream come true to play for the club he loved.

Another player who crossed the red/blue divide was a certain Terry Curran. Now Curran was hated by Blades fans who affectionately

called him the greasy gyppo. The reason for this hatred was simple: not only was Curran a great player who was idolised by the blue half of Sheffield but he scored a goal in the 4–0 Boxing Day Massacre in 1979. Wednesday fans bring that day up as if it was yesterday. Move on, saddos, it's nearly 30 years ago. After Curran had scored, he ran up to the masses of Blades fans and taunted them until a golf ball just missed his curly head. Curran was never accepted by Blades fans and his first touch in a Blades shirt was greeted with a chorus of boos.

Only a few players have managed to make the switch a successful one; recently, Alan Quinn, Derek Geary and Leigh Bromby have made the switch a success with all three playing a major part in the club's return to the Premiership. In the past, Simon Stainrod, Imre Varadi and Jeff King have all nullified the initial scepticism that rival fans had to the switch.

Wartime Blades legend Jimmy Hagan, who many view as the greatest player to ever play for United, ensured he kept his place in Blades folklore by refusing to sign for Wednesday for £32,000 which would have been a British record transfer fee, citing his reason that he could never pull on a Wednesday shirt. Hagan finished his United career, having played 442 games, scoring 151 goals in the process.

Hagan later went into management and was eventually offered the post of managing a great Benfica side that contained Eusebio, one of the world's greatest footballers.

Hagan died in a Sheffield nursing home in 1998. Two years later, United organised the unveiling of a bronze statue of Hagan that would have pride of place in the United Hall of Fame. The great Eusebio was guest of honour at the event, which was attended by over 450 guests. I went along with Sean Bean and Gary Armstrong, and Eusebio put on the United tie that I gave him.

Speaking of Beany, he caused uproar recently after ruffling the feathers of the Owls when he referred to them as 'fuckin' pigs'. Sean had been promoting a book called *Sheffield United, the Biography*. After doing an interview for Radio Hallam (near Hillsborough), he then headed for Radio Sheffield, whose studio is on Shoreham Street. He

actually said live on radio that he was glad to be back at this end of town as he'd just been up the fuckin' pig end. The snorters were outraged that a film star could belittle their club like that and the radio phone-ins were jammed with irate Wednesday fans. Imagine Sean's next voiceover: 'More reasons to shop at fuckin' Morrisons'!

It's not only players that feel the wrath of the Steel City divide; managers have also had to listen to 90 minutes of constant abuse about their former teams. Ex-Wednesday players like Gary Megson, Nigel Worthington and Trevor Francis have had to run the gauntlet of hate when managing opposition teams at Bramall Lane, with Megson hated with a passion.

When Blades fan Micky Adams took his Leicester side to Hillsborough, he was subjected to 80 minutes of abuse. I say 80, because some Wednesday fans alleged that, after Adams got a bit fed up with the abuse, he turned to them and pulled his nose back and made grunting sounds at them. They went shitpot-crazy and around 10 fans complained to police; they could give it out but, as soon as they got some back, they went crying to the OB, tossers. It was the same when Simon Tracey suffered abuse at a derby game; but, when United scored, Tracey ran around the back of the net doing an airplane impression in front of his tormenters and the grunters reported Tracey to police.

ONE SEASON, THREE DERBIES

SWFC V SUFC, HILLSBOROUGH, NOVEMBER 2000

The Worthington Cup had drawn United and Wednesday together, which meant that, during this season, there would be three derbies, a copper's nightmare. United's firm met in Crookes, which overlooked Hillsborough and was around a 20-minute walk to the ground. Around 400 lads turned out, many of whom had tickets for the Wednesday stands, as United had sold their 7,400 allocation in hours leaving many fans with no option other than going in the Wednesday areas of the ground.

The police had launched the biggest operation Sheffield football had ever seen, and warned, 'Anyone arrested and convicted will face an automatic life ban from football grounds.' The warning was well intentioned but everyone knew that the courts would make any decision and these words were simply trying to send a warning out to the fierce rival hooligan groups.

The police escort for the 400 United lads marching down from Crookes was unreal, but, by the time we had reached Hillsborough Corner, the group was that spread out that the first 50 of us had no police with us at all. Then, unbelievably, *more* United lads rushed to join us and we had pushing 200 lads that had broken free from the stretched escort. The only people still under escort were the beer-heads and singers.

A few police in cars realised we had broken free and tried to hold us as we reached Penistone Road but it was like trying to stop the

tide coming in. The BBC saw a large group of Wednesday fans gathered outside a pub across the road and the roar went up as they charged across the carriage way. The Wednesday fans scattered in a panic but the charge stopped as quickly as it began as United's lads realised that they were just 'normals'.

The United army arrived at the back of Wednesday's Kop with 10 minutes to kick-off. The streets were packed with fans as Wednesday fans gathered in hundreds as they queued to get through the turnstiles, but they needn't have had the worried looks on their faces as we were on the lookout for the OCS and no one else. Everyone split and went to various parts of the ground to take up their seats.

Twenty Darnall Blades had bought tickets for Wednesday's North Stand. They had been drinking up Hillsborough and had been independent from the main United firm. Wednesday sussed the mob and came up the seats towards them. They paused just before trading distance and Darnall saw their chance and steamed in. A stunned Wednesday firm backed off over the seats, one falling over and pulling two more snorters backwards over the seats in panic.

Boney M lost the plot and couldn't contain himself as he frenzied up in a battle against his most hated. Unsurprisingly, he was arrested but this fact didn't stop him aiming kicks at mouthy Wednesday lads as he was taken out of the stadium. Una had been sitting on his own near the front and a few Wednesday saw him and started giving him the verbals. Una stood up and beckoned Wednesday on with outstretched arms. He then improvised by pretending to pull a shotgun from under his coat, cock it and then fire two shots at the bemused Wednesday lads who were by now heading over the seats to him. He planted his back foot ready for war but the two Wednesday who were nearest him didn't fancy it until police came and dragged Una out.

Despite the warnings of life bans, as the teams took to the field, fighting broke out all over the ground. Around 500 United supporters had taken over a large area of the North Stand towards the away end. Wednesday won the game 2–1 after extra-time, a total of 36 fans had been ejected from the game and six arrests were made. Afterwards, United marched around 300 lads back into town.

SUFC V SWFC, BRAMALL LANE, DECEMBER 2000

Due to Sky TV's live coverage of the game and police advice, the game was scheduled for an 11.30am kick-off. This prevented fans from drinking prior to the game but it also left the rest of the day, which was a long one for the South Yorkshire Police. As we already knew, Wednesday's firm would not be coming to the game, although a little mob of 20 waifs and strays were escorted up Bramall Lane by a sea of high-visibility jackets. Fair play to that little group, they came to the game when Wednesday's main actors were sat in the Hillsborough pubs watching the game.

The large United firm were left disappointed but the day was young and, deep down, everyone knew that, if there was to be any trouble, it would be later in the day. The potential flashpoint would be later on in town and, after the 1–1 draw, 300 United met up in the Stonehouse in the city centre. Around the same amount stayed on London Road as rumours did the rounds that Wednesday were planning to go down there, so it was essential that a reception committee lay in wait just in case the highly unlikely rumours proved to be true.

The massive police presence in town made the threat of any violence between the two groups highly unlikely but excitement levels rose when news came through that 100 Wednesday had left Hillsborough on the tram. United were now on the bottom of West Street in the Walkabout pub. As the United lads tried to vacate the Walkabout and get on the streets, the police beat them back, it was obvious that Wednesday were indeed around and hand-to-hand combat broke out with riot police. The pub suffered substantial damage as United's lads tried to smash their way out and, eventually, a large group managed to smash their way out of the back.

The police lost control of the situation and were now faced with the problem that the United hooligans were split into two groups, with one group trying to get on to West Street. The other mob were still fighting with police in the entrance of the Walkabout. The group who had managed to get away then caught sight of the Wednesday mob on Division Street and it was game on. Police managed to get in between the two groups but the United firm

were in determined mood and broke through the police line. The OB used CS gas to try to quell the situation. United charged at the Wednesday firm who scattered, leaving just two of their old-school game lads to stand on their own before having to run, with one being captured and pulled to the ground. More gas was used, as the situation was out of control. The police had to do something and elected to start locking up the United lads in groups, and, in total, 50 BBC were lifted with one 30-strong group locked up en masse and released the next morning without charge.

It was a very violent day which proved that it didn't matter how many police were on duty; if determined groups of lads wanted it, they would get it.

SUFC V SWFC, HILLSBOROUGH, APRIL 2001

The third and final meeting of the season saw United return victorious from Hillsborough after a 2–1 victory. The derby season had ended all square with Wednesday winning 2–1 in the League Cup with a 1–1 draw sandwiched in between this victory.

The BBC had again met up in Crookes, this time around 300-strong. Nothing happened, just the usual escort, and this time the plod had got their act together by stopping the walk every 500 yards, which made the 20-minute walk take an hour and the kick-off was missed as the police pissed on our bonfire.

It was a different story for the Darnall lot, however, as they did their usual trick of travelling to Hillsborough on their own. The 30 or so met at a pub up Halifax Road deep in the heart of Wendy-land. They timed their arrival at Hillsborough so that it gave them maximum chance of a tear-up, and, 10 minutes before kick-off, they again infiltrated Wednesday's seats. Before they could group up inside, a few Darnall were sussed and Wednesday were moving in. The cavalry arrived and fronted up to Wednesday, and, although Wednesday undoubtedly had the numbers, they didn't have the quality. Wednesday steamed in, but two were dropped to the floor, causing the rest to hesitate.

'Wednesday, Wednesday,' the chant went up but battles aren't won or lost on a chant.

Darnall ran in, causing Wednesday to back off and run. Two Darnall got lifted.

Later that night, the mobiles were red hot as rumour had it that Wednesday were going down Darnall to seek retribution. Over 200 BBC turned up in a fleet of taxis to help their fellow club men out. Wednesday never showed; shame really.

THE TIDE IS TURNING!

That headline is a favourite saying from our blue and white rivals. Well, this tide never seems to come in. The United and Wednesday rivalry will go on and on with claim and counterclaim of who did what, who should have done this, and 'there were only 50 of us and 52 of you'. It never ends and, to be frank, it bores the arse off me nowadays, especially as the internet has seen a rise in cyber-warriors. You can get sucked into arguing the toss with complete pikelets on the net. After one of our lads was killed, a Wednesday lad came on the United site spouting things he would never have dreamed of saying to the deceased lad's face. When I used to go on the internet, everyone knew who I was; I didn't hide behind an alias.

So, when I got into a heated argument with this insulting cyber-pig, I lost it. To cut it short, he said he knew me well and I was a wanker and that he would do me in. We came to an arrangement, but I turned up and he didn't. Then he sent me a private message apologising for his behaviour, so I posted it for all to see. It's easy to tap on a keyboard, and I don't bother with the net any more.

Yes, we hate each other with a passion but, for too many years now, both Sheffield clubs have concentrated on each other rather than the opposition from other cities. I know it will never happen, but I don't know why both sets of top lads don't get together and call a truce, pretty much like the one in the early 80s when United and Wednesday would sometimes drink side by side in the Blue Bell in town.

Yes, it was strained and when the clubs met it was murder, but the week in week out bollocks that goes off now has had the OB laughing little apples.

United's firm have held court, and still do, in our great city, but I'm sure the tide could turn one day, just as it did when we took over in the mid-80s. Wednesday treated our up-and-coming youngsters with complete disdain; they couldn't see this threat developing right under their noses and, like a cancer, we spread and grew stronger. Before Wednesday knew it, we had taken over. The danger is that United could adopt that same attitude and get complacent.

The last time I had a bit of trouble with Wednesday was over three years ago when 30 United were in town celebrating a lad's birthday. We later split up and I ended up in the Barcas with 15 others. Wednesday were around as we'd seen them through the club windows, walking up and down outside, having a sly look but not daring to venture inside. Near the end of the night, there were only eight of us left, but a very high-calibre eight at that. To be honest, I was that shit-faced I'd forgotten about our foe until Drib came over and said, 'We'd better get together before we leave, Wednesday are still around outside.'

Sure enough, as we left the club, around 15 young Wednesday lads bounced towards us, hoods up and caps pulled so low that they virtually covered their faces. We walked calmly into them but they shot off, leaving two captured lads screaming. United showed their class that night by just holding the Owls lads and tormenting them a bit. They never got touched really but one was relieved of his P&S cap.

I was a bit embarrassed by the events as the lads I was with were all touching 40 and some of the lads we were chasing were young enough to be our sons, but what do you do when they come for it?

In truth, United's firm has dominated Wednesday off the pitch for over 20 years now and that looks like continuing for years to come. Sure, Wednesday have had the odd result but by and large it's been one-way traffic.

The gulf between the two groups was highlighted after Wednesday's

home game against Leeds United at Hillsborough in 2006. Wednesday were out in numbers celebrating a well-known lad's stag night. Also on Ecclesall Road, another celebration was taking place as around 15 United lads were out celebrating the birth of Fozzy's first child. Unbeknown to the Blades firm, Wednesday were drinking just 100 yards from the pub they were in. Five United lads moved on to the next pub which made the rivals only 50 yards apart, which was when the alarm bells started to ring and a Blades lad rang a Wednesday boy to ask where he was. As usual, Wednesday denied where they were but they soon exited the Nursery Tavern as they knew they had been rumbled and headed down the road. Stood in their way were five of United's main lads. Despite being severely outnumbered, United's lads stood solid and fronted the Wednesday firm. Wednesday couldn't budge the Blades lads and, apart from one lad copping a sneaky sidewinder, which resulted in a black eye, they were relatively unscathed.

The OB came and a couple of United lads got lifted. In short, it showed the gulf in class between the firms. If the boot had been on the other foot, Wednesday would have never stood their ground. Next day, on the internet (now home to too many Billy Bullshit merchants), Wednesday tried to gloss over the events. They made lame excuses like they thought there were more Blades in the pub, and so what if there had been? Are they not into football for the purpose of having it away, or are they in it to chant 'Wednesday' and dance around like they did when the five Blades stood strong?

'The tide is turning' comment started to gather momentum after Wednesday had a bit of a result against the Beeb after a home game with Rotherham three years ago. United got it terribly wrong that night. Thirty United lads were drinking in the Mulberry Tavern when they got news through that Rotherham were holed up in the Brown Bear which is only 200 yards away, and around 15 of the younger lads went for a nosy. The Rotherham firm was actually Wednesday and the 50 Owls attacked. United still had lads in the Mulberry and by the time they had got their shit together United were on the back foot.

Havo picks up the story.

By the time we'd realised it was Wednesday, it was too late, no excuses like, we were just slow on the uptake. Our pups had put up a fight but, by the time we headed around the corner towards the Crucible Theatre, we were on the hop. Despite our shouts of 'STAND', Wednesday had got too much momentum. We split as we ran and around 10 of us got chased by the main bulk of the Wednesday firm right into the Bankers. This is where our fortunes changed, or should I say *we* changed our fortunes. The 10 of us picked up stools and glasses and defended the doors. Wednesday were in the street going demented while they attacked the doors. We'd had enough and surged out into them. One was splattered as a wood-to-skull blow sent him reeling. This was enough for us to get them on the move. I couldn't really believe it but they just turned and ran. We followed and one grunter was caught and suffered a real mashing, while his so-called mates didn't look back, despite us shouting for them to come and help him. He was sparked. There's a fat Wednesday lad who's supposed to be a main actor with them; well, that cunt ran like fuck without a glance back.

Wednesday regrouped near the Crucible but we had tasted blood and went through them again. The thing that night was, they ran us, then we ran them, but to hear them go on over the next few days it was like they had won the Battle of Little Bighorn but we knew that, after the torment they had suffered over a long period of time, then they would take any crumb of comfort.

Wednesday started making big noises that the Beeb were finished and the tide had finally turned. I've seen Paul Stancliffe or Nigel Pearson turn quicker than this tide. Another incident that proved that Wednesday were desperate to try to claim any result came after around 15 United older heads had to retreat back into TP Woods after 50 Wednesday attacked them. Wednesday posted CCTV coverage of the brawl all over the internet claiming the result.

All it showed was the 15 United lads came out to confront an equal number of Wednesday. The Wednesday lads backed off but, unbeknown to the Blades lads, another 30 or so Wednesday came running up behind United and they backed off into the pub. Big deal. One Wednesday youngster was rumoured to be dead after being sparked outside the pub. Later, Wednesday were full of it. The tide has turned!

The so-called Wednesday upsurge coincided with the OB being intent on banning as many of United's lads as possible. The government had ploughed money into funding civil bans, a new way of getting lads away from football.

One fight proved that the Wednesday claims that the Beeb were on the back foot were as false as Jordan's tits. After Wednesday had returned from an away match at QPR in 2004, they plotted up 30-handed in the Yorkshire Grey. Not many United were out in town but, when a Wednesday lad rang his Blades mate, nine United lads left the town-centre pub and headed towards Wednesday. The Owls firm knew they were coming but didn't know the numbers heading their way. CCTV followed the nine Blades, and the crystal-clear pictures showed the events unfold.

United walked across the car park, giving the waiting Wednesday firm plenty of time to get out, Wednesday stayed put but grouped up around the doors. As United attacked, they just defended the entrance. One United lad put a few windows through with a telescopic cosh. Six of the nine were later arrested; the *Sheffield Star* ran the front-page story of how, according to witnesses in the pub, Wednesday hooligans had 'stationed men around the doors, they were on their mobiles and shouting to each other that they were coming and to barricade the doors'.

The six United lads escaped football banning orders because the judge reasoned that there was no evidence that it was connected to football but they copped for large fines and curfews. No Wednesday were arrested, which was not surprising really, as they had sat tight, despite having far superior numbers. It was further proof if anyone needed it that United's firm were not only gamer but also that they wanted it more than their Wednesday rivals.

There was no disputing the result the Beeb had later on that year when both mobs met head on; United, who were outnumbered two to one, sent a main Wednesday firm scattering to the winds. One of United's younger lads describes the events.

AUNT SALLY'S

The last League game of the season saw a few of us making a trip down to Vicarage Road. United were comfortably within the playoffs, and this was just a trip down for something to do, have a few beers and a laugh. About seven others and I were booked on a coach that runs from one of the boozers near Bramall Lane. The usual clientele were a mix of lads who weren't afraid to have a go when it came on top, some pissheads and a few shirters.

A lot of our lads were hanging back in Sheffield and drinking up Ecclesall Road. The pigs were at home to Walsall, and it's kind of traditional to try and meet up for one last tear-up before the season ends (although in all honesty there's scrapping all year round).

The trip south passed off without incident, and United lost 2–0. On the way back, we were checking up to see what had happened back in Sheffield; not a lot was the reply, but that we should try and get back as soon as we could.

We landed back in Sheffield at about half-four and met up with the rest of our lot on Ecclesall Road. There were about 50 or so lads out, largely made up of the youth with a few of the big hitters knocking about as well. They had already seen some action as the 50 of them had shaken off the plod by going out of the back doors of the Pomona and taking a nature walk, and they had tried to meet Wednesday near the top end of Ecclesall Road.

The plod had managed to stop United's charge at Wednesday and a few Blades lads were nicked. Later, back at the Pomona, a couple of young pigs were spotted having a pike around and were soon sent packing. A few minutes later, riot vans turned up, with the rozzers decked out as though they were quelling a military coup. We sat in the boozer having a few more pints, and a bit of the old marching powder.

A couple of hours passed and we hadn't moved, but we were getting calls from the pigs saying they were making their way to town. The rozzers were still sat outside, and it looked like we wouldn't be able to shake them off. A few of our lads called it a day and buggered off home. Slowly, we were getting down to about 30 lads, still largely youth. Again, the pigs were on the blower saying they were drinking 50-handed about a 10-minute walk away, up towards the hospital. Something had to be done, and some fucker came up with a plan so simple it was brilliant. We'd just go off in dribs and drabs, jump in a cab in the rank outside the boozer and meet up in a pub closer to the pigs. But we wouldn't tell them that.

Sure enough, it worked a treat. As our numbers dwindled on Ecclesall Road, the rozzers began to scratch their heads, and they left what was left of us to our own devices. We made our way up to the boozer; by the time we got there, probably 30–35 of us had made it.

We sipped a pint, and the old adrenaline got going. One of our lads was scouting out on the road, looking for signs of movement from the pigs who, according to their calls, thought we were still on Ecclesall Road.

The shout went up and we left the boozer and waited in the car park. The road along which the OCS were coming was about 6ft higher up than the pub car park, but the boundary wall was a good 7ft tall on their side and about 15ft on our side, so they couldn't see us. The boozer must've just had a refurb, cos there was a skip outside, packed with handy-looking bits of wood. As far as we were concerned, we were outnumbered two to one, so getting tooled up was only fair. A few lads brought bottles and pint pots out of the pub. However, the best tool to come out was one of those large shovels they use to get pizzas out of the ovens: a big flat metal sheet with a wooden handle. A little pep talk from one of the older lads called Tap and we were chomping at the bit. We waited for them to get within a decent range, and then we fucking went for it. The look of total fucking surprise on some of their faces was worth it alone; with

the barrage of glasses and bottles and the noise, a few of their young hangers-on (which made up most of their mob) shat it, turned and ran straight back where they came from. We couldn't believe it. Some of their older lads stood, but got a good hammering and were left well battered. Whatever credibility the fledgling ITI and OCS youth had given themselves, we shattered it inside three minutes.

The job had been done, but the rozzers were closing us down quickly, so we turned and did one back to the boozer. Unsurprisingly, they weren't too happy that we'd made monkeys of them and let a few of ours know about it when they were trying to get back in the pub. One of ours, to try and appear innocent when the OB came in the pub, actually sat down with a family who were just tucking into a roast dinner and tried to make friendly banter. I went through the car park and met up with a few others, and we made our way quietly through a couple of estates and back to Ecclesall Road. We were buzzing our tits off, and well chuffed that we'd just completely destroyed the OCS while so outnumbered. That was probably the last time we met our cross-city neighbours in decent numbers, and they just did one leaving a couple of their gamer lads to get shovelled (literally) in.

The young United lads look like carrying on as top dogs. As for me, I don't hate Wednesday like I used to. I don't know whether it's because I'm getting old or the fact that I don't bother with the bollocks any more. I actually get on with quite a few of Wednesday's old school; to me, they are sound lads, although I didn't think that years ago when I was at it with them. Maybe the youngsters at it today will have the same view in years to come. One thing's for sure, I know I've got better things to do than run around town under the gaze of cameras trying to win a war that was actually won over 20 years ago. I was in that group of young lads who turned things around and I've played my part in the history of the United and Wednesday conflict. I really don't know where, when or if it will ever end but I do think it will one day lead to a fatality,

as the hatred between the two groups holds no bounds. For everyone's sake, let's hope that doesn't happen, but the more the code of conduct is ignored, particularly by the younger element, then that scenario is a very distinct possibility.

LOCAL WARS

Sheffield is a weird city when it comes to the red/blue divide. There are areas all over the city which are strongholds for both clubs' lads and fans. Some of these areas are often on each other's doorsteps, for instance, the area where I live is predominantly United but the surrounding areas are mixed with a fair few Wednesday lads only a stone's throw away. I've always been a believer in keeping hostilities away from your own doorstep but my blue and white pals are of a different view. Many a time in the past, they've dropped into areas unannounced, showed off and then left without so much as a goodbye. To me, it's a cock's game; anyone can mob up, go to a pub, kick off with a few individuals and leave claiming some sort of shite result.

Anyhow, this is how local wars can get out of hand and I confess to seeking out a few local rivals when they paid my local a visit mobbed up looking for two brothers who don't even drink around our way.

One such story of how things can boil over if you're not careful happened around four years ago. One of United's younger lads worked behind the bar in the English Cedar pub that was situated in our village. He and his brother had been having bollocks with a few Wednesday lads from the next village. There had been a few rumours about Wednesday turning a firm out to sort these lads out but confirmation came via one of their own lads who thought it was out of order for a firm to turn up at the young United lads' place of

work and kick off. He'd actually given us information before and was sort of a spy in the enemy's camp.

That Sunday, my local football team had clinched a place in the cup final and, as usual, we celebrated with a Leo Sayer. I was blindo by the time we walked through the English doors. Kippins (the young Blade) was behind the bar and there was around 10 local United lads waiting for any attack on the pub. I wasn't arsed really; for one, I didn't think they'd turn up and, two, I was shit-faced. Around half-an-hour later, in walked 15 of United's firm. I assured the nervous landlord and landlady that these lads hadn't come to cause trouble but to protect the pub from attack. The pager behind the bar informed us that Wednesday were indeed on the move towards us. Within 10 minutes of the United lads turning up so did the OB, and two vans parked outside.

That was the end of the chance of a bit of a dance, I thought, but how wrong I was ... I was sat near the doors and around six or seven of our lot were outside around the doorway. The OB drove off and, around a minute later, I heard one of our lot outside shout, 'They're here.' I couldn't understand it, though, as I could see up and down the road and couldn't see anyone at all. It soon became evident that they were, in fact, here when our lot backed into the pub doors under a hail of bricks and bottles. I placed my drink down and ran to the entrance door and then careered outside. I immediately thought what a dumb cunt I was for not taking the glass out, as around 30 tooled-up Wednesday bounced towards the pub.

Our lot came rushing out and, along with a few others, I ran at Wednesday. The first lad to greet me was a smallish, unshaven scruffy-looking cunt; he held out a bat and swung it around as I approached while ducking and diving under the missiles. I didn't slow down and his face was a picture as he pulled back his arm and actually threw the bat at me before hot-footing it back from whence he came.

I'd actually run past Wendy's frontline who were by now backing away from our lot. I ran across and sidewinded one to the floor; another copped a pint pot on the noodle as he retreated, sending him to the canvas, then the roar went up and Wednesday were off at

a rapid rate. A couple were caught as the rest of their lads were diving through prickle bushes in a blind panic to get away. They had actually come from the fields at the back, so local knowledge of the area was apparent.

Two Wednesday were laid sparked out in the car park, and one was under a tree totally unconscious. What made it even more amusing for us was the sight of Merts coming out of the darkness with a baseball bat in one hand and Mr Bones, his massive Great Dane, straining at the leash in his other. Merts used to live near the English Cider and, while walking the dog, he'd spotted Wednesday tooling up and saying to each other what they were and weren't going to do. I imagined the look on their faces as we chased them back into the fields only for Merts and Mr Bones to scatter them as he came face to face with the fleeing snorters.

The OB screeched back up, and during the three or four minutes they'd gone, so had Wednesday; business had been dealt with.

We went back into the pub and I picked up the pint I'd left on the pool table. The OB came in and looked the familiar faces up and down. After a few minutes, I went outside to phone home, as I was meeting our Gertrude later and I wanted to cancel our rendezvous for obvious reasons. As I stood in the doorway, an ambulance drove into the car park to tend to Mr Sparko. Two plod in a car pulled up opposite me and one leaned out the window.

'Don't suppose you saw what went off, did you?' one said with more than a hint of sarcasm.

'No, I was snapping one off in the toilet at the time,' I replied.

The bizzie was just about to move on when Gurder came out of the pub. 'Don't suppose you saw anything, did you, Gurder?' the bizzie asked.

Quick as a flash Gurder replied, 'Yeah, mate, saw it all, that lad went up the tree to get some conkers. He slipped on a branch and nearly broke his neck.'

I had to turn away as I cracked up laughing at Gurder's explanation for the unconscious lad.

'I think you'll find it's not conker season, Gurder,' the plod replied, smirking.

'Even worse, then. He must have been up that tree nicking birds' eggs, serves him right then, dunnit?'

I cracked up and, to be fair, so did the plod.

Gurder walked back inside with a wry smile. Gurder has been around for three decades now and his quick wit and sense of humour never cease to amaze me. His sharp edge has got him out of a lot of scrapes.

Before I left the Oak, I had a quick chat with Tap. 'Go steady on the net, Tap, you know the OB will be reading everything you put,' I said.

'I know, I'm not putting anything on,' he replied.

Next morning I checked out the United hoolie site and there, in all its glory, was Tap's rant about the day's events. He'd posted it at midnight while still pissed. Still, I suppose a nice little result had to be told.

A couple of weeks after the English Cedar sketch, Gaz, a United fan who is not a hooligan, was jumped by three Wednesday as he staggered home from one of our locals. Prior to the attack, Gaz had a big cob the size of half a golf ball just above his eyebrow, which required surgery to remove it. During the attack by the Wendy boys, he'd been booted in the head and, when the swelling went down, the lump had disappeared, much to everyone's amusement.

'Had to cancel the operation to have it removed. I must get that Finchy [a Wendy lad] and his mates a drink next time I see em,' Gaz laughed.

Local rivalries can get silly. A typical example of one that got out of hand happened in the mid-90s, when three brothers who were Blades fell out with two brothers who were Wednesday. The tit-for-tat attacks got so out of control that a coach of Wednesday actually stopped off at the Blades brothers' local in Hackenthorpe on their way home from Coventry. Things simply escalated and, one Saturday night, rumour got around that Wednesday were planning another attack on the same pub.

Within half-an-hour, 100 BBC were plotted up and waiting. When nothing happened, a few went looking for Wednesday at

Frecheville. Fifteen BBC attacked the Sheriff pub and one of the Wednesday brothers was badly beaten up in the toilets. A week or so later, he had a heart attack and his brother blamed it on the beating he'd received.

The trouble between the two groups went on for years; one of the Blades brothers was even attacked while shopping with his wife in Meadowhall. To me, it's just stupid to cause trouble on your doorstep. Sometimes I've been dragged into things I felt I had to deal with locally but to me the rivalry should be left to match days and town.

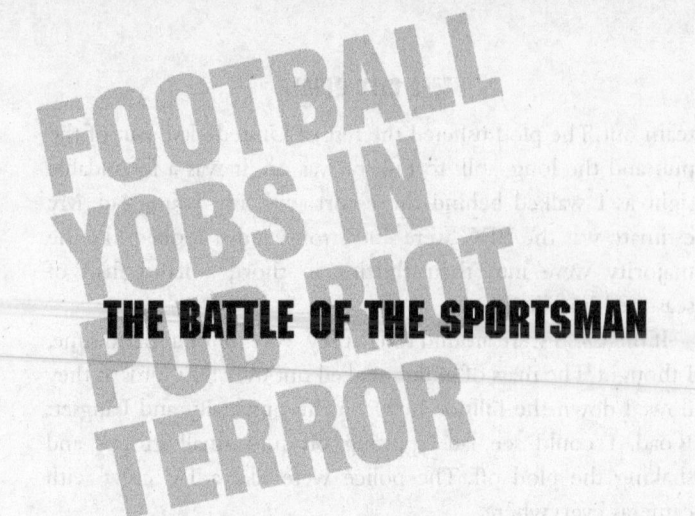

FOOTBALL
YOBS IN
PUB RIOT
TERROR

THE BATTLE OF THE SPORTSMAN

In my opinion, South Yorkshire Police should hang their heads in shame after an incident that happened late at night after the derby match at Hillsborough. I wasn't there – fuckin' glad I wasn't too – so I'll let the people who were tell their story.

This was it, Sheffield Wednesday v Sheffield United at Hillsborough, in short the big one. This fixture wasn't one to miss and holidays abroad weren't booked until the fixture list was published. The workplace and pubs became different places as the red/blue divide argued their case. It also saw the rival hooligan groups plan their day. The September game meant we didn't have to wait long before we got it on with the Owls mob. United's lads had started the season in very active mode and had already been involved in major disturbances in Coventry, Derby and even the pups had been at it on Skegness seafront.

On the day of the match it was a bit of a rush due to the early kick-off time and the fact that my son was playing football that morning.

I got a call from my mate Andy, who was in the Hanover pub around half a mile from Bramall Lane. So, me and the lad went down to the Hanover to meet him. On arrival, the street outside was teeming with lads. Designer clobber everywhere and it soon became apparent that United had turned a massive

team out. The plod ushered the rest of United's lads out of the pub and the long walk to the sty was on. It was a formidable sight as I walked behind the escort with my young lad. My estimate was the BBC were 400-strong and it looked like the majority were into their thirties, in short, a nasty firm of seasoned hoodlums.

If the OCS were around today, they were in for a torrid time, I thought. The mass of bodies snaked out over 500 yards as they flowed down the hillside between the university and Langsett Road. I could see lads splitting off into small groups and shaking the plod off. The police were like a TV crew with cameras everywhere.

It was evident the plod had no chance of keeping this torrent of lads in order as they tried to keep the bulk together. Eventually, the majority of the firm were stopped at the bottom of Langsett Road, The plod were trying to fathom out what to do with such a large group. I had no problem in moving through the police blockade, as I had my young son with me. As I got through, it started to get a bit heated, as the Beeb pushed forward and lines of plod tried to stand firm.

I eventually got to Hillsborough Corner only to be greeted by another blockade of police. The scene was more akin to a war-torn republic as a dozen police on horseback were backed up by riot police and dogs, while the helicopter hovered just above street level. As I neared the ground, I saw a group of around 20 OCS surrounded by police. If only they knew what was heading their way, I thought.

I learned through the mobile that United were at it with the police and a group of around 60–80 lads had broken away and got into Hillsborough Park.

The game itself saw United batter Wednesday, only to unbelievably lose 2–0. It was later in the day that this game would go down in Sheffield's football-hooligan folklore. There was always sporadic fighting during the day and evening of a game, but what happened later was nothing to do with our rivals.

Lad X picks up the story.

We'd been to Hillsborough with a huge mob and we'd basically had nothing but a few baton marks to show for our efforts. The elusive OCS had managed to vanish into thin air after the game. It's the fourth time I've been to Hillsborough in the last eight years and I've yet to encounter our rivals.

We show, they don't, end of. That's why the plod are always on our case but I didn't expect them to go as far as they did later in the night. We are obviously the fox and the plod are the hounds and, yes, they ripped us apart. The Sportsman Inn is a supporters' pub 100 yards from United's ground, and there was no sign of trouble. In fact, only around 60 United lads were still out, so the pub was mainly, as we call them, shirts. Around another 100 United boys were in the Cricketers.

Wednesday had been up to their usual tricks, that being phoning us up and telling us they were in one place when, in fact, they were nowhere near. After a couple of wild goose chases, everyone settled down.

Just as I thought there was going to be no action that evening, I got a call from Billy. He and his pal had just been attacked by Wednesday down near the Leadmill. Two taxis had headed off to check if the Wednesday lads were in the Ball. We phoned them and they turned the taxis around and headed back down to the Leadmill. Around a dozen of us set off on foot. We met the lads that had been attacked outside the Royal Standard pub.

We were informed that around 40 Wednesday were in the Dodgers pub near the train station. The two taxis arrived and we were now 20-strong. The rest of United's lads were on the blower and informed us they were on the way. We wanted to get it on, so headed straight for the Dodgers without waiting for back-up.

Unfortunately for us, some police in an unmarked car spotted us. The plod soon had us against a wall. We weren't having it and kicked off with the plod. That culminated in five

more of us getting nicked. One of my mates was accused of assault on the inspector; total bollocks, but at least he didn't get charged at the station. I headed back to the Sportsman. Inside, it was still full with mainly fans; I got a drink and went outside. There were around 20 lads outside, just drinking, when the OB screeched up mob-handed. The riot police politely told us to move inside. From what I saw, everyone was slowly heading inside, when, without me having any idea how it all started, it had kicked off with the police.

There was a crush to get inside, as the batons were brought down on our heads. The lads inside were trying to attack the plod but we were stuck in the middle getting battered. Lads were going down and getting dragged inside by their collars; it went up as the besieging police were pelted with bottles, flying glass, chairs, everything, including the kitchen sink.

My back was burning due to several strikes with batons; I had six welts across my back. The police were backed away from the pub doors as everyone surged forward as the roar went up. I peered outside; there must have been around 100 plod in the road. Stalemate: we weren't going out and the plod weren't coming in. The stand-off lasted an hour. Then the riot squad formed what I can only describe as a tunnel of death. We were let out one at a time, filmed on video then, it seemed, if you gave a wrong look or said anything, the batons were wielded.

I went out and braced myself.

'Run, you fat bastard,' the first copper said.

I don't run for no one, so I walked through the line of 30 police. I copped another four or five blows to my legs and arms. I was fuckin' black and blue but my pride and spirit remain intact.

Two weeks later, 25 United fans were arrested and charged with various violent-disorder charges for the battle of the Sportsman. Of the arrested, 10 were jailed for between 14 and 22 months. Even a family bloke aged 43 with no previous convictions copped two years.

I believe the police went way over the top during the whole

incident, and that they actually got away with it, as the courts ignored massive amounts of evidence from the fans that were there and on the receiving end of overzealous plod. But I guess it is no surprise to most of us that they accepted the police view that they were doing all they could to prevent an outbreak of serious public disorder, and ignored the fans.

In my opinion, it was the worst piece of police brutality Sheffield had ever seen; a few miners may disagree with that statement but, to me, the worst hooligans that day were the plod. I hate them with a passion now. My mate got 22 months; he is now banned from Sheffield city centre and banned from England games. The worst of it all, though, is he's banned from Bramall Lane for six years.

The police have been sued and hit with complaints by various people because of the events of that day. I don't understand how the courts can give jail sentences to people with one hand then pay out with the other.

THE SHEFFIELD DERBY, 2002

Before the United and Wednesday derby at Bramall Lane, I agreed to do an interview for *Look North* (a local BBC news programme). I'd also asked Paul Heaton if he would say a few words about the hooligan scene. I met Paul and we went and had a quick drink with the United firm who had gathered in the Moorfoot Tavern. Outside was swarming with OB, inside was chocka with United's hooligans. One of the lads came over and tipped me off that the OB had mentioned my name, as one of the lads was at home listening to the scanner. Me and Paul walked up to the Lane to do the interview.

It was quite surreal as they filmed me leaning on the corner flag, pretending to read my own book. After the real BBC had got what they wanted, we headed back to the Sportsman pub. Rumour had it that Wednesday were for once turning a decent mob out and would be coming to the game for a change. With 10 minutes to kick-off, police escorted around 30 to 40 lads up Bramall Lane. I tagged behind for a nosy. Once they got level with the Cricketers they started singing football songs, a bit childish like.

The OB had them well under wraps, and United's firm, who were looking on at the side of the pub, had no chance of a dance. I managed to get through the police blockade, as Wednesday were ushered to the turnstiles on Bramall Lane. It was then I saw a couple of their main actors. They gave me a wave and a nod. I tried to talk to one of them called Dinga but the mufti squad gave me a shove.

Then this tall bone-headed dresser started with the 'Cowens, you're a wanker.' He's surrounded by OB and giving it the big 'un. I stared him up and down, trying to see what clobber he had on so that I would recognise him later. The OB gave me another shove so I was off in the ground.

G and H block in the South Stand were absolutely rammed. It was a great atmosphere. Wednesday took the lead through Alan Quinn, who was soon to swap trotters for hands. (Quinny later redeemed himself after he had switched teams in our city and scored the winner in a dour encounter against Wednesday at Bramall Lane in 2005. Incidentally, Quinn is the first player to score for both clubs in a derby.)

We replied in style and ran out 3–1 winners, making me and thousands as happy as Larry. Saying that, Larry wasn't that happy after getting a six-stretch for a fight in town. He's a United lad and had been bottled in a nightclub in town, so he had waited outside the club for the lad to come out. The assailant was then attacked himself with a glass and Larry found himself locked up. During the trial, the local paper ran the story and Larry got four years for the assault, and the judge gave him another two years on top for shouting that he was BBC to all and sundry as he waited for the bloke who had attacked him.

'I'm giving you a further two years for admitting you are part of an organised football gang' rang in Larry's ears as he was led of to the cells.

Anyhow, back to the match. During the game, three distress flares were fired into the away end, and two United fans were subsequently jailed for their part in the firework display. This, coupled with a few other incidents, gave the police all the ammo they needed to enforce the closure of G and H block in the South Stand. A £100,000 fine hung over the club. With the closure of G and H, the atmosphere at the Lane did suffer. That area of the ground had become a no-go zone for police and stewards and the police openly admitted that they couldn't look after the area.

As the South Stand emptied on to Bramall Lane, there were United lads everywhere. The 40 or so Wednesday won't be singing now, I

thought as I walked. Outside the away end, hundreds of hooligans were waiting and so were the OB with the batons, dogs and horses. Just inside one exit stood around 15 Wednesday surrounded by OB; this was the remnants of what was left of their firm.

To be fair, you have to give those lads credit, as the previous season Wendy simply hadn't shown and got so much stick for it. At least this time they had come, even though the reports of them turning a couple of hundred out were way off the mark. It was bedlam on Bramall Lane as the OB tried to move the waiting hordes on. It was then I saw a face that had me thinking, Where have I seen him before?

Despite seven pints of Nelson Mandela before the game, it registered: it was big mouth from before the game. He'd put on a baseball cap and was trying to slip away in the crowds. I tucked in behind him and followed. As soon as we're away from the plod, he's copping one, I thought. I followed and he was nervous as he looked this way and that, trying to get away from the ground unscathed. Past the petrol station, I thought, This is my chance.

I walked quickly past him then turned to face him. 'How do, big mouth.'

His face was a picture but, to be fair, he was thinking on his feet all right, as he bolted to the side of me pulling a passer-by into my path as he ran. Then, dink, in his panic, he'd run across St Mary's roundabout and a car had clipped his back leg. He fell but was back up and off like an Olympic sprinter.

I turned to walk back towards the Lane. There were mobs of United everywhere. In the darkness, I spotted a group of around five young lads, 16–17 tops. They were obviously together but were trying to walk separately.

Following behind them were Brian and a few other United hoodlums; they'd sussed this little group of young Wednesday and were closing in. As the young Owls realised they had been rumbled, they just stood at the roundabout like startled rabbits in the headlights.

I went over to them. 'Come with me, lads.' I beckoned them across towards the church.

They wouldn't move and looked terrified.

This sounds a bit knobheadish but I took one by the arm. 'Look, I'm not going to touch you. I'm Steve Cowens. Come with me and I'll make sure you're all right, lads.'

Brian and his posse realised how young these lads were, as I pointed it out to them and they watched as I took the young lads across the road and to safety. Not one of the Owls pups said a word, but the tallest lad just nodded my way as they disappeared towards town.

A bit later, the OB had around 10 lads wrapped up. These were a few of Wendy's main actors and what was left of their firm. I leaned through the plod and shook hands with Dinga and Lewis, two of Wendy's more game lads.

'Fair play for turning up but watch yourselves,' I offered.

The OB didn't seem to know what to do with them as large groups of United were everywhere and the atmosphere was ugly. The plod took the few Wednesday towards town.

They were completely surrounded by Beeb, and across the road the Darnall lot made a charge at the police escort. The OB struck out with batons as they were nearly overwhelmed. I had to laugh at Tap; he was stood toe-to-toe with one of United's football intelligence and, as the copper tried to hit him, he's bouncing around giving him loads. Sometimes there are lads who are too game for their own good and Tap comes into that bracket. He's banned now and the same copper filed his report with the usual bollocks in it.

A few United lads were forced over a bridge directly above the excuse for an escort. Then the loudest bang came from the middle of the escort and had the police horses jumping up on their back legs, bucking bronco-style. That was no firework, I thought. United saw this as the chance to have another surge at the startled police. Dogs and batons kept United at bay. I later found out the explosion was an army stun grenade and I now know who threw it, nut case.

I'd kept out of it all and just walked behind watching and taking it all in. My phone rang and it was Paul asking where I was. He was outside the Sportsman way back at the Lane and asked if I'd heard the bang and what it was. I turned to walk back to the

Sportsman and got a wry smile off Harold, who is another United football officer.

He's been on the scene years now and I'll never forget the first time we encountered him and football intelligence officers. It was at Hull and 50 of us had settled in a town-centre pub when in walked two geezers with green Barbour coats on. They tried to have a drink and blend in but they were that obvious they may as well have had their helmets on. I and two others hid in the women's toilet while the rest of our mob were put on a bus and taken to the ground that day. The thing with Harold is he's actually a big Blades fan and, from what I've seen since, he's by far the best plod that's kept an eye on our thugs.

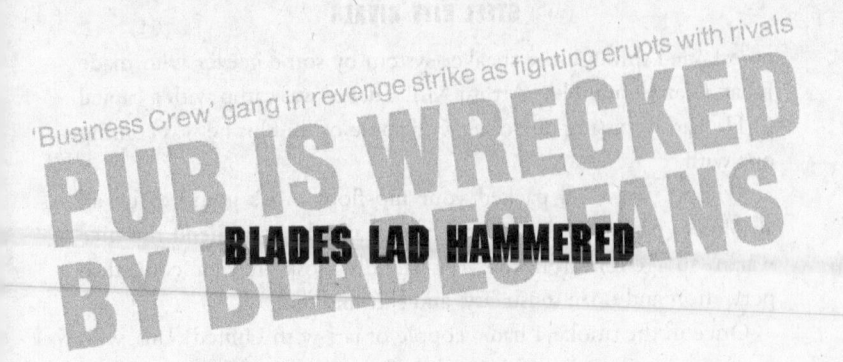

BLADES LAD HAMMERED

West Ham away was a fixture that had shivers running down your spine in the 80s and early 90s. A tough area, some tough geezers and a well-respected firm, known to all as the ICF. God, how it's changed. To be fair, a lot of grounds have lost the intimidation factor for one reason or another. United's own ground had the life sucked out of it for a couple of years as the plod and authorities banned anything that moved or was seen in a stoney coat. It does my nut in when you go away and the stands at the side of the away end are full of nuggets in Aqua caps gesturing all game. We had G and H shut at the away end of the South Stand, why? Simple, the OB couldn't control it. They wouldn't step foot in it, as sometimes there was as many as 1,800 lads in there for games like Leeds, Wendy and Liverpool. Bramall Lane was an intimidating place to visit. Three sides of the ground making one hell of a racket. This coincided with our best home form in years; the fans were like a goal start. This season's return to the Premiership has seen the Lane's great atmosphere return.

West Ham was the same; only promotion via a playoff win over Preston has breathed life into a ground that was like a morgue but it used to be one deafening, intimidating place to visit. I think their boardroom have sucked a lot of passion from the place.

Anyhow, West Ham away 2003, a chance to meet up with Cass, a good day on the pop and hopefully three points. I travelled down on the train with a few close mates. On the journey down, we were

entertained through the speaker system by some geezer who made Julian Clarey sound like Arthur Mullard. He was camp with a capital C. He had us pissing ourselves with some of the shit he was coming out with.

'I hope you've all packed your flip-flops as it's going to be an absolutely gorgeous day in the capital' and 'I recommend the nice warm sausage rolls from the very friendly kiosk, they are cooked to perfection and ooze sensuality,' and shit like that.

Once in the smoke, I had a couple of jars with United's lads, who were supposed to be taking a big firm. That big firm ended up numbering 50–60ish.

Boro who were at Arsenal that day had a firm further up the road and a couple had asked one of ours if I was around and I was welcome to join them for a beer. We split from our firm and went for a drink on our own. Later, as I walked down the side of the ground, I saw a figure that I recognised instantly, West Ham's own one-eyed Bob. Bob's a well-known face around Upton Park and he's a sound geezer as well.

I ran across at him and his mates. 'Come on we're here.'

Bob's mates looked a little startled then he realised who the spaceman was and came and shook my hand. I'd met Bob at a film premiere in London. Tony Rivers, one of the Cardiff lads who wrote the *Soul Crew* book, was there as his mate Gareth was starring in the film. They were spot-on lads and we had a great night, apart from a few Andy Warhol types knocking around but I suppose you get that with these sketches.

(When I went for a piss at the film premiere, I nearly zipped my cock off as a transvestite lobbed his knob out of his tights at the side of me, fuck that!)

The game was a dull 0–0 draw. I tried to get West Ham midfielder Don Hutchison's attention as he came over to the corner where we sat. I'd had a couple of great nights out with Don when he was at Sheffield. He's a great character and I liked the fella. I've a few stories about our nights out but I'll keep them to myself.

After the match, myself and Wilb turned right outside the ground and Sheffield's football spotters stopped us.

'Where you off to, Steve'?

'Off to the same place we've been before the game, I'm going for a drink,' I said.

They let us go and we went in the pub to be joined by around 20 non-hoolie mates.

The last train from St Pancras was 9.30, and we headed to King's Cross and met up with some other lads in a bar opposite the station. I got a drink and sat in the window and was promptly entertained by a Charles Bronson look-alike. Charlie B went around and around the pub on a bike with a huge smile on his face; he must have gone around 40 times until a taxi nearly skittled him.

One of the lads' mobiles went. 'It's Wednesday,' he said as he answered it.

I switched off and went into the land where little fairies in suspenders chase goblins about – oh yes, I was stoned.

My stoned-ness was interrupted with the words: 'You fuckin' clowns, what you doing down there when we're at West Ham? It's not even our boozer, hang around until we get back, you fuckin' plum.' It was Claws giving a Wendy lad the verbals.

It turned out 100 Wednesday had settled themselves down in the Moorfoot Tavern which, although it's not a Blades pub, it's close to London Road.

Everyone's mood changed. Getting back to Sheffield was now priority number one. As we walked towards the train station, I bumped into a well-known non-hoolie Blade called Shred (the best, most loyal Blades supporter that has ever lived). He made me laugh as he said, 'Oh no, not again.' He was referring to when he had helped us repel an attack from Grimsby's boys on the platform of the station. He'd suffered a bad beating that day and was arrested with the rest of us, but that's all been documented in the *BBC* book.

On the train, more news came through on the blower from Tap, one of the BBC's main actors.

'Have you heard about Mally?'

'No, what's up with him?' I asked.

'He's been battered by Wednesday, fuckin' on his own in the

Moorfoot, and they've proper smashed him up. He's in hospital,' he went on.

It turned out Mally was in the Moorfoot when Wednesday had gone in. To be fair, some of their main lads had told him to go which at first he was going to. Now Mally is one of the gamest lads around, but the daft cunt went back and gave out a bit of the verbals. Wednesday smashed him up; some clown thought that smashing him in the face with a bottle would be fun. They then threw glasses and stools over the bar at the terrified bar staff while chanting 'Wendy, Wendy'. I know a lot of their top boys were suitably embarrassed by the whole affair, but, I'll tell you this, if the boot had been on the other foot, a few clips would have been dished out to the chaps. If they think that's what football is all about, then they want to call it a day.

The train journey home wasn't dull; a couple of Blade-on-Blade fights, singsongs and, from what I saw, there was enough coke snorted to keep Escobar and his henchmen high for a few weeks.

It was gone midnight when we eventually got back in Sheffield. Wilb and I headed for a pub, where there were around 25 United boys outside who were on one big time. They had been scouring town in cars checking out if Wendy were around. The club they usually went in had been checked but to no avail.

Mally then turned up at the pub straight from hospital. He was in a bad, bad way, and it was clear he'd suffered a severe beating. Everyone went on one now they'd seen the state of Mally.

All Mally kept saying was: 'They can't hurt me, the blue 'n' white bastards, I fuckin' hate the cunts.'

In truth, he had been badly hurt but I admired his attitude.

'See what they do! Fuck it, the gloves are off. No rules, fuck the code. If you see one on his own from now on, he gets it,' Tap argued. Turning to me, he continued his rant. 'See, Steve, this is our payback. You leave them when the numbers aren't right and this is what you get in return,' he reasoned.

Tap was right and I thought about an incident from a month earlier when I'd been on Ecclesall Road celebrating my pal's stag night. Later that evening, around 40 of us had gone in a club that Wednesday sometimes go in. The 40 were mostly Blades but I have

quite a few pals who support the grunters and they are sound lads and good friends. We'd been in the club around half-an-hour when one of my mates came over.

'That Dweeby is in the corner with a few Wednesday.'

I knew Dweeby from the days when he used to drink around our way; he could be a trouble-causing cunt at the best of times and always seemed to be getting twatted but he didn't really bother me.

I'd even sent him a book up to Leeds, where he lives now, at the request of one of his family. Trouble was, in the Leadmill a couple of months earlier, he'd spat at a girl who goes in our local and thrown his drink on her because she had a United pendant on her gold chain.

I waltzed over, and he stuck out his hand to shake mine. 'All right, Steve? Thanks for the book.'

SLAP! 'Fuck the book,' I said, as I slapped him hard across the face, girly style.

I sometimes think a slap is more degrading than a punch. I didn't want to hit him anyway as I knew the fella but he and his six mates had to know he was out of order.

'What are you doing spitting on girls, you pleb? We're all rivals but you cunts always have to take it too far,' I said.

'I made a right idiot of myself that night,' he explained.

SLAP! 'Say it again,' I said, which he did. 'There's no need to go off like that. What chance have we got with the code of conduct when nuggets like you are pulling strokes like that,' I argued.

He nodded and I went back to enjoying my night.

Some United boys came in later and when they realised that a few Wendy were in the corner they went for them. I ran across and jumped in the way. Dweeby had picked up a chair. I suppose he had to really as they were backed up in the corner and there was nowhere to go.

'Put that fuckin' chair down,' I told him before turning to the handful of United that had gone over. 'Leave it out, there's only a few of them.'

Our lot left them and left the club; the bouncers thanked me. I went back to my pals and our night continued.

So you see that's why Tap was right. I'd helped a few Wednesday out and then this happens to Mally. He was right and maybe next time I'll step to one side and watch it go off.

This wasn't the end of it. Next day, a pub was targeted by the BBC. Fifteen main lads went to the Hall Inn on Sunday afternoon. The Hall Inn is a Wendy watering hole and is also camera'd up.

This didn't stop United's lads storming in, and the few OCS that didn't manage to get out the back got mullered. One of these was an older respected Wednesday lad. He was hospitalised as were a couple of other lads. One lad who copped it was a Wednesday fan but not a thug. He copped a bad beating in the beer garden and suffered a perforated eardrum amongst other injuries. This is rather unfortunate when things go this way, as he was a nice enough lad but he liked to be in the company of bad lads. It cost him this time, unlucky really. I used to work with him at the DIY store where I worked for 18 years.

Anyhow, I got to hear about what had happened later that day. At last orders, 30 Wendy went to a pub I drink in, what for I don't know. Wendy knew that I'd had nothing to do with what happened earlier in the day and it wasn't my style. I puzzled it out. Why had Wednesday gone to the pub when they knew the United boys who'd attacked the Hall Inn were on London Road; it was a cop out.

I was on one big time and searched out a Wednesday lad who's the mobile organiser for their crew. When I eventually got him on the blower, he explained that I wasn't the target but, to be honest, I haven't a clue who the real target was, as no lads from around our way had been involved in the earlier attack. I'd only gone home with my wife an hour earlier so I'd fortunately missed them. I was well fucked off. The OCS knew where the Beeb were: eight miles away on London Road. At 11.30-ish a few OCS pulled up on London Road in two cars and threw a couple of bricks through the pub windows and drove off.

Things in Sheffield were tetchy for a while with rumours of visits to rival pubs. Things got out of hand simply because over-the-top bullying had occurred. No one was arrested for the attack on the

Hall Inn, despite police announcing that the perpetrators would be dealt with.

Around three weeks later, I had a phone call from a good source saying that Wednesday were planning to come to a pub in the village and kick off. On the night in question, around 20 local United lads waited in the pub. I didn't involve the BBC as I didn't think we'd need them. By 11.30pm, there was just five of us left in the pub, as the others had gone home as a chance of a ruck looked unlikely.

Then Claws got a call that Wednesday were making their way to a meeting point not far from us. I was well oiled by this time but in no mood to take this shit.

'Right, let's go and greet them, but I'm warning you I'm not going anywhere no matter what the numbers are. If you come, then you have to stand,' I said.

Claws is game as fuck and he nodded.

We made a phone call to get transport and eight of us went to their meet. They weren't around so we went looking. Somehow, our two cars got split up, and then the news came through that they knew we were about and wanted to meet us on a quiet road outside an abattoir. I thought, Sound, a great place for a dead pig to be laid to rest.

The car I was in headed straight there without waiting for the other one. Outside the meet, a car was parked up with five lads in. We pulled up alongside. The look on their faces was a picture. As we started to get out of the car, a Wednesday lad called Qauz screamed, 'GO, GO, GO.'

The car reversed down the road at breakneck speed. Our other car was speeding up and tried to cut off their escape. The cars collided and I watched, as they sped off into the night. We again waited in vain, then drove around for an hour searching, but to no avail. It had been a silly night and I wondered why I had got so involved but, if Wednesday feels the need to cause bollocks on the doorstep, then they have to be met head-on.

Four months after the assault on Mally, 150 BBC were section 60'd and turned away from Burnley town centre, two of the three coaches decided on an impromptu stop off at Hillsborough on their way

home. A Wednesday lad was chased but not caught and Wednesday had the cheek to moan about the Beeb stopping off in Hillsborough, arguing that they knew that Wednesday would not be around, while conveniently forgetting that they had terrified innocent pub workers and that a United lad had been badly hurt in an attack which included the use of bottles. They labelled the BBC as bullies and snidey for turning up when they knew we wouldn't be around, hypocritical muppets.

SONGS SUNG BLUE, EVERYBODY KNOWS ONE

In 1981, I ended up in a full-scale riot in Steely's nightclub over the song 'Hi Ho Silver Lining'. United and Wednesday fans used to substitute the words 'silver lining' with our clubs' names: 'And it's hi, ho, Sheff United' and, of course, Wednesday did it using their name. Lungs were almost burst to see who could out-sing the other and this often led to violence, as it did that night in Steely's. Wednesday have recently used the song as a sort of anthem for the team to come out to. United's own anthem is an adaptation of John Denver's 'Annie's Song'. Both clubs have songs that aim at slagging or pulling the other club down. One such song is:

Hark now hear, United sing, the Wednesday ran away (again)
And we will fight, forever more, because of Boxing Day.

United fans started singing it not long after the 1979 Boxing Day Massacre. Wednesday soon jumped on the bandwagon but I've never understood why they sing it; why do they have to fight forever more because of Boxing Day? They won 4–0, the thick cunts.

Anyhow, here are a few more songs that Blades fans sing:

No pig fans in town, no Hillsborough to sadden my eyes
Jack Charlton is dead, and the pig fans have fled
Every year is 1889.

STEEL CITY RIVALS

Forever and ever, we'll follow our team
Sheffield United, we are supreme
We'll never be mastered
By no Wednesday bastard
We'll keep the red flag flying high.

If I had the wings of a sparrow
A dirty black arse of a crow
I'd fly over Hillsborough tomorrow
And shit on the bastards below.

My old man said be a Wednesday fan
I said, 'Fuck off, bollocks, you're a cunt'
He said, 'Come on, let's go to the game'
I said, 'Fuck off I'm going to the Lane'
And so I went down to John Street
And found myself a good seat
Saw the lads go two-up at the break
Then went to the bar for a pint of Magnet
And a meat pie filled with steak.

I was walking down Shoreham Street, swinging a chain
Went up to a Wednesday fan who called me a name
So I kicked him in the bollocks and kicked him in the head
Now that pig fan is dead.

HILLSBOROUGH CORNERED

As you've read, it doesn't always go United's way in battles with our foe; sometimes we've come unstuck but it's usually when the Beeb's gameness has backfired. One of our young guns describes these events from October 2003.

Do you know when you have one of those really good ideas while pissed, and when they actually happen they're a bit shit and poorly thought through? Well, this is one of those. It was a spectacular failure.

After some nondescript home game in the autumn of 2003, about 15–20 of us were out on the lash around town. We'd been getting the usual calls off the pigs ('We're coming into town; we're 50-handed,' etc, etc) all night and it was beginning to piss a few off. They hardly ever show in town when we're out in any kind of numbers, and when they do they're always picking off a few Blades and claiming a result.

It was getting on a bit and I was in a decent state of fucked-ness when a brilliantly simple plan struck me like a bolt of lightning. We'd go to them fuckers on Hillsborough Corner and take it to them. A quick 'get in, do the business, get out' type of thing. So simple, what could go wrong?

I looked around and put the word round that we'd be going up once everyone had supped up. There were probably 10–15 who said they were up for it, and I was happy that

would probably do. I rang up a couple of the older lads; they were otherwise engaged and called me a mad fucker, but fair play.

We boarded a tram and made our way up there. There were only about 10 that made the trip; a few had cried off and said it was a suicide mission and that the pigs would be on to us straight away and in large numbers.

When we got to the Deep End, the bouncer on the door wouldn't let us in, so we crossed over to Legends. The place was empty, so the 'straight in, do the business, get out' plan was going wrong already. We settled in for a couple of pints, and I got chatting to the bouncer who recognised me from the Mulberry:

'What the fuck are you lot doing here?'

'Thought we'd come up and say hello.'

'Are you fucking stupid?'

'Looks like it.'

It took a while but, after about 20 minutes, the first couple of pigs came sniffing. One of our lads worked with them, so went out to have a word. He was out there for about five minutes before another one of ours went out, walked up to them and twatted one. That was it then. The rest is a bit of a blur. We all piled out and waited for the rest of the pigs to come after running the two lads off. They went into the Shakespeare pub and about a minute later a few more lads came out. They backed us off to the bridge; I took a few hits but stayed on my feet. Then the whole fucking pub emptied, along with what seemed like all the Blue Bell as well. We were fucked, no two ways about it.

We stood there and gave them the big 'un. Then I ran into them. I can't really remember much else until I came round with four bobbies round me and an ambulance siren blaring. My phone was ringing, but I was in no fit state to answer it. The swelling and bruising took a good month to go down. I know I was up against some railings at one point, trying not to go down, but the numbers were too much.

By all accounts, there were about 50 pigs that came out of the boozers, and I'd run straight into them shouting, 'Come on then.'

Most of the lads I went up with did one, which, given the numbers, is fair play. Those that stood know who they are and I have full respect for them.

THE SHEFFIELD DERBY 2007

After going to Hillsborough for the Derby in January 2007, I vowed never to return again. It was supposed to be a quiet meet-up with a few Blades for a drink in Walkley before the game. The few turned into over 200! The OB still outnumbered us and took the piss as usual by making us miss the first 20 minutes, despite us setting off on the 15-minute walk to Hillsborough one hour before. I'd just got in the ground when a mix-up between our goalkeeper Paddy Kenny and defender Chris Morgan saw Wednesday's Steve Watson lob the ball into the empty net. Then the ref unbelievably sent off United's Matt Killgallon for raising his foot above waist high; despite there being no contact with anything in a blue and white shirt, the player went down like a sniper had got him and 8000 grunters, squealing like the begging bastards they are, saw the ref send Killa for an early bath. Despite only having 10 men we were the better side, but we lost 1-0. After the game, United's lads left early but were captured and put on a tram to town. Myself, Plumpy and an ex-United player decided to walk and have a drink on the way to town. No such luck. Fifteen OB captured us after 200 yards and got a bit heavy as they shoved us back to the tram stop.

I nearly got nicked because I was pissed-off at the heavy handed plod. With the final whistle gone, United and Wednesday clashed at the tram stop as pissed-off Blades waded into piss-taking Wednesday lads despite a large police presence. It was nothing major, but two Blades lads got lifted for their troubles. We were then forced onto the tram by the police and it was rammed. You couldn't shift. After 30 minutes we still hadn't moved; no one could breathe and a lot of lads started kicking the tram windows through. This led

to another 30-minute wait while the not-so-intelligent police tried to ID the unidentifiable!

I stood on that tram thinking, 'This is it, I've been to Hillsborough 11 times and this is my last.' We got off at West Street and went in the pubs, the OB were everywhere and were giving out Section 60 search orders like Smarties. Around 30 of us had got tucked up in a backstreet pub off West Street. Then the OB piled in and started a fresh round of Section 60's; me and Plumpy sneaked out the back, climbed over a wall and went into another pub. I've vowed never to return ever since that day, but who knows?

Earlier that day, United's banned lads were escorted from Walkley to Sheffield town. As they passed a pub they bumped into Wednesday's banned lot, including their TV star. A few verbals were exchanged but the OB presence blocked any combat. It did kick off one hour later as United's lads got a taxi back up to the pub; Wednesday came unstuck and their star ended up in intensive care for four days. The game at the Lane that season also saw Wednesday turn up with a paltry 15 lads surrounded by 40 police; it had been the same poor turnout for their last three visits and a lot of United's lads had stopped even hoping for combat.

THE SHEFFIELD DERBY 2008

The following year (2008-9 season) I'd arranged to go to my mate's place in Spain for a few days with my son. It coincided with United's game at Hillsborough, but I wouldn't have gone anyway. I couldn't believe it, but in the airport bar was none other than their TV star. Now, no disrespect, but I hadn't heard of him until he'd been on *Danny Dyer's Real Football Factories*, nor had any United lads and a lot of Wednesdays for that matter.

I walked over to him when I'd got my drink. 'Alright, Steve,' he said.

'Yeah, sound. What you doing, getting out of the way after last year?'

To be fair to him, he said he'd asked for it as he'd gone on TV shouting his mouth off. We had a chat and I was surprised that he was quite a decent geezer really, as he'd come across so badly on *RFF*. I wished him well as we left for our flight.

While I was away, United's lads had planned to do something

different this game. It was a great idea they'd come up with and, bang on 11am, taxi after taxi pulled up outside Legends on Hillsborough Corner. The first taxi full contained Tap and a few others, who walked up to the few Wednesday sat around and said, 'Leave now, today this is a Blades pub.' There was a bigger insult in making them leave their own pub than battering them; it was also more stylish, come to think of it. More Blades arrived and, by 11:05am, over 100 lads were inside. Wednesday knew United were there but the OB didn't. It took 20 minutes for the police to suss things out. Wednesday should have at least got some sort of challenge together, especially as a large BBC flag was hung in the window. Eventually, 150 lads were searched and either Section 60'd and sent back to town or escorted to the game. Even after the game a small firm of Beeb pups got to Hillsborough Corner and squared up before police intervention.

Wednesday had to come up with some sort of effort at the Lane after United's cheeky turnout at Legends. Before the game, around 100 lads and fans were escorted from West Street. United were frustrated again but, after the match, around 40 Wednesday had got just past the Cricketers and it looked like game on until they started singing. As the large OB presence started to wrap them up (they didn't need much – they were as tight as George Michael's Fila shorts in the 80s), a few United lads ran into them and punches were exchanged through the police. I watched the whole thing happen; Wednesday's firm of 40 included a lot of old faces, some game lads from years gone by and a few grey-hairs to boot. The BBC were not around in any number as they had plotted up near St Mary's underground. This didn't stop the few Beeb and norms having a dig; the escort was broken into as United attacked and Wednesday defended. Fair play to Wednesday though, they had come for once and deserve a bit of credit for it.

THE 2008-9 SEASON

During 2009 nine United lads were jailed for fights with Wednesday, with seven going down in one week while no Wednesday had even been nicked. (But then I suppose you have to

actually *fight* to get locked up, eh?) One Wednesday lad had even grassed yet they still have him amongst them now. One of the fights had been captured on CCTV and I've seen it: only seven or eight United lads were involved as Wednesday backed into the pub doors, but three United lads got jailed for their part. The film shows what happened and, without going into major detail, it's embarrassing from Wednesday's point of view. Wednesday even resorted to turning up at Bramall Lane while United were away at Crystal Palace; I know two Wednesday old-school who said they were embarrassed by that.

United were still in with a chance of automatic promotion at the end of the 2008-9 season and a win at Palace on the last day could see us up automatically, depending on another result. United sold 9000 tickets for the game. Neil Warnock (by now Palace's manager) did what we thought he'd do and gave us no favours as Palace scrapped for everything, leaving us frustrated at the 0-0 scoreline. As we slowly edged our way out of the capital, news came through that 100 Wednesday were acting up in empty pubs around Bramall Lane. The race was on, but we knew that it was another two to three hours before we got back to Sheffield, so there was a good chance that the Wednesday toilet writers would have jogged on.

We were around an hour away when news came through that Wednesday were now on Ecclesall Road. To cut it short, the first van back steamed into Wednesday outside a pub. They had no intention of waiting to get mobbed up; for all they knew, Wednesday could have still had 100 lads in there, but this didn't stop a van of 12 steaming Wednesday. Wednesday backed into the pub but two or three got badly beaten, with rumours going around that one had been stabbed. The car I was in just got on Eccesall Road as the fight was finished. Two lads were laid out on the floor and police began taping off the area as ambulances arrived. By all accounts, only around 25 Wednesday were left in the pub as the rest got twitchy, knowing that United would be back anytime now.

It just showed the gulf between the two firms. Wednesday were content to go into empty pubs writing 'OCS' on toilet walls while United were in London, while the first van back carrying 12

BLADE VERSUS OWL

United lads thought nothing of taking on Wednesday, not knowing what they faced. It's a massive difference between the mindsets of the two groups.

CONCLUSION

At the end of the day, the great United and Wednesday debate will roll on and on. Both sets of fans will argue their corner over everything and anything, whether it be who has got the best team, best ground, most loyal fans, both sets of supporters will argue over anything, even the colour of a fart. The only thing that really unites both set of fans is the universal hatred of the hugely arrogant club that resides 32 miles up the M1 motorway, Leeds United. There's only one match in the fixture calendar that both Sheffield clubs don't mind if the other one wins and that's against dirty Leeds.

Neither side will give the other an ounce of praise, the first question asked as the fans leave either ground is: 'How's the pigs gone on?' I find both sets of fans totally different in views and outlook. Wednesdayites love the words 'sleeping giant', 'massive' and 'remember when'. They see themselves as having a right to be up there with the best, even though they are far from that status at the moment.

A lot of Wednesday fans are still clinging on to the fact that they spent a few semi-successful years in the Premiership during the 90s. During that time, they won the League Cup which was named the Rumbelows Cup at the time, or, as Blades prefer, they won the washing-machine cup. Wednesday fans in general blow around like a crisp bag in the wind: win three games on the trot and they are going to take on the world, lose three and it's the end of the world. Granted, we Blades have fans who will slag the team, manager or

whatever one week, then the following week they are the best thing since sliced bread, and it infuriates me.

Wednesday fans are generally drawn from a larger fan base than just the Sheffield area, and have fans in areas such as Doncaster, Chesterfield and Barnsley, while Rotherham seems to be more of a Blades stronghold.

United's fans are predominantly from Sheffield, the pride and passion shows the affinity that we have for our club and our city. United have always had a more Sheffield feel about the club. From the early nickname of 'The Cutlers' to the present day name of 'The Blades', the club's name epitomises our city's history as the heart of the once-thriving steel industry. Similarly, Sheffield's heritage is embodied in the club's badge. In past years, the actual Sheffield coat of arms was used as a club crest, which adorned the chests of the likes of Tony Currie. Over the last two decades, the Sheffield coat of arms has been replaced by the crossed swords placed below the Yorkshire rose, still showing the club's pride in and attachment to the area. Wednesday on the other hand have a bedraggled Owl as a badge, or daft parrot, as I prefer to call it.

Unitedites are generally much more realistic about where they see their club. They are used to being let down and their outlook on our club confirms that. Our glass is half-empty while Wednesday's is half-full. The reason for that viewpoint is simple: we have been the nearly men on so many occasions in recent times, plus it took us 12 years to finally get out of the Championship and into the Premiership, and only one season to get back down again! Losing three playoff finals to Crystal Palace in the last minute at Wembley and to Wolves at Cardiff, then losing more recently to Burnley at the new Wembley stadium, was bitterly disappointing and a massive blow to the club.

Couple those disappointments with defeats in FA Cup semi-finals to both Newcastle and Arsenal, not to mention a 2–1 defeat at the hands of Wednesday in the same competition, plus a League Cup semi-final defeat to Liverpool, then you can see why the club's fans keep their feet on the ground.

Wednesday's only argument now is the fact that they have good

crowds, with local newspapers frequently publishing letters from our blue and white friends, whose only subject is that they think they have more fans than us. United have dominated proceedings for over 11 years now on the pitch and over 24 years off it (in hooligan terms). This fact has left Wednesday fans clutching at straws as to why their club is better or bigger than United. It's true that Wednesday have some very loyal fans and they consistently turn out crowds of over 20,000 and that is fair play to them. A lot of them are still clinging to the fact that they are a big club, or 'massive', which is the term that they prefer.

United's fans have been equally loyal, if not in the same numbers; we have stuck by the club and we had a few crowds of over 20,000 people in the Fourth Division Championship campaign in 1980–81.

A few seasons prior to United's drop into the English basement league, Wednesday escaped the same fate by one point and consistently played in front of crowds of under 8,000, with one attendance being as low as 7,310.

The potential demise of Wednesday at this time saw the infamous fundraising appeal from Sheffield's (non-biased) newspaper the *Star*! The appeal was aimed at raising funds for Wednesday and called 'SAVE OUR OWLS'. Everywhere you went in town, some twat was rattling a blue and white tin with a daft parrot on the side of it, while shouting 'Save our Owls'. Indeed, the *Star* even had that headline emblazoned across the top of its front page, fuckin' bin dippers.

The Owls were at an all-time low on and off the pitch, they had just gone six consecutive games with sub-10,000 crowds and were in deep trouble at the bottom of Division Three. It left a bitter taste in United fans' mouths, even more so when the *Star* didn't launch a similar campaign when United went into the Fourth Division a few years later. I'm glad really, as we didn't want to have to get a mongrel out of the free ads and sit on street corners begging. I still know Blades who will not have anything to do with the *Star* because of that and their view that the paper is biased towards Wednesday. I must admit that, in my opinion, that argument carries some weight.

To me, the great crowd debate is a no-brainer; not only in its

pettiness but also because the facts point to both clubs having around the same in terms of support, with Wednesday perhaps shading it and figures through the years prove this. It all depends on how successful each club is through the decade.

Ever since Sheffield has had two League clubs, United have had more fans through the turnstiles on 53 occasions out of 107; hardly a big gap, is it?

Indeed, in the mid-60s to the early 80s, United averaged 3,500 fans per game more than the snorters.

The fact that United have an average over 27,000 for the last three seasons does not mean we have more fans than Wednesday, who are averaging just over 22,000 in the same term; we just aren't as stupid as they are when it comes to shooting our mouths off. The new fans that have suddenly appeared at the Lane will disappear with relegation, we all know that; just like the Third Division record crowd of 49,309 that packed into Hillsborough for the Sheffield derby in 1979, that crowd turned into 13,200 for Wednesday's next home game, despite their 4–0 win in the aforementioned game. Speaking of that game, I went with my dad, granddad and three cousins, and we were all in tears when we got back to my auntie's for Christmas dinner. Sat at the head of the table and decked out in United hat and scarf was the only Wednesday fan in our family, my uncle Dave.

He used to play for Wednesday but is a sportsman and wants both clubs to do well. He works for United as a scout now.

When Wednesday gambled on big wages in the Premiership with the likes of Benito Carboni and Paulo Di Canio on their payroll, United were in crisis. Years of boardroom turmoil involving chairmen and directors who had anything but the club's interests at heart had ripped the life and soul out of the place. The behind-the-scenes activities were like a soap opera. First up was Reg Brearley (1981) who at first looked like he was going to make a good fist of things and guided the club to two successive promotions from the Fourth and Third Divisions, respectively.

Then came the blow of Sheffield Council's decision to refuse Brearley and the club planning permission to convert Bramall Lane

into the best athletics stadium in the country. Sheffield Council hierarchy were predominantly Wednesday fans at the time and United fans have always believed that the main reason that the club's plans were thrown out was because of the pork-ular ones on the council.

This argument carried added weight when the Sheffield taxpayer had to fork out millions to have the Don Valley athletics stadium built for the World Student Games a few years later. The council had scored a dramatic own goal.

When Brearley decided to relinquish his post as chairman, the result was pure pantomime. The club was within a gnat's cock of having Iraqi businessman Sam Hashimi placed in charge of the club. The Iraq war was just around the corner but this would have been the least of our worries as one year later Sam returned as Samantha following a sex-change operation, and you can imagine the field day Wednesday fans would have had.

A local businessman stepped in and saved the club from the he-be-she-be, but even that involvement was short-lived and United were forced to look elsewhere just a week before they were due to play their FA Cup semi-final at Wembley against the snort beasts from Hillsborough.

Then, in 1996, a businessman and Manchester City fan from Glossop called Mike Mcdonald took over affairs. At first, he too looked like he was going to make a good fist of things and, under the managership of Howard Kendall, the club looked to be going places. But, halfway through the season and with United in prime position for promotion to the Premier League, the club sold strikers Brian Deane and Jan Fjortoft on the same day. A month or so later, Carl Tiler, Don Hutchison and Mitch Ward all followed. The fans took years to get over the way we had thrown promotion away when it was within our grasp.

The reasoning behind what happened was baffling and it seemed to some of the fans that, for whatever reason, the people behind the club simply didn't want us to go up. What followed in seasons to come was a poor team on the pitch that were heading for the Second Division after a succession of failed managers saw Adrian Heath left in charge; crowds were dwindling, there was no money and no

prospects, and the club had an air of despair about it. Wednesday, on the other hand, were living the dream and looking down on us like shit on the bottom of their shoe. Those years were hard to take as a Blade but I really think it helped galvanise the fans.

Mcdonald also held preliminary talks about merging the two Sheffield clubs together! The club would be called Sheffield City, play its home games at the Don Valley athletics track and our club colours would be red and blue stripes. Ingenious! It showed he had absolutely no idea about the strength of feeling in Sheffield. He soon departed but is still a major shareholder at the club.

Enter Neil Warnock, who under the chairmanship of Kevin McCabe totally changed the club around. The improvements on and off the pitch have seen the ground transformed into a modern compact stadium that is now a better ground than the dated open waste that is offered at Hillsborough. Hillsborough has recently been chosen as a World Cup venue over Bramall Lane, should the event be held in England in 2018, which is a joke. Bramall Lane is in the city centre, surrounded by hotels, bars and transport links; it is a far better, more modern ground, close to the city's train station. The FA's wig-wearing pig, Mr Richards, came out with the biggest load of crap I've heard when he told of his reason: Hillsborough has better transport links! Eh? He may as well have said, 'Look, I'm a Wednesday fan so I've said Hillsborough.' He even started round two of his quest by saying it's better than Elland Road, which has also been chosen to compete with Hillsborough as Yorkshire's chosen World Cup ground.

In the meantime, Blades fans have kept their feet firmly on the ground and our season's hopes have been on survival only. Warnock has done an unbelievable job with the tools he has had at his disposal. All we Blades fans expect of our team is players who will give 100 per cent for the shirt and, under Warnock, the players have run themselves into the ground for the club. We love tryers and prefer them to fancy-Dan big-time Charlies.

Sheffield Wednesday, on the other hand, are now 27 million quid in debt. Unless someone comes along with big money to throw at the club, they will continue to struggle. Their only hope of raising a

bit of capital is to try to sell their training ground which is actually owned by Sheffield City Council.

We Blades will enjoy being number one in Sheffield while it lasts. We are realists and know that fortunes can change. As always, we will continue to follow and support our team with the pride and passion that we have in our club. Bramall Lane is a special place with an atmosphere that is rarely mirrored and Sheffield United are indeed a very special club.

You fill up my senses, like a gallon of Magnet
Like a packet of woodbines, like a good pinch of snuff
Like a night out in Sheffield, like a greasy chip buttie
Like Sheffield United, come fill me again.

Up the Blades.

EPILOGUE: WEDNESDAY DOWN, 2010

The build-up to the Sheffield Derby was reaching fever pitch. Alan Irwin had changed Wednesday's fortunes at first after replacing Brian Laws, but with three games to go a terrible run of results had put a serious dent in their hopes of avoiding the drop.

In contrast, United's season was dwindling out to what we always knew it would, mid-table mediocrity. In essence our season now rested on the demise of Wednesday. A few weeks prior to the game, 12 Wednesday lads had been jailed for a total of 36 years for an assault on five blokes sat innocently on a train, who just happened to be Leeds fans. Now Sheffield's hatred of Leeds is well known, but what could be seen on the CCTV footage of events from that day was not pleasant viewing, in fact it was embarrassing to a Sheffielder. United's youth had been pretty active during the season and had established themselves as a serious force, especially in our city. There had been a few incidents which were mostly caused by Facebook and other shit social network sites ('grassing sites' is another term you could use). Anyhow, a few Wednesday had been bigging themselves up and dropping a few names of various Blades youth and incidents. In short, they were grassing. Just why people go on those sites is beyond me – get a life!

(One such lad who had been mentioning names was caught and dealt with by a couple of Blades youth.)

Wednesday's chairman – who is hours of fun, by the way – had given United just under 2000 tickets for the game, arguing that

Wednesday only got that amount at the Lane. What we and everyone else knew was that when they had sold the initial 2000 he would sell the rest, and by the time of the game we had 5,200 fans in the Leppings Lane end. I, for my part, was making history by being stuck in Spain due to an ash cloud! I ended up sat in my mate's bar, listening to the game on the internet during my six extra days' holiday.

Even though we were abroad, we still got news through that 50 United lads had got into Hillsborough Corner for the second year running and they had just run 20 or so Wednesday that had come to greet them. Taxis had been used again. Trouble continued into Hillsborough Park, but the police had things under wraps after a couple of arrests.

The game itself saw United come away with a 1-1 draw and, more importantly, it left Wednesday still well and truly in the mire. So it all came down to the last match between Crystal Palace and the Snorters, with Palace only needing a draw to stay up. They should have been well and truly safe but administration saw the club docked 10 points. The game itself was a tense affair and, when Darren Ambrose scored to make it 2-1, the writing was on the wall. Darren Purse equalised, but in truth Wednesday didn't deserve anything from the game and when the final whistle blew, 2-2, Wednesday were down.

A few joyous Palace fans were celebrating on the pitch in front of the away end with their players, when they were attacked by Wednesday's angry fans. The scenes saw young Palace fans attacked and even a 50-year-old woman was punched in the face. Palace's Clint Hill was attacked as he left the field. Arrests will no doubt follow – knock, knock.

The pub I was in was bouncing around, as a hundred Blades deliriously celebrated Wednesday's relegation. Now Wednesday were on the receiving end and boy, they didn't like it. It was okay when United lost to Burnley and they were sending texts and gloating like the knobs they are. But now the boot was on the other foot, and I thought of the dicks that sent me texts after we lost to Burnley in the playoff final. I also thought of how they had rejoiced at our

shortcomings in previous seasons. It was payback time, but not from me: I didn't text one person or even take the piss, I've got a bit of class. Wednesday fans well and truly spat the dummy out, but what goes around comes around. United fans celebrated well into the night, and who could blame them?

So what now for our two rival clubs? Both are in deep financial trouble at a time when everyone is tightening their belts. Wednesday will probably push for a place in the League One playoffs, and United will probably struggle to finish in the top half of the Championship. Neither side has anything to gloat about really, on the pitch anyhow. The two hooligan groups will continue to hate each other and so will the shirters.

Wednesday's hooligan group are a totally different breed from United's. It's amazing that we share the same city. I know and respect a lot of Wednesday's old-school lads, and they must cringe at times at this new breed that aren't fit to lace their boots.

United have been above Wednesday in the league now for 11 years, off the field they have held court for near on 25 years and things don't look like changing for a while. But as the story goes on and on, the tide will turn!

When the kids are UNITED, they will never be divided.